Mom —
This book is about
Joe Dunn, Frank &
Mamie's son. The
beginning mentions lots
of familiar places.
We hope you enjoy.
Love —
Alice & Mike
December, 2006

The Search for Canasta 404

✳✳✳ ★ ✳✳✳

THE SEARCH FOR CANASTA 404

Love, Loss, and the POW/MIA Movement

Melissa B. Robinson

and

Maureen Dunn

Northeastern University Press

BOSTON

Published by University Press of New England
Hanover and London

Northeastern University Press
Published by University Press of New England,
One Court Street, Lebanon, NH 03766
www.upne.com

© 2006 by Melissa B. Robinson and Maureen Dunn
Printed in the United States of America
5   4   3   2   1

Library of Congress Cataloging-in-Publication Data
Robinson, Melissa B.
p.   cm.
Includes bibliographical references.
ISBN-13: 978-1-58465-486-5 (cloth : alk. paper)
ISBN-10: 1-58465-586-4 (cloth : alk. paper)
1. Vietnamese Conflict, 1961–1975—Missing in action—United States.
2. Vietnamese Conflict, 1961–1975—Prisoners and prisons. 3. Dunn,
Maureen, 1940–   4. Dunn, Joe (Joseph P.) 5. Missing in action—
United States. 6. Prisoners of war—United States.
I. Dunn, Maureen, 1940–   II. Title.
DS559.8.M5R63   2006
959.704'37—dc22   2006008075

 University Press of New England is a member of the Green Press
Initiative. The paper used in this book meets their minimum
requirements for recycled paper.

This book is dedicated to my
mother, Helena, and my husband,
Clay. Thanks for keeping the faith.
—*Melissa B. Robinson*

This book is dedicated to Joe Dunn
for showing me true love is forever.
—*Maureen Dunn*

Contents

Preface

On an ordinary weekday afternoon in April 2002, I was talking to a few people I knew from Boston, sources and the like, in a Capitol Hill hearing room when I noticed a woman sitting in a chair near a door. Thinking she was part of the local crowd that had gathered for a congressional hearing into the ties between the FBI and Boston's criminal underworld, I approached her, notebook in hand, like a typical reporter.

"Hi, I'm Melissa Robinson, I'm with the Associated Press," I said.

"I'm Maureen Dunn," she replied. In town for an entirely different reason, she had stopped by the hearing room in a U.S. House office building to catch up with some Boston folks she knew would be there.

"I've got nothing to do with this," she said, referring to the subject at hand. "But I've got my own great story about government secrecy to tell you, if you're interested."

I was. So began my friendship and professional association with Maureen Dunn.

Over the next few months, Maureen sent me clippings and documents. In return, I sent her samples from my portfolio.

Maureen got to know my work over an eclectic career path that has taken me from my very first summer job in journalism, typing box scores for my hometown newspaper's sports department, to my most recent position as a New England reporter for the Associated Press. In turn, I learned about her husband Joe, a twenty-five-year-old Navy pilot who had been shot down in an unarmed plane eleven days after the scheduled end of his Vietnam tour. I also found out how Maureen had sought the truth despite a prevailing culture of keeping silent about the men who had vanished in the war or who had survived, only to be captured and tortured.

I was quickly mesmerized by a story that was rooted in rural, turn-of-the-century Ireland, the birthplace of Joe and Maureen's courageous mothers, who were influential in forming their children's spirited, resolute characters. From there, the story moved to the streets of Boston, where Maureen and Joe were raised, through the burning skies over war-ravaged Vietnam, and along the coast of a tropical Chinese island.

I'm too young to have covered the Vietnam War, and I worried that would be a drawback. In a way, I longed to be one of those sports writers, war correspondents, or beat reporters whose books emerged as natural outgrowths of their daily coverage. Then again, my background was an ideal fit for Maureen's story. I graduated from Boston College and knew Boston, having covered everything from fishing to politics for over a decade. I also had traveled the length of Vietnam from Hanoi to the Mekong Delta, publishing stories on religious freedom and on the fate of a soldier whose POW/MIA bracelet I'd worn as an adolescent.

In the end, Maureen and I decided it was fate. We launched our project. She handed over videotapes, government records, personal correspondence, and newspaper clippings. I pored through it, did more research, conducted interviews, and prayed my old laptop would hold out. (It did, more or less.) After four years, one agent, hundreds of telephone calls, weeks holed up in Randolph and on Cape Cod, the birth of a child (my third, in 2003), and a publishing contract, we had a book.

Acknowledgments

There are a good many people whose help and generosity were instrumental in my ability to pull together this book. First, I'm grateful to everyone who agreed to share with me their deeply personal memories of the war and its aftermath, especially Joe's squadron mates in VA-25, and members, past and present, of the National League of Families of American Prisoners and Missing in Southeast Asia. Thanks, too, to the League, Pentagon, and military officials and advisers who patiently explained over thirty-five years of policy and helped me get my facts straight.

A warm thanks goes out to the members of Joe and Maureen Dunn's families for opening up their homes and hearts to me, sometimes over multiple visits and many hours. A special thanks to Dan Gallagher for allowing me to draw upon his excellent research on Joe's case. I want to single out my employer, the Associated Press, for granting me a sabbatical to work on this book and for giving me permission to quote from old AP stories in writing it. Thanks, too, to the *Boston Herald* for allowing me to quote from the many historic newspapers in its lineage. I owe a debt of gratitude to my agent, Lane Zachary, for her consistent vision and reassurance, to my editor, John Landrigan, for his sound judgment and calm steady guidance and, of course, to Maureen Dunn, for trusting me with her and Joe's story.

On the personal side, thanks to my brother-in-law for driving two box loads of files from Massachusetts to Maryland, and to my close friend, Judy, for tracking down a newspaper clipping in Boston. Thanks to all my family and friends for being patient when I had to miss parties, birthdays, weekend swims, and other fun in order to work. I am especially grateful to my three lively, wonderful kids for encouraging me when I felt tired, to my mom, for always believing in me, and to my husband, for picking up the slack at home and providing a critical mix of unflagging support, good cheer, and superb frontline editing.

Melissa B. Robinson
Silver Spring, Maryland
November 2005

✳ ✳ ✳

Thanks to Lane Zachary, my literary agent and friend, for always believing in this story. To Melissa B. Robinson, my co-author, for surviving this book, both physically and mentally, and to her family for allowing her to be absent so much! Special thanks to University Press of New England for agreeing to publish a story many did not want told. To Sheila Burgess Hill for all her copying of documents.

Thanks to all the wonderful friends and concerned citizens throughout the country who have worked so hard for an honorable accounting of the MIAs, God bless you all! Special thanks to my neighbor and dear friend, Anne Barkhouse, who became my computer specialist (everyone knows I am not!) throughout the years for all the POW/MIA events.

I don't know if just saying thank you is enough to my family who have supported and encouraged me all these years but thank you, I love you all. Special thanks to my nephew, Dan Gallagher, who was determined to resolve the mystery of Joe's fate, and for going with Joe-D' to China. To my sisters, Anna Hoey, Mary Driscoll, Agnes Gallagher, all avid readers, wish you were here to enjoy the book. To my mother, Helen Hoey, for making me strong enough to survive it all. To Mamie and Henry Dunn, Joe's mother and father, for giving me Joe. My love to Hennie and Fran Kelly, Joe's sister and brother-in-law who introduced me to Joe, who became the love of my life.

Most importantly, to my son, Joe-D', thank you for bearing with me and assisting in the search for your father (especially the emotional trip to China), and for making me write this book because you believed it was a part of history and had to be told. I am so proud of you, and I know Daddy is too. I love you, the other Joe who became the second great love of my life.

Maureen Dunn
Randolph, Massachusetts
November 2005

Prologue

On Valentine's Day in 1968, Maureen Dunn was thinking about fixing spaghetti for dinner when she stepped outside to grab the evening newspaper from the mailbox of the cozy white house she shared with her older sister and small son outside of Boston.

Maureen had been out of sorts all day. She felt jumpy and forgetful. When she didn't leave in time that afternoon to give a niece and two nephews a ride home from school, as she'd promised, another sister attended to it on her way home from work.

Maureen wasn't sure what was wrong. She figured she was just preoccupied by the fact that her husband was due to leave Vietnam any day now. The day before, Joe Dunn, a Navy pilot finishing up a tour aboard USS *Coral Sea,* had called his wife from Cubi Point Naval Air Station in the Philippines, where he had gone to pick up an airplane for ferrying back to the carrier. He still didn't know when they would be departing the Gulf of Tonkin. Maureen was anxious. She had already picked out a new blue outfit to meet Joe's plane at Lemoore Naval Air Station in northern California, where his squadron was based. Her sisters had agreed to look after her toddler son, named for his father and known as Joe-D', while she was gone.

Joe would already have been on his way, except that North Korea had attacked USS *Pueblo* three weeks before, taking the captain and surviving crew of the intelligence-gathering ship hostage. That meant that USS *Enterprise,* which was supposed to relieve *Coral Sea,* got diverted to North Korea. With no word on when they would be going home, Joe and his squadron mates kept flying missions and waiting to hear.

Maureen unfolded the newspaper from the mailbox. The front page featured a cute photo of a five-year-old girl holding a valentine for her Dorchester classmate. But the large headline running above the photo and the story to its right stopped her cold.

"China Downs Lost U.S. Plane," it read. "Unarmed, Propeller-Driven Craft Strays; 2nd Escapes."

Maureen's stomach lurched. She quickly scanned the story, which was reported by the Associated Press out of Washington: "An unarmed propeller-driven U.S. Navy plane was shot down by Chinese Communist MIG aircraft after it 'inadvertently strayed into air space' off Red China's Hainan Island, the Defense Department announced today."

Maureen kept reading: "The Pentagon said the incident occurred Tuesday night when two unarmed Navy A-1 planes 'experienced navigational difficulties' while on a ferry plane trip from Cubi Point in the Philippines to the aircraft carrier *Coral Sea* in the Gulf of Tonkin."[1]

Maureen stopped. She felt a cold sweat breaking out on the back of her neck and forehead. Her heart pounded as the familiar names swirled in her head. Cubi Point. A-1. *Coral Sea.*

It had to be Joe. But why hadn't the Navy called?

It was fifteen minutes before five o'clock, and Maureen knew she didn't have long before government offices would close for the day. She dialed the Navy's Chief of Information (CHINFO), but the office referred her to Lemoore, where no one answered the telephone. She went back to CHINFO, then back to Lemoore. She was getting nowhere. As her nineteen-month-old son darted around the house, shrieking and laughing, she thought of whom else she could try. The Navy put out a report on casualties every day. Maureen grabbed the telephone directory and looked up the number for the First Naval District office, which she knew was located in the Fargo building in downtown Boston.

"Who are you calling for?" asked the young man who answered the phone. He sounded young and inexperienced.

"I'm calling for my husband who could possibly be in this shootdown," Maureen said, explaining her concerns about the details in the newspaper story.

"They would have notified you," the man said.

"Could you just do me a favor and look at the names?" she asked. "Is it Joseph Dunn? Is he on there?"

The young voice paused for what seemed like a very long time.

Finally, he spoke up.
"What's his middle initial?"

This is the true story of how Maureen Dunn's personal tragedy helped launch a national movement. When Maureen's husband Joe was shot down by China during the Vietnam War, she was stymied in her efforts to find out what had happened to him. Was he dead? Was he a prisoner? The U.S. government had little to offer. The Chinese were hostile to inquiries. With nowhere else to turn, Maureen looked to her family and friends for help. She started the local "Where Is Lt. Joe Dunn?" committee, one of the first publicly active POW/MIA organizations in the country, and later emerged as a leader in the National League of Families of American Prisoners and Missing in Southeast Asia, a nonprofit POW/MIA advocacy group. Within two years of its founding in 1970, the League went from a fledgling group of relatives hungry for information about their missing and imprisoned men to a political force with entrée at government's highest levels.

Though this book re-creates Joe's point of view, it does so by relying on his own letters and on extensive interviews with those who had direct dealings with him, including his family and fellow pilots from his attack squadron in Vietnam. And while Melissa B. Robinson wrote the book in the third-person, she did so with the involvement of Maureen Dunn, who provided countless hours of interviews and voluminous materials accumulated over thirty-seven years of activism, including an invaluable videotape of a family fact-finding trip to China.

The book opens in the early 1960s, but its themes of love, war, and coping in the aftermath of unthinkable loss are universal and all-too-familiar. This is Joe and Maureen's story.

✳✳✳ **1** ✳✳✳

Love

On a chilly night in April 1963, Maureen Hoey walked away from the shuttered information booth to the pay telephone at the far end of the dim, grimy T platform and dialed Hennie's number. It was nearly nine, and just a few people were waiting at the Park Street station, where the trains run beneath the bustle and bright lights of Boston's Downtown Crossing shopping district. The busy station cut a wide swath underground, running under a corner of Boston Common, down the hill from the gold-domed State House and a block away from Filene's and Jordan Marsh.

Maureen figured she'd been waiting long enough for this blind date. Tall and slender with beautiful blue eyes, she was beginning to attract attention. One man even suggested they get together if his date didn't show. Not only that, she didn't want to run into her girlfriends. They soon would be getting off the trolley to go to the City Club, where they would dance and drink rum and cokes. It was their Friday night ritual and Maureen, though she wasn't a drinker, was usually a part of it. She didn't want to have to explain to them why she was hanging around the T alone at night in her good red coat with its mother-of-pearl buttons.

The phone rang, and Hennie picked up.

"Hennie, it's Maureen. What is the deal with this guy?" she practically shouted at her friend. "He's still not here."

Hennie laughed.

"He couldn't find any socks. He's on his way. Don't leave."

Maureen hung up. He couldn't find socks?

The youngest of ten, twenty-two-year-old Maureen had spent virtually every Wednesday afternoon of her young life in the Mission Church on

Tremont Street in Boston's Roxbury neighborhood, saying a series of special prayers to the Blessed Mother by her own mother's side.

The church famously enshrines a copy of a miraculous icon of Mary and Jesus known as the Mother of Perpetual Help. Since the late nineteenth century, thousands have flocked there to pray for a cure through Mary's intercession, leaving behind crutches, braces, and canes as testaments to the power of faith.

Maureen's mother, Helen McManus Hoey, never missed a Wednesday, even though she wasn't troubled personally by physical afflictions. But she worried about her children, especially one daughter with uneven legs and a slow gait and a son with a knack for getting into trouble. Helen's most fervent desire was that her children be healthy and good. So each week, with Maureen in tow, she made her way to Mission Church to say a novena to Mary.

Maureen had a good rapport with her mother, a courageous woman who had fled crushing poverty in Ireland, thrown out an alcoholic husband, and worked three jobs to support her brood. Even though Helen was strict and sometimes critical, Maureen was content to live at home and work as a hair stylist at the Village Beauty Shop in Roslindale Square, where every woman who came in wanted to look like glamorous Jackie Kennedy.

Maureen had been a decent student. When she graduated from the all-girls Holy Trinity High School in Roxbury, she was offered scholarships to Mount St. Vincent's and Our Lady of the Elms colleges. But she turned them down and went to hairdressing school so she could earn money.

She had no regrets. Styling hair was fun and creative, and she was able to take occasional classes in government and political science at Boston State and Boston College, the university started by Jesuit priests for the city's Irish Catholic immigrants. The classes fed an interest in politics that had begun when Maureen was a kid leafletting for Democrats whom her brother, Francis Hoey, was trying to get elected. Maureen knew she had arrived when, after a few years, Francis finally decided she was seasoned enough to tag along with him to the G&G deli on Blue Hill Avenue in Dorchester, where all the politicos went on the night before Election Day.

With five older brothers and a mother guarding her honor, Maureen wasn't allowed out unless someone in the family met her date. On this particular night, her brother Freddy Hoey had agreed to stick around until eight o'clock to greet Joe Dunn, Hennie's youngest brother. But when Maureen got a call from Joe, asking her to meet him at the T because his car wasn't working, she broke the rules. Freddy had his own plans. After he left, Maureen slipped on her coat, shut the front door of the triple decker behind her and headed down hilly St. Rose Street in Jamaica Plain to Saul's drug store to catch the Arborway trolley to Park Street.

Joe Dunn, meanwhile, was having his own problems. They started with meat.

Earlier that day, Joe's father, Henry Dunn, had thrown him out of the house for telling his mother that Henry had bought the roast for Sunday dinner at Roxy's, a local grocery. Joe's mother, the proper Mary Conneely Dunn, preferred a butcher in the market district. She'd chewed Henry out and he'd taken it out on Joe, who left so fast after his father got mad that he forgot socks. He made it to a friend's house in the city to change, but there his green Pontiac had died, forcing him to take the T to meet his date, a friend of his sister.

Fortunately, Joe wasn't one to get discouraged easily. Fearless and optimistic, as a kid he had found work at Paragon Park testing the old wooden roller coaster by standing in the first seat, arms outstretched. He never lied or backed down, not even when one of his brothers pinned his arm behind his back during a fight, taunting him to give in. Joe got a broken arm instead.

Joe's one soft spot was reserved for Mamie, as his mother was known. They shared the view that what was right was right, and what wasn't right was best avoided. Joe's fun-loving side came from his father, a free spirit who worked as a steamfitter at the Boston Navy Yard. As a younger man on Nantasket Beach, Henry's powerful build earned him the moniker "Dynamite Dunn." On Sundays, he would delight the crowds by walking into the surf on his hands, much to his wife's consternation.

Now twenty, Joe was about to graduate from the Benjamin Franklin Institute of Technology, where he had studied electronics. But that wasn't what he wanted. Joe had decided to become a military pilot the day he saw his first air show at the South Weymouth Naval Air Station. Transfixed by the sight of planes looping and diving through the bright blue sky of southeastern Massachusetts, Joe vowed, "That's what I'm going to do." All that was left now was to lose ten pounds and get into shape so he would be accepted into preflight training.

At Park Street, Maureen paced along the platform. It had been a hard week. First, she had wanted to hear President Kennedy speak last Saturday at

Boston College's centennial ceremonies but had to work. Later, she'd read in the paper how he had charmed the crowd with humor about his accent.

"It is a great pleasure to come back to a city where my accent is considered normal, and where they pronounce the words the way they are spelled," he had joked.[1]

It was getting awfully late to be just heading out for the night, and Maureen was thinking that she should head home and catch *77 Sunset Strip* on television. But as she turned for the stairs that led outside to the street, she suddenly saw a guy in a dark overcoat running down the steps.

When he got closer, she noticed that he looked like a lot of other tough Irish kids from the city, except for a certain babyish softness about his features that was set off by his dark turtleneck. His skin was fair but his eyes were very dark, and his hair was a deep auburn. He wore tweed slacks, a white oxford shirt, and brown penny loafers. Maureen could see the lapel of a camel-colored jacket under his olive raincoat.

He walked right up to her.

"Maureen?" He grinned.

Maureen found the grin slightly annoying. You'd think he would apologize, considering how he had kept her waiting.

"Yeah."

"I figured you must be Maureen, since you've got the red coat."

"Look, let's just get this over with," Maureen told him. "I like your sister. I like your brother-in-law. But I've never waited for anybody before and I won't again."

Joe didn't flinch. He looked her up and down.

"Yeah, well. You don't exactly look like Elizabeth Taylor."

Maureen stared at him.

"Excuse me?"

"Kathi told me so much about you, I figured you'd look like Elizabeth Taylor."

Maureen was speechless. Hennie's daughter Kathi apparently had been talking her up.

Joe paused for a beat and turned toward the stairs.

"Come on, let's go."

Maureen followed him. This was turning into some night.

"OK," she said. "Where are we going?"

"To Hennie's. We're going to use her car."

Maureen followed Joe to the trolley to Dorchester's Fields Corner neighborhood, where they caught a bus that wound its way down Granite Avenue to Milton, where Hennie lived with her husband, Francis Kelly, and their five kids. Joe walked up the front steps and knocked, and his dark-haired, dark-eyed sister, a natural prankster, opened up, grinning. It was clear she was genuinely happy that Maureen and Joe had finally met but also amused by the image of proper Maureen pacing the subway, waiting for her cocky, happy-go-lucky brother.

Maureen walked in and her eyes were immediately drawn to Mamie, who recently had been diagnosed with Hodgkin's disease and was resting under an afghan on her daughter's couch. The doctors were fairly optimistic, saying she could live for many years. Mamie knew Maureen, who had babysat for Hennie a few times, and she pounced as soon as Joe and his sister slipped into the kitchen.

"So what do you think of my Joseph?" she asked.

"He seems very nice, Mamie," was all Maureen could think to say.

But before Mamie could press for details, Hennie walked back in, her brother trailing her. "Why don't you guys go over to the Arbiter Club?" she suggested. The Jamaica Plain club was a popular local spot, and Hennie's husband, a musician, was playing there in the Kelly Brothers Band.

"You love to dance, Maureen. And Joe loves to dance."

"That would be good," Maureen said, giving Joe a quick glance. She was relieved to have a plan. They could listen to music for an hour or so, and then Joe could take her back home, which wasn't far from the club.

"Let's go," Joe said. He grabbed the keys from Hennie, walked over to kiss his mother goodbye, and the two of them headed out.

As they drove, a landmark caught Joe's eye.

"Boy, many's the Wednesday night I spent in that place," Joe said, as much to himself as to Maureen.

Maureen sprang to attention. "What?"

"Yeah, Mission Church. My mother has a tremendous faith in the Mother of Perpetual Help," he said.

"You gotta be kidding me," Maureen said. "I went with my mother every week to the novena."

It was an odd coincidence, being in the same church on the same day all those years, Maureen thought as Joe pulled Hennie's sedan up in front of the club. As she climbed out, Maureen could hear music and laughter coming from inside. She started to relax. Any guy who prayed the weekly novena with his mother couldn't be all bad.

The club was hot and smoky, and Joe got a beer for himself and a soda for Maureen, who'd never acquired a taste for alcohol. A few minutes passed in awkward silence. Then Joe spoke up.

"So would you like to dance?" he asked.

"Sure," said Maureen.

The band cranked up some rock 'n' roll, and Maureen and Joe started dancing, twisting and turning their arms and legs in sync with the music and one another. One song followed another, and Maureen was about to say she was ready for a break when the band leader announced a contest for the twist. They took off, twisting low to the ground and back up again. When it was over, they had won a $5 prize.

By the time Joe and Maureen left the club, it was after 1 A.M., and Joe had a few hours to kill before heading to the *Boston Herald,* where he made extra money delivering the weekend editions. They were eating breakfast in a diner near the Franklin Park Zoo when Maureen, sipping her tea, caught sight of a clock on the wall.

"Oh my God," she said. "It's 2:30."

"So what?" said Joe. "You're gonna turn into a pumpkin or something?"

"You don't know my mother," Maureen said. "She will be distraught. I've got to go home. Now."

Outside in the damp, early morning air, Maureen hurriedly got into Joe's car. She turned her head to speak when Joe leaned toward her, grabbed her face with both his hands and pulled her close. Their lips brushed, and then they kissed more deeply. Maureen could barely breathe, and the pounding in her chest and head made it hard to hear.

When they pulled up to her house, Maureen knew Joe better leave fast if she ever wanted to see him again. "I don't even want you to walk me up the stairs," she whispered. "I wouldn't want you to meet my mother this way."

As Joe pulled away, Maureen climbed the steps to the front door. She was almost at the top when the lights in her family's flat came on. She froze as the door swung open.

"Jesus, Maureen, where have you been?" Freddy was in the doorway.

"The time got away, Fred."

"Maureen, you are lucky she didn't have Hennie's number."

Maureen walked in. Helen, arms crossed, was standing directly in front of her in a bathrobe.

"I hope that date was worth it, Maureen," she said. "Because you won't be leavin' the house for the next month."

"Look, Ma, I'm sorry, but," Maureen spluttered.

"I don't want to hear a word about it. That's it, Maureen. I'm going to tell you right now, if you want to live in this house, cancel everything for the next month," Helen scolded her. "It's three o'clock in the morning. What do you think of yourself?"

The weeks passed slowly, and when Maureen saw Joe next he was standing in her house in a white dinner jacket. She had on a yellow gown, and a sparkly tiara rested on top of her silky smooth pageboy. It was prom night at Joe's college, and Maureen had happily agreed to go even though her mother wasn't crazy about letting her out again with someone who had kept her so late the first time.

But Maureen was crazy about Joe. Ever since that first date she had thought of him as the guy she wanted to marry.

About a month after they had met, the intensity of Maureen's feelings caught her off guard. Climbing into Joe's Pontiac with a bag of paper plates, napkins, and other Memorial Day picnic supplies she had picked up for her mother, Maureen looked over at Joe, who was grinning in the driver's seat.

"Oh my God, I love him," she thought. The next thing she knew, she blurted out, "Joe, I love you."

Joe was silent for what seemed like forever. Then he turned to Maureen and said, "Please know that I care a lot about you and I care so much about you that I'm not going to say 'I love you' because I'm not sure yet. But I care more about you than anyone I've ever dated."

Maureen thought she would throw up.

Two weeks later, Maureen met Joe at Hennie's for a night of babysitting. They hadn't seen each other much lately because Joe was studying for his final exams. On the way over, Maureen thought this might be the last night she would ever see him. She was falling more in love with him all the time, and if he wasn't feeling the same way, she wanted to break it off before it got too painful.

Hennie and Fran's rambunctious kids adored their Uncle Joe, who would play and wrestle with them for hours. When the kids finally went to sleep, Maureen collapsed on the couch.

"I don't know if I could handle this all the time," she said.

"But you want a lot of kids?" Joe asked.

"Oh yeah, I do," she said.

"Me too," he responded.

"That's good," Maureen said.

"You hope the person you're going to be with makes the same decisions," Joe continued.

Maureen wasn't ready for the words that followed.

"Because today I decided that I love you."

"You did?" Maureen said, stunned.

Joe cupped her face and kissed her.

"I love you," he said.

Joe and Maureen were together from then on. When summer came, they economized so Joe could save money and repay Mamie the $800 he owed her for tuition. They took walks along the Charles River, split the $1.19 all-you-can eat special at Howard Johnson's and hung out on the South Shore, where the Dunns had moved when Joe was a teenager.

The family had been living in Fields Corner when Henry spotted a house on Spectacle Island in Boston Harbor, where the city dumped garbage. Henry paid $10 for the house and had his sons and son-in-law take it apart, move the pieces by barge and reassemble it in Hull, where they had spent summers. Somehow, they had gotten all the plumbing and wiring to work, and soon after the Dunns moved to Hull year-round.

The Hull house was lively and chaotic, as Maureen discovered. Mamie's brothers, who like her had emigrated from Inisheer, one of the Aran Islands off Ireland's western coast, were often there, as were Joe's brothers, Jackie and Paul Dunn, and their families. On Saturday nights, Joe sometimes would drop Maureen off after a date and head back into the city to deliver the papers. Maureen would sleep in the extra twin bed in Mamie's room. On Sunday morning, she, Joe, and Mamie would go to Mass.

When they weren't together, Joe went running to get into shape for the Navy, and Maureen continued to work at the beauty shop, where for $37 a week plus tips she shaped her customers' hair into flips, pageboys, and bouffants.

Caught up in their romance, neither Joe nor Maureen paid much attention to the worsening news out of Vietnam, where President Eisenhower had made a commitment in the 1950s to help South Vietnam maintain its autonomy from the communist North.[2]

In the summer of 1963, while Joe and Maureen were falling in love, Vietnam's deepening political turmoil burst into public view when a Buddhist monk burned himself alive in the streets of Saigon. The suicide, widely publicized, horrified the West.

Kennedy, who was following through on Eisenhower's pledge, had thousands of U.S. advisers in Vietnam, but events were overtaking his strategy of propping up South Vietnam under the autocratic and repressive leadership of President Ngo Dinh Diem. The Buddhist protests had revealed the extent of the opposition to Diem, which reached a climax when his military turned on him. On November 3, Diem and his brother and closest adviser, Ngo Dinh Nhu, were murdered in a coup.

About three weeks later, Maureen was washing a woman's hair at the beauty shop when the barber next door ran in.

"Did you hear?" he shouted. "The president was shot."

Maureen looked up, shocked. Another beautician turned on the radio, and Maureen pulled her customer's head out of the sink and began rolling it up in big curlers as everyone stopped talking and listened closely to the announcer. More women came in, but Maureen told them the rest of the day's appointments were cancelled. She didn't care if she got fired, she just wanted to go home.

Just as Maureen was finishing up her work, the radio announcer broke in with the heart-stopping bulletin that Kennedy was dead. Maureen sat down in disbelief as images flashed through her mind.

The first time she had seen him, she was a girl in the Sacred Heart school color guard, and he was a Boston congressman marching just ahead of her with Jackie in South Boston's St. Patrick's Day parade. She remembered how he'd shaken her hand while they were lining up. In 1960, she had campaigned for Kennedy with her brother Francis, the Democratic activist, passing out flyers and going to rallies at the Boston Garden and State House.

She had even voted for the guy before turning twenty-one, the legal voting age. At the polling place, Maureen had passed herself off as Barbara Hoey, a sister-in-law who lived on the same street and was in the hospital after having a baby. Maureen didn't think of it as breaking the law. She figured she was just voting in the place of a Kennedy supporter who couldn't get to the polls herself.

Maureen left the shop as fast as she could and took the usual bus to the Forest Hills T station near her home. The bus driver seemed distressed and spacey, and the ride very long. Cars were stopped in the road, and people were rolling down their windows and yelling, "Did you hear? The president's dead."

In the streets, folks milled about, talking and crying. It was as if no one knew what to do. Any shop with a TV drew a crowd, as people crammed together in doorways and craned their necks to catch a glimpse of the news. In one TV repair shop in Roslindale Square, passersby ran in and convinced the owner to find a working set and turn it on so they could watch.

Shortly after Maureen arrived home, her brothers, sisters, and mother began trickling in from their own jobs. They embraced one another and sat in shocked silence and sorrow around the 19-inch black-and-white console television. Helen went into her bedroom to kneel and pray for Kennedy's family. That was her habit whenever a friend died. Then she went into the kitchen and started making tea and roast beef sandwiches, as if she were hosting a wake for one of her own sons.

Maureen found much the same scene down at Joe's house over the weekend. A grief-stricken Mamie, who remembered horrible tales of Irish teachers being scalped by the English back on Inisheer, never thought she would see such a tragedy in America. Like Helen, she laid out food while Henry poured shots of whiskey.

Maureen knew that, after the assassination, she would never feel quite the same. A 1950s kid who had led a carefree, sheltered life in her tightly woven cocoon of family and friends, her only worries were how the Red Sox were doing and how she was going to get 25 cents together for a movie and popcorn at the Rialto.

There were serious times, like when Maureen's brothers left home to fight in World War II and Korea. But young and optimistic, she knew they would be OK. And a year before, the family had mourned a close friend, Jackie Gallagher, a Boston police officer who had been shot to death in a robbery. Still, this felt different. Kennedy had been one of them, and someone had hated him enough to kill him. If that could happen, no one would ever be invincible again.

Less than two months later, Maureen was driving Joe to catch his flight to Pensacola, Florida, where he was to report for preflight training. Joe had been thrilled by his acceptance, even though he wasn't looking forward to being away from Maureen, whom he truly loved. As for Maureen, she was just grateful that she couldn't see too well out of the windshield as she maneuvered the car through the snowy roads toward Boston's Logan Airport. It kept her mind off Joe's departure.

They had gotten a reprieve the day before when Joe's flight was cancelled due to bad weather. Not that it was much fun. Most of the day was spent at the hospital with Mamie, who had fallen off the front steps of her house into a snow bank, hurting her shoulder. Maureen knew she wouldn't get a second break, but she still couldn't fathom daily life without Joe. She could still picture them sitting by the Christmas tree weeks before, exchanging gifts. She had bought him a nice sports coat from Remick's in Quincy, and he had given her a beautiful dresser set. But she couldn't ask him to stay either. Joe would be miserable if he abandoned his dream, and then what kind of future would they have?

Joe turned to Maureen at the gate to try to lift her spirits. He was as sure of her as he was of the Navy, and he didn't want her to be too sad.

"I may be leaving, but I'm leaving my heart with you," he said, pausing for a moment before he turned and walked down the jetway, where he disappeared from view.

Down in Florida, Joe found that he couldn't spend a lot time worrying about Maureen's happiness, his mother's health, President Johnson's policy in Vietnam, or much else. He was just trying to survive.

On the flight down, he had struck up a conversation with a guy who had found out the hard way that he wasn't cut out for naval aviation. The guy had just gotten out of the hospital after suffering a breakdown due to the rigors of training.[3]

It didn't take Joe long to understand how such a thing could occur. His days were programmed from 5:30 A.M. until 10 P.M. without so much as an extra minute to smoke a cigarette. Even though he was a former lifeguard, he found the swimming practices grueling, especially when they were followed by hours of drills with heavy M-1, 30-caliber rifles. There were classes to master in naval orientation, meteorology, and weapons. Meals were eaten in ten minutes or less. Then there were the rules. Endless rules and regulations.[4]

Joe asked Maureen to pray for him. He wanted to make it so badly.[5]

"So you see they are trying to make us crack and they will make some of us crack," Joe wrote to Maureen less than two weeks into the program.

"Unless I shape up more than I have wich [sic] is quite a bit I'll probably crack," he wrote. "Listen to this. When you lock your locks your combination always has to be left on 3. All shoes in the closet have to be laced up at the top and a bow tucked inside. You put your razor away and take the blade out of it. Thousands upon thousands of little details. Honey, you wouldn't believe the way I have had to change my ways. I hope it's for good."[6]

Joe managed to write to Maureen, but just barely. Late at night, before falling asleep, he would lie on the floor and quickly scrawl a few lines. One night, he heard an officer approaching and leapt into his bunk so fast that he left a letter on the floor. The officer walked right over it, leaving a footprint on the back of the sheet. "Don't mind the foot prints honey," he told Maureen. "He almost caught me."[7]

As for mailing the contraband correspondence, Joe and his buddies were clever. While marching to breakfast at 5 A.M., they passed their letters down the line. When they came to a halt at the mess hall, the last guy in line was always standing next to the mailbox. He would drop them in when the officer in charge wasn't looking.[8]

Maureen, meanwhile, wrote to Joe every day and lived for his replies. They ran up huge telephone bills and, in February, got lucky when Joe caught a free ride home for the weekend on a military plane headed to South Weymouth. Most nights, though, Maureen had to make do with huddling under her bedroom pillow, hoping her mother wouldn't hear her chatter.

"Do you think I'm stupid?" Helen finally called out one night. "Put that thing down! Wasting all your money . . ."

There were the intense bouts of loneliness. They hit Maureen sometimes when she was alone, or when she spotted a happy couple or young family.

". . . last night when it quieted down and I was watching TV & everyone else was asleep, Freddy was out; I was thinking of you & I started to cry for the want of you near me," Maureen wrote in one of her letters to Joe in March. "Do you think this will ever get better? This tremendous lost and lonely feeling I have quite frequently? After almost 2 months I don't think so; but I keep praying for courage to face the following months & years to come."[9]

Such moods didn't dissuade Maureen from wanting a life with Joe, even though she realized that there would be more difficult separations ahead if Joe stayed in the military. The two weren't yet engaged, but neither had any doubts that they would be together, so Maureen began squirreling money away for their future.

"Went to the bank, we now have $30 in savings account, $6 in X-mas club, $10 in bank at home for trip to Florida," Maureen told Joe about a month into his preflight program. "So, honey, we're worth about $50. Wow, well it's a start."[10]

In July, it became official. Joe didn't have a ring, but he proposed on a sunny afternoon in Boston's Public Garden as they rode the Swan Boats. Excitedly, Maureen turned to their fellow passengers and announced, "He just asked me to marry him!" Everyone applauded.

Later that day, strolling along the Charles River paths where they had courted a year earlier, Joe carved their initials into a giant shade tree. A self-timing camera captured a passionate kiss that sealed their pledge to one another.

Now facing life as a military wife, Maureen started to pay more attention to Navy news, reading magazine articles about jets and aircraft carriers. And Joe, who had finished preflight and was continuing to train in Milton, Florida, regaled her with tales of daredevil exploits in the clouds. It was all terribly exciting to Joe, but it scared the hell out of Maureen. Vietnam, when she caught wind of the conflict on the evening news, seemed so remote from her own life that she didn't give it a second thought. But the vision of Joe guiding a rapidly descending plane onto a slippery landing deck in the middle of a big, dark ocean was another story. It made her so nervous that she told Joe to never tell her when he would be making a carrier landing.

Joe refused to listen. Exasperated, he told Maureen that she had the "worst possible outlook to have." His chosen field was risky, and he didn't want her fear to escalate until she either left him or forced him to quit. Worse, she might cause him to lose confidence.[11]

". . . if it did affect you this way and you got me to be nervous of it, it would probably be my downfall," he said. It was time for Maureen to face reality.[12]

"I hope you realize that it is impossible to hide from the truth (as it always is), and that you will proceed to get a thorough knowledge of what is involved in Navy flying," Joe told her. "I will not marry you until I'm confident that you realize what is involved and what you can expect in the future. I must know that you can take whatever fate brings our way in stride."[13]

But Joe wasn't thinking about war. He thought flying, in fact, wasn't nearly as dangerous as some books made it out to be because modern planes were safer than older models. Plus, as he told Maureen, "There isn't a war on."[14]

But on that very day—August 7, 1964—the United States was set on a course of military involvement in Vietnam from which there would be no turning back.

While Joe composed his letter, Congress passed a resolution giving President Johnson sweeping authority to do whatever he thought necessary to fight communism in South Vietnam.[15] Months before, McNamara had told Johnson that the situation had worsened considerably, with the Viet Cong in control of forty percent of the countryside in the South. In some areas, the percentage was much higher.[16] After reports of attacks on the USS *Maddox* by North Vietnamese patrol boats, the Gulf of Tonkin resolution passed Congress with just two dissenting votes.

As Johnson weighed his options, Maureen delved into the details of wedding planning. The ceremony would be in the fall of 1965 in her home church, St. Thomas Aquinas, a landmark in the historically Irish St. Rose Street neighborhood. After the ceremony, there would be dinner and dancing to Fran Kelly's Kelly Brothers Band at the Morrissette American Legion Post in Quincy. As she made plans, Maureen's thoughts often turned to family, especially to her mother and Joe's.

Helen, who had clashed with Joe from the start and was accustomed to having Maureen around, would have a big adjustment. It would be easier for Mamie. Although she idolized Joe, her youngest child, she had warmed to Maureen early on. But Mamie was in such poor health that Maureen didn't know if she would live to see the wedding.

The answer came a few months later. In November, Mamie's health took a turn for the worse, and Joe flew home on emergency leave. Hennie's husband Fran picked him up at the airport and took him straight to Dorchester's Carney Hospital, where Maureen met them.

Maureen stood in the doorway, watching as Joe walked over to the hospital bed. The fluorescent lighting gave the room an eerie glow, and it was very quiet. Joe looked down at his mother, a once-forceful woman so weakened by illness that she could scarcely draw breath. Then he gently climbed into the bed next to her and lay down, taking care not to disturb any tubes or equipment. In his full dress blues, Joe tenderly gathered up his mother's frail weight in his arms and held her close.

Mamie had been in and out of consciousness for days. But she knew Joe was there and put her hands up to the sides of his face.

"I'm here, Mamie. I'm here," Joe said, his tears running through her fingers.

"Joseph, my manee," she said, using an old Irish endearment for a boy. "My Joseph, my manee . . ."

From the doorway, Maureen could see that Joe remained deeply connected to his family, despite his career drive. No matter where the Navy took him, that would never change. Maureen felt comforted. Her own father had been absent in her life, and she wanted a husband she could count on.

Mamie died soon after Joe's visit and was buried high on a hill in Hull overlooking the ocean. She had always loved the spot because it reminded her of her long-ago home on the Aran Islands. And though Mamie had never been a drinker, Joe and his brother Jackie didn't think it right to let her go without a send off. The night she died, they hit every pub in Dorchester, raising glasses to their mother's memory.

In the months that followed, Joe focused on learning to fly propeller airplanes and on his coming marriage. He missed Maureen terribly and wished she could greet him after a long, stressful day. But the flying was going well. With every new accomplishment, Joe gained confidence and his competitive nature flourished. Even after he and an instructor were poisoned by exhaust-generated carbon monoxide during one flight, and were so groggy and dizzy that they could barely land the plane, he groused about being grounded until he was sufficiently recovered.[17]

"Lewis my roommate is pulling ahead of me," he complained. "That really ticks me off because I was 2 hops ahead of him and we started form at the same time. He is supposed to fly a four plane formation hop from here to Jacksonville Saturday and RON (remain over nite) and come back Sunday. It kills me to think that it should be me instead of him."[18]

By the spring of 1965, as Joe trained and dreamed of a long, loving life with Maureen, Vietnam was steeped in violence and turmoil. The insurgency had intensified to the point that Viet Cong were brazenly attacking U.S. interests, spurring Johnson and his aides to make critical decisions to escalate U.S. involvement. By the year's end, the number of U.S. troops in Vietnam would approach two hundred thousand.

As Joe approached the end of his training, he grew more aware of the mounting conflict in Southeast Asia but didn't have a sense that it would affect him personally. He had more immediate concerns, such as completing his flight requirements so he could make it home in time for his wedding. He hoped to finish by Labor Day. Then again, "it should start raining down here soon which might slow things down. There's a possibility we might have to move up the wedding date. It'll be awhile before we know anything though."[19]

As it turned out, Joe earned his wings in Corpus Christi, Texas, where he'd trained since January, just two weeks before his wedding. Maureen didn't go to the ceremony. She thought Henry should have the honor of pinning Joe's uniform. Knowing that Henry worked in the Boston Navy Yard, and had had two older sons enlist, she knew how much it would mean to him to have an officer—an aviator, no less—in the family.

Joe could hardly believe that he'd made it. He'd had some tough days over his nineteen months of training, like the time last month when he had flown a night hop, gotten up at 5:30 A.M. for four hours of ground school, flown an afternoon hop, had a quick supper, and then flew again. He was so tired that night he fell asleep writing to Maureen.[20]

The separation from Maureen was also wearing Joe down. "I'm just sick and tired of these incomplete days," he wrote a month before their wedding. "No matter how good a day I have it's not half good enough because I don't have you. I wonder if you really realize how much I need and want you. I can't think of anything I want more or have ever in my life wanted more than I want you. I wake up mornings missing you and wanting you and go to sleep at night wishing oh so bad that you would be beside me."[21]

Now things were looking up. He and Maureen would be married, and he had received decent orders to report for duty as a flight instructor in propeller aircraft.

Joe wondered if many of the guys from flight school would end up in

Vietnam. The war was heating up, and President Johnson seemed hell-bent on helping South Vietnam fight communism. When Joe thought about it, he figured it was a worthy enough goal, helping people secure the right to live as they pleased. But he had no particular plans to play a role. As he and his father toasted the future in the officer's club, his new wings pinned to his chest, Vietnam seemed very far away.

"Things have been looking bad as far as Vietnam is concerned lately," he'd told Maureen six weeks earlier. "The only difference (from Korea) is I think we're better prepared to fight that type of war now. The U.S. military learned a lot from that war. Actually, we're fighting the same people all over again just in a different country. I don't think it will affect you and I in any way in the near future."[22]

Nearly two months later, Maureen stood in front of her bedroom mirror, checking her pink lipstick one last time. Her dazzling white gown had an empire waist and satin skirt that flared out just slightly. Its long sleeves and bodice were of white lace, and the single strand of pearls around her neck grazed the edge of a scalloped neckline. There was a delicate lace cap on her head, and behind it a stiff veil of white tulle hung to the middle of her back.

It was September 18, 1965. Maureen and Joe would be married in just a few hours. It had taken so much maneuvering to get to this point, she could hardly believe it was really going to happen.

Three times the wedding date had to be changed to accommodate Joe's schedule. When Maureen thought it was going to be on a Friday, she had sought a special dispensation from the Cardinal. She wanted to serve roast beef and mashed potatoes at her reception, and Catholics were banned from eating meat on Fridays. Then the wedding was moved to Saturday, only that meant that they couldn't use the main church because the Host was being venerated all weekend on the altar, so the wedding would have to be in the church basement. Maureen kicked up a fuss, so the priests scheduled a special procession to move the Host downstairs to the lower chapel an hour before the wedding so Maureen and Joe could be married in the grandeur of the main church with its high, painted ceilings and magnificent pipe organ.

Then there was the question of Helen.

Maureen first realized she was in big trouble when she walked into her house the day before her wedding and saw her mother sitting in a rocking chair in the kitchen, arms crossed, while Anna Hoey, her oldest sister who also lived home, ironed Maureen's bridal veil.

Maureen had spent much of the night before and that morning with Joe, who had just flown in and needed briefing on all the ceremonial details.

"I can't believe you're ironing that for her," Helen said loudly to Anna as soon as Maureen was within earshot. "She's out all night and day, she can do it herself."

Maureen could tell Helen was genuinely annoyed, so she tried to smooth things over.

"Ma, do we need to go up to Hanlon's and get your shoes?"

"Why would I be needing shoes for something I'm not attending?" Helen retorted. "Why would I want to go to a wedding for someone you've been out all night and day with?"

Maureen sighed. She'd seen this stubborn, difficult mood before. She called her sister Agnes "Aggie" Gallagher, a kindly mother of eight who reassured her that their mother would come around. Maureen was worried. But the next day, she woke up resigned and philosophical.

"I'm getting married at six," she told Anna. "If she's there, she's there. There's nothing more I can do." That afternoon, when Maureen got back from helping her florist twirl white flowers and green ivy around the huge candles she wanted along the center aisle of the church, her mother was waiting for her at the front door.

"I have to go to Hanlon's and get my shoes," she said.

As Maureen stood in the back of the church, surrounded by eight brides-maids and junior bridesmaids in royal blue gowns and hair bows, holding baskets of daisies and baby's-breath, it seemed as if nothing else possibly could stand in the wedding's way. Most of the guests were seated, and Maureen could see a gaggle of her mother's old Irish lady friends clustered together toward the back.

Just then, Helen arrived, looking elegant in a blue dress and matching pillbox hat. Her dark hair was peppered with gray, and she used a cane to steady herself after hip surgery and a subsequent infection left her with a limp.

"Ma, you can go down with Franny," Maureen whispered as Hennie's husband extended his arm to escort Helen to her seat at the front of the church.

"I'm going down the aisle with my sons," Helen said.

Maureen Hoey and Joseph P. Dunn were married on September 18, 1965, at St. Thomas Aquinas church in Boston's Jamaica Plain neighborhood. (Photo courtesy of Maureen Dunn)

"Ma, you're going down the aisle with the ushers," Maureen said.

"No, I'm not," she said.

But before Maureen could protest again, the church lights went out and the altar boys began lighting the candles along the center aisle. Maureen had been adamant about walking down the aisle in candlelight.

"What in the name of God? Are the lights out?" Helen asked. "Didn't they pay the bills?"

"No Ma, I'm going to have the candles on the altar and the acolyte candles down the aisle . . ." Maureen started to explain.

"Look at Mrs. Kelly," Helen said, noticing a friend who had come to see the ceremony. "How embarrassing that the light bill hasn't been paid so my daughter can get married."

Maureen, thinking fast, motioned to one of her nephews, John Gallagher, who was serving as an altar boy.

"Johnny, Ma wants you to light the lights. After you've finished lighting the candles, go back and flip the lights on."

"That's right John," Helen said.

But as soon as Helen looked away, Maureen tugged on her nephew's arm.

"Johnny, when she's halfway down the aisle, cut the lights off," she whispered.

"OK."

Minutes later, as Maureen's attendants were straightening her gown and pulling her veil over her face, she heard the hymn that was to accompany her mother's entrance.

"Oh, thank God," she murmured.

Then she looked closer.

There was Helen walking down the aisle on her sons' arms. With the confusion over the lights, and so many people bustling around, Helen had managed to get two of her sons to the back of the church, where they waited behind the refectory doors until it was time to escort her in.

But Maureen had the last word. The lights cut out as soon as Helen got near her seat, but by then it was too late to complain. As Mendelssohn's *Wedding March* played, and with blazing candles lighting the way, Maureen walked slowly toward the altar where she could just make out the figure of Joe waiting for her in his crisp white uniform next to his best friend from high school, Eddie Slavin. Even in the darkened church, Maureen could see the gleam of Joe's gold wings.

✳✳✳ **2** ✳✳✳

War

Joe scanned the murky bluish green water off South Vietnam's craggy coast from the window of his A-1 Douglas Skyraider but didn't see anything suspicious, just a few fishing sampans out for the day's catch. The beach seemed to stretch on forever, a skinny, dull brown strip of sand and dirt along the water's edge. Inland, the terrain quickly changed into a deep green patchwork of grassy plains, forested hills, and bamboo groves.

It was the first time Joe had ever done "coastal VC-ing," as the guys in the squadron called the practice of flying up and down the coast looking for military targets. Anything that looked like an enemy outpost was a candidate for bombing.

On this particular day in August 1967, Joe and another pilot from his squadron, Lt. Cmdr. Rosario "Zip" Rausa, had spent hours flying up and down the coast at a couple of hundred feet without spotting so much as a questionable hut. They were about to turn back when Joe's eye caught something on a distant rise.

As the A-1s approached for a closer look, Joe saw the outline of what appeared to be a lookout tower with an antenna on top. Joe didn't know what it was but thought it could be some sort of surveillance post used by the National Liberation Front, the southern communist forces commonly known by the slang term "Viet Cong." Certainly, it was the most promising target they had seen all day. They decided to make a run on it.

The A-1s came in low off the water, flying in zigzag formation to evade the enemy fire that could erupt at any moment from directly below. Flying faster and faster, the A-1s climbed until they were nearly on top of the tower. Then they dove, unleashing a torrent of rockets and 20-millimeter gunfire that burst through the air. The tower exploded into flames as the A-1s quickly gained altitude and pulled away. Behind them, smoke billowed from the ruined tower into the treetops.

"What a feeling it is to pull away from a target like that and get out over the water where you know you're safe," Joe told Maureen. "It's really the biggest challenge I've ever faced in my life."[1]

Except when he was with Maureen, Joe was happiest when he was flying. It was the lure of flying the A-1 Skyraider propeller airplane that had brought him to Vietnam in the first place.

"That's flying a real plane," he had told Maureen.

As he flew over verdant countryside and wide expanses of ocean to his aircraft carrier *Coral Sea* stationed off the coast of Vietnam in the Gulf of Tonkin, Joe's thoughts often would turn to Maureen. He couldn't believe they had been married for nearly two years.

Their marriage had gotten off to an inauspicious start. Three days after the ceremony, they were awakened by an early morning telephone call to their dumpy motel room near the Dallas airport. A seat had opened up on the first flight out to Corpus Christi, and Joe had to get to the airport fast. He didn't have time to think. Unable to get out the night before due to bad weather, he was due back on base that morning. So he quickly packed a bag and took off, leaving Maureen crying in her peignoir. Twenty minutes later, the phone rang again.

"There's another seat," Joe said. "But you have got to be here in fifteen minutes. Just get in a taxi and get here!"

Maureen hung up and looked around. The walls were a shade of institutional neutral. The bedspread was garish and crumpled. The burnt-orange shag carpeting had been ground down by years of wear. There was no reason to stay and no time to waste. Dumping everything into two suitcases, Maureen threw on her trench coat, and left.

She made the flight, barely, and breathed a sigh of relief only when she was finally on board. Joe, seated toward the back, smiled when he saw her get on. But as she started to take off her coat, still looking back at him, she saw a startled and anxious look spread across his face. She looked around, wondering what could be wrong. Then she looked down, gulped, quickly wrapped her coat back around her and sat down. She smiled nervously at her seatmate. He nodded pleasantly. "I can't believe it," she thought. She had left so fast she had neglected to change out of her filmy white negligee.

And that wasn't all she had forgotten. In her rush, she had left the big blue bubble hair dryer she had lugged from home on the motel room floor, foiling her plan to earn a little money on the side by doing hairdressing. But Maureen was happy just to be on the plane, and she chalked up her losses. Anyway, she knew it wouldn't be the last time her own needs and aspirations came in second to Joe's duties.

The couple's time in Texas was brief, and soon they moved to Pensacola, Florida, where they had fun setting up their first home in a rented beach bungalow. Money was tight, so Joe threw a quilt over seats taken out of the middle row of their navy-and-gray Volkswagon bus to make a couch. They refinished an old metal bed and draped fishing nets filled with seashells across the den ceiling.

They quickly fell into a routine. Joe went to school in nearby Milton to become a flight instructor, and Maureen cleaned the house, cooked, ran errands, and read on the beach. When Joe took a Russian class at the University of Florida, Maureen signed up for a course in political science, her long-time interest. She also worked as a substitute teacher in the local public elementary schools. On Friday nights, they would head to the officer's club, where Joe would have a few drinks and Maureen would drive home. Sometimes, they would get all dressed up and crash the Navy weddings that were announced on base.

Disagreements were inevitable, but they weren't about lifestyle.

Much to the amazement of family and friends, who knew Maureen as an outspoken woman who valued education and political activism, she went along with Joe's desire that she be a traditional homemaker. Mamie had worked as a cook, and Joe wanted his own wife to stay at home with their children.

Maureen didn't mind becoming the family's chief "cookie baker," as she put it. Despite her spirited nature and outside interests, at her core she emulated her mother and two of her sisters who had large families. Maureen had always said she wanted ten kids, which wouldn't allow much time for outside work. She and Joe struck a deal. He would provide an income, do home repairs, and help discipline the kids. She would take care of the house and the kids and prepare meals. If there was time, she could earn extra money as a beautician.

Maureen accepted this separation of duties. When she and Joe did clash, it wasn't over his career or her housekeeping. It was a classic clash of wills between two headstrong people who, as the youngest in their respective families, were used to getting their own way.

One beautiful afternoon, shortly after they were married, Joe and a pregnant Maureen were cruising the sun-drenched streets of Pensacola in a borrowed Porsche, watching the palm trees blowing in the gentle breeze. The Porsche was a loaner from a friend who had borrowed their VW bus for a few days.

"I know how to drive this," said Maureen, who was supremely proud of her driving skills, as they neared their house.

Maureen had first learned to drive at twelve. Back then, she, her mother, and her unmarried siblings, including Anna, Aggie, James, Freddy, and Edward, lived upstairs in a house they called "the castle" in the Forest Hills section of Jamaica Plain, a residential neighborhood of two-family homes bound by Hyde Park Avenue and Forest Hills Cemetery. Downstairs lived Maureen's sister, Eleanor, and her husband, Eddie Sheldon, who would let Maureen back his black sedan into a nearby dead-end street. Maureen thought it was the greatest. When she noticed that her sister Aggie's beau, John Gallagher, had the exact same car as Eddie in yellow, she pestered him to let her drive too. By the time Maureen got her driver's license seven years later at nineteen, when Anna got the family's first car, she figured she already knew more about driving than most others on the road. So she wasn't about to let Joe get the better of her as he navigated the Porsche through the streets of Pensacola.

"Do you really?" said Joe, calling her bluff. "OK, why don't you give it a try?"

They switched seats, but when Maureen went to move the sports car into first gear, she found its standard transmission didn't handle like those of the cars she was used to.

The Porsche stalled over and over, but Maureen was too stubborn to let Joe resume driving.

"I'm walking home," he said finally, hopping out and leaving Maureen to deal with the car. When she couldn't get it moving after a couple more minutes, she left it in the street and followed Joe home on foot.

When Maureen arrived, Joe got so angry that she'd left the car that he locked her out of the house.

"Go back and get the car," he said, talking to her from the other side of a glass-paned front door.

"You go back and get it, it's your friend's car," she said.

"You're the one who left it there,"

"You better let me in," she said, pulling on the front door handle.

"Maureen, go back and get the car," Joe said as he turned away and walked back into the house.

Upset about the car and roiled with pregnancy hormones, Maureen raised her foot and kicked the door with all her might, shattering glass everywhere. Then she carefully stepped over the broken shards and went in, but Joe had already slipped out the back to retrieve the car.

Hours passed. When Joe called that night, he told her he was at the "O club," as the officer's club was called, and wouldn't be coming home. He was too angry. But he wanted her to know where he was in case something happened with the baby.

"I'm only doing this because you're pregnant," he said, referring to the call. "I'm going to stay here. That was a stupid thing to do. You endangered your life and our child's life."

Maureen knew she was wrong. She blamed not only her heightened emotional and hormonal state but the difficult adjustment she'd had to married life far from home.

The truth was, as much as Joe and Maureen loved each other, they hadn't known each other for very long before they had gotten married. They had been dating for just eight months when Joe left for the Navy. For nearly two years after that, there were only brief visits before their wedding. They had never had to compromise, except over inconsequential matters such as which movie to watch or where to eat. But after they were married, they had to read each other's moods and cope with the ups-and-downs of daily life. And Maureen was homesick. Joe had Navy friends and colleagues but Maureen felt isolated. Besides Joe, her entire world was her family and, except for a neighboring Navy wife who would go to the beach with her, she had made no new friends.

Gradually, Maureen faced the fact that her life had to consist of more than waiting for Joe to come home from work and wondering what her sisters were doing a thousand miles up the coast. The days of living within spitting distance of hordes of relatives were over. If she didn't adapt, she would have one lonely life as a military spouse.

So as time passed, and Joe and Maureen learned to live together, Maureen reached out. They went to parties, picnics, and potlucks organized by

Joe's squadron, and Maureen became friendly with other Navy wives. They went to the beach and water skiing on the Blackwater River. While Maureen still missed her family, she began finding pleasure in her new life.

Joe, meanwhile, was getting acquainted with what was at stake in Vietnam, where President Johnson appeared utterly committed to staying the course.

"Tonight the cup of peril is full in Vietnam," Johnson told the nation in his 1966 State of the Union address. "We will stay until aggression has stopped. We will stay because a just nation cannot leave to the cruelties of its enemies a people who have staked their lives and independence on America's solemn pledge—a pledge which has grown through the commitments of three American presidents."[2]

After Joe became an instructor and joined the VT-3 training squadron at Whiting Field in Milton, Florida, in 1966, he and Maureen relocated from Pensacola. While Maureen painted the nursery walls yellow, borrowed a small crib, and bought a Hedstrom black-watch plaid stroller for the baby due in July, Joe trained pilots for the Navy and Marines—and for South Vietnam.

One of Joe's jobs was to teach South Vietnamese Air Force pilots how to fly the T-28, a propeller training plane known as the Trojan that had been produced in 1949 by North American Aviation, Inc., for the Air Force. After the design proved successful, the Navy ordered its own, and the aircraft went on to see action in Southeast Asia and North Africa.[3]

Teaching South Vietnamese students gave the war a personal dimension that it previously had lacked for Joe.

The cadets impressed him. Even with limited English, their commitment was apparent. Some of the other pilots on base saw the Vietnamese and, allies or not, blamed them for American deaths in Vietnam. Maureen, hearing Joe talk about such animosity, wondered if any of the cadets were being targeted unfairly as communist infiltrators.

Joe didn't see troublemakers or communists. He saw well-educated men who had left their families thousands of miles away in a war zone to receive specialized training so they could go back and fight communism. They were men with everything at stake.

"You know, these people are being persecuted and being denied their rights," he told Maureen one night after dinner. "Every man is free, is independent, has the right to make his own decisions. For someone to say, 'You can't do this and you can't do that,' it's wrong."

One day, Joe even brought two of the cadets home for coffee. They seemed uncomfortable off the base, and Maureen wasn't sure how to put them at ease, but it didn't much matter in the end. They seemed to appreciate the gesture, and Maureen hoped the visit would help them trust Joe.

Such episodes raised the couple's awareness of the escalating war, but Joe still didn't see a role for himself. As he said when he watched an evening news report from Vietnam, "It'll be over before I get there." They would be in Florida three years, he reckoned, and the war had already been going on for two.

So Maureen put aside thoughts of the war and went about her daily routine until 6 A.M., July 4, 1966, when she woke with abdominal pain. Unsure of what to do, she did laundry. Then she woke up Joe.

"I'm starting to get cramps," she said.

"How close are they?" he asked.

"They're close," she said. She actually had no idea how close they were. She hadn't bothered to time them. But they felt close enough.

"When they get really close, call me," Joe said, turning over. "I want to be wide awake and good for the day, so I'm going back to sleep."

Maureen hung the wash. The pain got worse.

"Joe, we've got to go."

As it turned out, they had time to spare. Maureen's labor slowed after she got to the hospital, and it wasn't until twelve hours later that she and Joe, who donned scrubs and a surgical mask, went into the delivery room.

"Do you see what we're doing?" Joe asked. "We're giving birth to another human being."

"No, Joe," Maureen said, gasping in between contractions. "WE are not giving birth. I'm giving birth."

Joseph Patrick Dunn II was born at 11:20 P.M. on the fourth of July. Maureen and Joe had never wanted a "Joe Jr." in the house, thinking it would rob the child of his own identity. Their son would be called "Joe-D'."

For the next few months, Maureen and Joe were preoccupied with baby bottles, diaper changes, and crying jags. Then in the fall of 1966, Joe came home from work one day with news.

"I'm going to Vietnam," he said.

"What?" Maureen asked. She wondered if she'd heard him right.

"Yeah, I'm going to go fly the A-1. There are only fourteen guys left that are going to fly the A-1 and I'm going to be one of them."

Maureen couldn't believe it. Joe had said many times that he wouldn't be going to Vietnam. Even now that he had volunteered, he thought it possible that the war could end before he ever got out of northern California, where his A-1 training was to start in January 1967 at Lemoore Naval Air Station.

What Maureen couldn't know, and what Joe may not always have realized, was how badly he wanted to fly one of the last, great propeller planes of the twentieth century before it was retired.

Joe knew that jets, fast and glamorous, were the future. But he idealized propeller planes, which had been flown by the great World War I and II aces. Jets couldn't match props for history or sheer challenge.

"When you fly a prop plane, you fly the plane," Joe would say. "When you fly a jet, the jet flies you."

When Joe heard that the Skyraider was going to be flown for the last time in Vietnam before being given to the Vietnamese National Air Force, he couldn't resist. He told his superiors that he was ready to volunteer for duty if another A-1 pilot was needed.

"I want to fly that," Joe responded once Maureen was able to think clearly enough to ask him why on earth he had volunteered when he had her and a small child at home.

It was a simple reason, deserving of a simple reply.

"That's nice," Maureen said. She couldn't think of one other thing to say. Setting the dinner table with her white plates trimmed with blue, Maureen thought about trying to change Joe's mind. But it was futile. Joe had always been single-minded when he set his sights on something, and this was no different. She turned her thoughts to packing for California.

Joe had six months to master the "Spad," one of the A-1's many nicknames, and he worked hard at it. On weekends, he and Maureen would go sailing under the Golden Gate Bridge in a mahogany sailboat he had won in a card game back in Florida. With a small baby to care for, Maureen had little time to worry or be lonely. Whenever she thought about the dangers of flying military planes over enemy territory, she pushed the thoughts away and focused on immediate tasks, such as how she would cope as a single parent after Joe shipped out.

Maureen didn't know a soul in California and had no idea where she and Joe would be stationed next. Then one day, when she went to buy groceries at the military commissary, she noticed two grim-looking officials knocking on the front door of a house on base. She imagined them delivering the worst possible news about someone else's husband and knew she had to get out of there. It was depressing.

"This is horrible," she told Joe. As long as he wasn't going to be in California, she really didn't want to stay there.

"There's no one out here," she said. "None of my family is here."

"Why don't you go home?" he suggested. Helen hadn't been feeling all that well, and it would be important for Maureen to have family support if he was going to war.

"The only thing is, you're going to need the car back there," he said.

The next thing Maureen knew, she was watching Joe-D', a robust one-year-old with dark hair and blue eyes, taking his first steps at the San Francisco airport. Decked out in his finest sailor suit, he was trying to greet his Aunt Anna, who had flown in to help Maureen drive back home.

Two days later, Maureen, Anna, and Joe-D' climbed into the VW bus and started their cross-country odyssey. Joe would fly home after his training wrapped up so he could say goodbye to everyone before returning to California to ship out. He even made plans to fly his old dog, Laddie, home to Boston to be with Maureen and Joe-D'.

As he prepared for Vietnam, Joe tried to assuage Maureen's fears by telling her that he had a good chance of surviving a shootdown over water. He was a strong swimmer, and as long as he withstood the initial hit he would parachute into the ocean with a life raft and enough food, water, and shark repellant to keep him alive until the Navy boat or helicopter arrived. Guys were being plucked out of the water like that all the time.

Admittedly, his prospects were grimmer if he got shot down over land, where if he survived the landing he could quickly find himself at the mercy of enemy forces. But the A-1 wasn't flying major attack missions over North Vietnam anymore because it was too vulnerable to the surface-to-air missiles (SAMs) that had proliferated there. The Navy didn't want to waste Spads where jets ostensibly could go with greater success, so by the end of 1966 the A-1 was restricted in North Vietnam to reconnaissance flights that steered clear of hot spots such as Hanoi and to the search-and-rescue missions that best suited its capabilities. Still, North Vietnam was armed heavily, and any flight there was highly dangerous. There was plenty of hazardous work in South Vietnam as well, where the A-1 flew combat runs in addition to its other missions.[4]

Used extensively in the Korean War, the A-1 was a big-bellied propeller plane with many nicknames including "Spad," a reference to a French manufacturer of World War I fighter aircraft. It was known for its ability to fly low for long periods of time, carry enormous weapons loads, and absorb heavy anti-aircraft fire. That made it ideally suited to providing close air support, which meant assisting its own troops with enemy forces close by.[5] In Vietnam, the A-1 was used to provide cover for helicopters when they went in to rescue downed pilots. The aircraft would fly low around the rescue scene, bombing or shooting anyone who attacked the helicopter or the pilot during the rescue attempt.[6]

That was the exciting part. Search and rescue work typically was characterized by long periods of boredom punctuated by bouts of terror and exhilaration.[7] An A-1 pilot could find himself flying in circles off the coast of Vietnam for hours with nothing to look at but a big, blue expanse of ocean and some boats. But once a call came in, he had to shift immediately from cruising the beach to speeding over hostile ground to a rescue site while being pelted with anti-aircraft fire.

All in all, given the Spad's role and his own abilities, Joe felt his prospects of surviving the war were good. As he told Maureen, "If I get shot down over water, I'm home safe."

While Maureen coped with her anxiety at Joe's imminent departure, she faced other challenges in her readjustment to life back home.

Space was tight in the small white bungalow in Randolph, Massachusetts, where Maureen and Joe-D' had moved in with Anna and their mother, Helen, after a week of diner meals, motel rooms, and diaper changes on the road from California. Helen had moved to Randolph from Jamaica Plain after her two youngest, Maureen and Freddy, were married and living on their own. Now they tried to make do, with Maureen and Joe-D' sharing an upstairs bedroom near Anna's while Helen stayed downstairs.

Maureen had noticed subtle changes in her mother, too. When she first saw her again, she thought Helen looked older than she remembered. Nothing was obviously wrong. But Maureen also thought her mother was moving more slowly and tiring more easily than she had in the past.

These worries were soon put aside. Four days before Joe's departure, there was a big blowout going-away party for him at the Dunn family home in Hull. The location was ideal for someone who had grown up on the beach and spent summers as a lifeguard, and the mood was upbeat. Friends and relatives who had come from nearby and out of state drank beer and whiskey and ate grilled beef with kosher salt, a specialty of Joe's brother, Jackie. They all wished Joe well. He told them not to worry. It's only a six-month tour, he'd say. I'll be back before you know it.

One of the guests, Joe's uncle, Coleman Conneely, had something on his mind, and he cornered Joe as the party went on all around them. Coley and his twin brother, Eddie, had emigrated years after Joe's mother Mamie, their older sister, and settled in Connecticut. Now Coley wanted to know how on earth his nephew could orient himself well enough between the night sky and the dark sea to land on an aircraft carrier.[8]

Joe patiently explained how the carrier's signals helped guide him onto the landing deck.

"Coley, I come in on the beam," he said. He seemed so relaxed and confident, so full of life, it seemed as though everyone around him breathed a sigh of relief. It was impossible to think that something terrible might happen to him in Vietnam.

Maureen felt the same way. Whenever her fears started getting the better of her, she would remind herself that Joe knew what he was doing. He was a good pilot, and he had an unbreakable will.

Still, she didn't eat much of her duck the next night as she sat across the table from Joe at Anthony's Pier Four, a fancy downtown restaurant. Joe knew what was on her mind.

"I promise you, I will come back," he said.

"What?"

"I know that you think that I won't be back," he said.

"It's not so much that I really believe you won't be back," she said. "I'm frightened that you won't be back."

"I promise you, I will be back," he said again. He was so sure that Maureen had no choice but to believe him.

The next night, Maureen took Joe to the airport, where she tried to be strong for his sake. As he had told her long ago, he couldn't worry about her crying on the ground while he was in the air trying to handle twelve tons of equipment under enemy fire.

"Six months will be gone before you know it," Joe said at the gate. "If we're smart and save our money you can come see me on 'r and r' in Hong Kong."

Maureen gave him a weak smile. Words were failing her. They kissed and Joe began to walk away.

Maureen cleared her throat.

"See ya'," she called out.

Joe stopped and turned. He gave her a big "thumbs up" and smiled.

"I love you," he said. "I will love you forever."

Maureen watched Joe walk all the way down the jet-way and disappear onto the airplane, just as she had done three and half years before when he'd left for preflight school. Driving home, she felt sad and worried and knew she had to get her mind off Vietnam. She went to her sister Mary Driscoll's in Hyde Park, where there was always a big spaghetti dinner on Tuesdays plus six kids to provide distraction. But driving down Mary's street, Maureen was overcome by a feeling of unease.

Mary greeted her youngest sister at the front door with a hug.

"Everything's going to be fine," she said. Right then and there, Maureen shook off her bad feeling and resolved to be positive while Joe was away. He would be back in six months. In the meantime, she would enjoy her family.

When Maureen finally got home that night, she was exhausted. She walked into the house and saw Joe's Navy portrait on the table where she had placed it so Joe-D' would have a constant reminder of his father while Joe was away. In the coming months, whenever Joe-D' would go near the picture, Maureen would point to it and say, "That's Daddy." When he got a little older, he'd lean in and kiss the glass. As soon as he could talk, Joe-D' referred to Joe as "Daddy," a term he never abandoned, no matter how old he got.

The house was quiet, and Maureen went to the kitchen to get a cold glass of water.

"Ma?" she called out.

"I'm out here, Maureen," Helen called from the back porch, where they had a glider. She enjoyed sitting there on summer evenings.

"Everything went all right at the airport?" she asked. "Are you all right?"

"Yeah, I'm OK," Maureen said. She got Joe-D' ready for bed, came back downstairs, then walked outside to sit with her mother, who had gotten a bad feeling as soon as she bid Joe goodbye. She was teary.

"Ma, what are you crying for?" Maureen asked. "You had five boys. Three of them went off to war. They all came back."

"I'll never see him again," she said.

"What?"

"Joe, I'll never see him again," she repeated.

"Well, that's a nice thing to tell me," Maureen said.

"No, I'm not telling you that you'll never see him again. I'm saying that I will never see him again."

Maureen shook off her mother's words, figuring she was just emotional because Joe had left.

Four nights later, Maureen walked into Helen's room to say goodnight and found Laddie lying at the foot of her mother's bed. He had been by Helen's side all day.

"Ma, let me get the dog out of here," Maureen said.

"Leave the dog, Maureen," Helen said.

Maureen couldn't figure out why Helen wanted Laddie to stay. If he started roaming around or whining during the night, he would disrupt her sleep.

"Ma, I don't want him here. If you get up, you'll trip over him."

"Leave the dog, Maureen," Helen insisted.

So Maureen did as her mother asked, leaving Laddie and walking over to the bed to kiss her goodnight. But just as her lips brushed her mother's, Maureen felt Helen's head slump away. Maureen pulled back. She looked at her mother and knew immediately that she was dead.

"Oh my God, Ma," Maureen gasped. She pulled the pillow out from under Helen's head, leaned her head back, pinched her nose and started mouth-to-mouth resuscitation.

"Anna," she called out between breaths. "Anna, it's Ma. Call the fire department."

Anna ran into the room. She stared, dumbfounded, then started to cry.

"Maureen, she's dead," Anna said.

Maureen realized it was hopeless to try to revive her. What she and Anna had to do now was call their brothers and sisters to come over immediately. As close as they had been to their mother, Maureen knew her siblings would have a hard time accepting the finality of her death unless they had a few minutes to say goodbye. The firemen got there first, but Maureen told them they would have to wait.

"You will not take this body until my brothers and sisters are here," she said. "My mother is not dead."

When Maureen called Joe to break the news, he offered to try to come home. But she begged him off. It would be too hard to say goodbye a second time, especially with her grief over her mother's loss so fresh.

Joe, who hadn't forgotten the heartache of Mamie's illness and death, knew Maureen would take her mother's death hard even as she put on a strong front. When she wrote and told Joe she didn't want to send any Christmas cards that year, he tried to boost her spirits, telling her that Helen wouldn't want her to be glum.[9] But beyond sympathetic letters, Joe couldn't do much. He had his own challenges thousands of miles away.

Joe's confidence was tested in his very first weeks aboard *Coral Sea,* where he was one of the junior pilots assigned to Attack Squadron 25 (VA-25). The carrier was part of a patrol known as "Yankee Station" about a hundred miles off the coast of Vietnam in the Gulf of Tonkin.

One night in August 1967, not even a month after he'd left Boston, Joe was watching the flight deck TV after a briefing, when a Spad's engine cut out as it approached the carrier for landing. Without power, the pilot, whom Joe knew and liked, tried to level the plane's wings and ditch. For awhile it looked good. But then something went wrong, and the Spad crashed.

"The plane sank and the pilot never got out," Joe wrote to Maureen that night. "It was really lousy to get so close to the carrier and have it quit. Another ten seconds and he would have been aboard."[10]

When Joe got a new roommate, an A-4 pilot, he heard the harrowing tale of how the guy had narrowly escaped a fire on the flight deck of USS *Forrestal.* He'd been poised for takeoff and had to taxi his aircraft through flames to get to safety at the front of the ship.

"He was lucky none of the bombs went off, as this did happen to a lot of the other planes," Joe wrote to Maureen. "He saw two of his buddies get blown up and couldn't do anything about it."[11]

Then there were the tales of warfare.

On *Coral Sea*'s last night in port in the Philippines, Joe listened in on the stories told by the squadron's seasoned combat pilots, those who had already done a Vietnam tour.

The night wasn't what Joe expected. He had always assumed a ship's last night on dry land would be a hell-raiser, but the mood was subdued. Most of the guys had a drink or two and then retired to watch movies or write letters. Joe, listening to the conversation, was taken aback by the pilots' descriptions of flying under fire. They sounded scared.

"From what they were saying I guess you really get fear put in you the first time you get shot at," Joe told Maureen. "I think if I was that scared, I'd turn in my wings tomorrow and get out of here."[12]

But Joe never lost his nerve or his wings, despite some close calls.

One night the weather was so bad, the control tower alerted Joe to the fact that he had just passed another pilot in his squadron. Joe never saw the guy.

"It's crap like that that kills people," he wrote. "I could have flown right through him and never have known it."[13]

Another day, he was low on fuel as he approached the carrier but couldn't land because the plane directly in front of him took too long to clear the landing area. The same thing happened on his second try. By the third attempt, "I was really sweating as I knew I had to get aboard this pass as I only had one more try and the deck was pitching pretty bad because of heavy seas."[14]

But despite their gripes about hairy landings, getting up early, flying in bad weather, and the rest, the aviators were an ultra-competitive bunch. No one wanted the next guy to get ahead of him in the race for the most flights. They would all bug the schedules' officer for extra hops and criticize "baggers" who tried to hog flights.[15]

As revealing and interesting as his shipboard lessons were, the sights of Asia proved even more surprising.

For all his ambition, Joe had arrived in Southeast Asia a sheltered guy who, except for his Navy training in Florida and Texas, had never ventured far from the Irish Catholic enclaves of Boston where he'd been born and raised.

His friends were all scrappy city kids like himself who stayed close to their mothers, rooted for the Red Sox, and went to Mass every Sunday. Many wanted little more out of life than a good dinner of roast beef and potatoes, a steady job at the shipyard or mill, and a cold beer on the weekends. When they married their high school sweethearts and had kids of their own, they raised them to be good citizens, good Catholics, and good to their families. Everything else would take care of itself.

In Asia, Joe encountered a world he'd never imagined. He was horrified by the poverty in the Philippines, where wages he figured at $1 a day or less forced young women into prostitution so they could help support their families. In Japan, the crowds and open sewers amazed him, as did the cars, houses, and portions of food that all seemed so much smaller than back home. One night in a Japanese bar, an embarrassed Joe thought he was in the wrong bathroom when a woman came in to wash her hands in the sink as he used the urinal nearby. She told him that most bathrooms in Japan were unisex.

"Can you picture you or your sisters?" he wrote jokingly to Maureen. "I can picture Mary or Aggie peeking in to see if there were any men in the room and then standing guard for each other."[16]

The one constant in Joe's life, besides his love of flying, was Maureen. No matter what he did, his thoughts were never far from her and how much he missed her and Joe-D'. When they were cut off during a telephone conversation from the Philippines, Joe tried for twenty minutes to get the operator back.

"I hated it because I wanted to tell you how much I love you and how much I miss you before we hung up," he wrote to Maureen later that night. "If I sounded different it was because of one or two things. First and foremost, because I miss you so much. It's hard for me (to) talk to you and keep back my emotions. I want to hold you and hug you and tell you how much I love you."[17]

About a month into his tour, Joe flew a familiarization flight of South Vietnam, his first real hop off the carrier. The next day, he flew his first mission, a rescue combat air patrol, or rescap. The more senior pilots were often bored by the tedium of circling off the beach for hours, waiting to be called in if someone got shot down, but Joe found the first time exhilarating.[18]

"It's awesome to sit there at 5,000 feet and look down at enemy land," Joe wrote. "You think of the people there, some of them don't even know what is going on. Yet some of them you know are sitting and waiting for you to give them a chance to shoot you down. It gives you a keen sense of life. And you know also that you will probably kill some of those people. It is a state of mind that you just can't imagine, no matter how much you hear about it, until you're in that situation."

That same day, he and Zip hit the lookout tower. Joe told Maureen it was the "beginning of the end. Now that we've started it won't be long before it's all over and I'll be back in your arms giving you a big hug and a kiss."[19]

Joe loved to fly, but he hated being away from Maureen. When he thought about how he couldn't see her that day or the next, no matter how much he wanted to, it drove him crazy with frustration. He had always been able to make things happen. Now he had no control. Near his second anniversary, Joe thought back to his wedding day: smoking outside the church with his brother Paul, dancing the twist with Maureen, watching his best man get drunk, and seeing Maureen cry as she said goodbye to her mother.

"I love you more than anything in the world," Joe wrote.[20]

The pain of his absence from Maureen and Joe-D' was leading Joe to a hard choice. He was thinking of getting out of the Navy after fulfilling his current commitment. He believed the Navy had been good to him, and for him, but he didn't want to spend half of every year away from home for years to come. Plus, he wanted to try to get a job as a commercial pilot while the airlines were still hiring people with two years of college. The only catch was, without an extension, Joe was less likely to get good orders after Vietnam. If he extended, he'd probably get to fly jets. If he didn't, he would more than likely have to bide his time in a dead-end job without much flying until his discharge.[21]

As Joe considered his future, he eased his longing for home by pasting half a dozen pictures of Maureen and Joe-D' on his bunk so they were the first faces he saw in the morning and the last before he fell asleep at night.[22]

The separation was hardest when he wasn't flying much. He was even restless on shore leave, despite playing tennis and shopping for bargains on clothes, stereo equipment, and toys for Joe-D'.[23] The time dragged compared with being in the air.

Once Joe learned the ropes in his initial weeks in the squadron, he evolved into an ambitious pilot who hated returning from a four-hour rescap with nothing to show for it. He complained about being teamed up with another pilot whom he deemed too risk-averse. If that pilot saw no action during a routine rescap, he would head back to the ship and jettison his rockets into the ocean. Joe didn't want to take crazy chances, but he didn't mind a bit of extra flying in search of some potential enemy targets, just as he and Zip had done on that first day of coastal VC-ing.[24]

But as much as he loved the thrill of combat flying, Joe wasn't oblivious to the reality that people were dying under the bombs, cannons, and napalm he dropped in his A-1. He believed he was doing his duty in fighting communism, which he saw as a genuine threat not only to the peoples of Southeast Asia but to his future grandchildren. And until a better way came along, he was prepared to keep doing it.[25] Still, that didn't mean that the killing rested easy on his conscience.

"It's probably good that I don't realize that the North Vietnamese have wives and kids," he wrote about halfway through his tour. "Because on account of me and all the other guys like me there is a lot of widows and fatherless children. I don't know how many I've killed, maybe 25, maybe 125, there is no way of knowing how many people were on the boat you just blew up or the junk you just sank or the building you scattered all over the countryside."[26]

He also thought he was lucky. He could destroy the enemy, blowing up their equipment, supply boats, and warehouses and killing their combatants, from high in the sky, not up close after some jungle ambush.

"Sometimes it's lousy at night when you think of the guys you blew up or shot to pieces," he wrote after a day of blowing up barges and fishing boats around Vietnam's northern islands.

"You know that they probably have wives and kids just like I do," he said. "But at least it's better being a pilot. We're sort of detached being in the air. You don't see all the bodies and mangled men up close. Although you know they're there."[27]

When Joe thought about it, it didn't make any sense that men were expected to return from war and talk about what they had seen and done. Really, how could anyone sit down and casually discuss all the men they had seen die, or those they had killed?

When Sister Mary Agnita, the former Mary Healy and a close friend of Maureen's, wrote to Joe to tell him that he was in her thoughts whenever she thought about war and killing, he didn't know what to say.

"I can think of better things I'd like to be remembered for," he wrote.

Then he told her about a guy he had known, a pilot with a wife and three kids with whom he'd shared a few jokes during a weather and intelligence briefing one day.

"The next time I saw him he was lying face down in a rice paddy with his A4-Skyhawk in a ball of flame not more than 100 yards away," Joe said. "I was flying at treetop level with the other guys trying to protect him until we could get a chopper in to pick him up. Meanwhile, the village right next to us is pouring anti-aircraft fire at us and automatic weapons, machine guns, etc. And they're also trying to get out into the field to get the downed pilot if he is alive."

When Joe and the other pilots saw that they had no chance of getting the pilot out, they turned on the village. They strafed it with 20-millimeter cannons and rockets not only to get the chopper out but as payback for killing the pilot and putting holes in their own aircraft.

"But that enemy village also had a lot of women and children who were helpless to defend themselves," Joe said. "How do you explain the feelings about a situation like this?"[28]

As Joe wrestled with the war's grim realities, Maureen passed her days in the company of her sisters and sister-in-law, Leona Hoey, who was married to her brother James. On warm days, the kids would play while the mothers sat outside and chatted about what Maureen would wear to meet Joe's ship and how everyone had to come visit their next duty station. During the winter months, a group often would head over to Maureen's for sledding and ice skating at a nearby pond. Sometimes a few of them would go to Woolworth's or Grant's, where Joe-D' couldn't resist letting the canaries out of their cages, much to the manager's dismay.

"I just can't imagine how Ma did it," Maureen said one afternoon on her sister Aggie's front porch. Helen had raised ten children, and Maureen felt worn out by one. But as much as she was weary of parenting Joe-D' by herself, she didn't want to complain. She knew her mother had had it harder, as did Aggie, whose husband worked two and three jobs to support their large family.

When suppertime rolled around, Maureen steadfastly avoided the evening news on TV. She cut off those who tried to fill her in on the latest reports from Vietnam.

"I don't want to hear it," she'd say. "If I do, I'll turn the news on."

Still, there were days when Maureen couldn't entirely escape her fear.

"Having lived with someone who I loved so much, I can't imagine doing without him and not having him here," Maureen told Aggie.

"Well, you don't have to imagine it," Aggie said. "He's going to come home. You'll be together. Then, he'll take you away again. And then you can start crying for us."

By late 1967, Joe was more than halfway through his tour and the U.S. commitment in Vietnam had swelled to close to half a million U.S. troops. There were no signs of abatement, even though the war protest movement had gained tremendous momentum during the past two and a half years, breaking out of the college campuses where it had taken root and into the broader public realm after the U.S. bombing campaign against North Vietnam began in early 1965. The first national anti-war march took place in April of that year in Washington, D.C., drawing roughly twenty thousand people. There was a conference on the war on the University of California's Berkeley campus, and more marches, demonstrations, and speeches followed. By 1967, young men were being urged to resist the draft. Hundreds were arrested at a demonstration at the Pentagon that fall. And while students had formed the core of the anti-war movement, it had gained more mainstream support along the way from entertainers, political and civil rights leaders, the pediatrician Dr. Benjamin Spock, the poet Robert Lowell, and many others.

Even so, Johnson was determined to stay the course. When his own defense secretary expressed doubts about the effectiveness of the administration's Vietnam strategy, Johnson decided to fire him. Vice-President Hubert Humphrey was dispatched to Saigon in October 1967 and made the White House position clear.

"Despite public opinion polls—none of which may I say have ever been friendly toward a nation's commitment in battle—despite criticism, despite understandable impatience, we mean to stick it out, until aggression is turned back and until a just and honorable peace can be achieved," Humphrey said. "That is the policy of the President of the United States, the Vice-President of the United States and the Congress of the United States. So let people understand that."[29]

What Johnson and his advisers didn't know was that the biggest communist offensive was yet to come.

As Joe's tour wore on, he grew impatient for home even as his work on the line intensified. He was happy to fly on Christmas Day so he wouldn't have as much time to dwell on being apart from Maureen and Joe-D'.

"I usually don't know what day of the week it is or what the date is," Joe wrote. "All I know is that I've been in this room for what seems like a lifetime of evenings missing you and thinking about you. Sometimes I feel like it will never end."[30]

Joe, though, soon found himself doing some of the most dangerous and thrilling flying of his tour.

When communist forces attacked the remote U.S. Marine outpost at Khe Sahn in January in a siege that would last for months, Joe and other Spad pilots were sent there for twelve-hour stretches to dive-bomb enemy forces.

The Spads were so loaded with bombs, rockets, ammunition, and napalm that they weighed in at nearly twelve tons when they went off the ship's catapult. And they had to fly much lower than the usual 3,000 feet, which was out of range of most machine guns and rifle fire.[31] "If you're a split second off you could kill 30 or 40 of our own Marines," Joe wrote to Maureen.

Johnson had put out optimistic statements about the war during late 1967. But in early 1968, everything changed. At the end of January, shortly after the attack at Khe Sahn, communist forces unleashed a massive offensive in cities throughout South Vietnam, violating the truce they had agreed to in observance of Tet, the lunar New Year. Commandos succeeded in attacking and infiltrating the U.S. embassy compound in Saigon, stunning Americans who saw the bloody and chaotic events unfolding on their living room television screens.

Joe's squadron was in the thick of battle, dropping more ordnance than any other squadron on the ship. "Things have really been pretty serious in South Vietnam," Joe wrote after one morning of bombing enemy troop concentrations near the Laotian border. He had achieved "centurion status" for making one hundred carrier landings and had earned a couple of citations. He was up for a few more but probably wouldn't get the one decoration he coveted most: the Distinguished Flying Cross of the Navy. Even so, Joe wasn't going to take any great risks just to get a medal with just weeks to go.[32]

With so much bad news out of Vietnam, Maureen worried. But she was also excited as Joe neared the end of his tour.

"Here I am again & in the best frame of mind I've been in for the past two weeks! And all because of a letter I got from you today!" Maureen wrote on February 8, five days after Joe's carrier was supposed to depart Yankee Station for the Philippines.

"Boy, they're really keeping after Khe Sahn," she wrote. "What a beating both sides are taking. The death losses are unbelievable. You've been in on most of it, honey, haven't you? I hope tomorrow is the last day of combat for you."[33]

But the day before *Coral Sea* was scheduled to depart, they received word that they had been extended at least until February 10. *Enterprise* was supposed to relieve *Coral Sea,* but instead had been diverted to North Korea in wake of the *Pueblo* incident. North Korea had seized the *Pueblo* on Janu-

Joe Dunn (second from the right) and fellow aviators stand before an A-1 Skyraider on the USS *Coral Sea*. Joe's attack squadron, VA-25, was the last to fly the A-1 before the Navy retired it in 1968. (Photo courtesy of Maureen Dunn)

ary 23 and would hold the ship's captain and surviving crew—one sailor died in the attack—hostage for eleven months.[34]

When the night of February 10 came, Joe's skipper announced that he still had no definite word on when the ship would leave.

"Boy was I disappointed today when I was thinking that possibly I had flown my last hop," Joe wrote to Maureen. "I know it's hard on you but it's no joke out here. Everybody is ship happy. We've been on the line since the beginning of January and we've only had one stand down day of rest in the whole time."

The skipper had said they would stay put for the next couple of days, until he received some notice from his superiors on the ship's schedule. Joe figured that, in any case, they had no more than a week or so left before they would be heading home.[35]

3

Last Flight

Four days later, a dozen red roses arrived at Maureen's front door from Clifford's Florist in Quincy. It was Valentine's Day, and Maureen was shaken up because she had read a story in the evening newspaper about an A-1 pilot who had been shot down over China and then heard that Joe was on the Navy's daily casualty report. More than anything, she was confused. If Joe had been shot down, why hadn't she received any notification from the Navy?

"These have come a long way, Mrs. Dunn," said the delivery man as he held out a long, white box.

Dazed, Maureen took the box and lifted the top. She saw a small, white envelope on top of the deep red roses and pulled out a card.

"I will love you forever," it read. "Love, Joe."

Maureen took the box inside and stared at the flowers. An hour ago, the young man at the Navy district office downtown had told her that Joseph P. Dunn was listed as a casualty for February 14, 1968. Now, Joe was sending roses. Having spoken to Joe before he left Cubi, Maureen knew he easily could have ordered the flowers early for Valentine's Day before leaving on his ferry flight back to the *Coral Sea*. Even so, the timing of the delivery, plus the fact that she hadn't heard from the Navy, made Maureen wonder if there hadn't been some mistake. Maybe Joe was really all right.

Maureen thought over what had happened since she first saw the newspaper story and started making telephone calls.

Shortly after hearing about the casualty listing from the district office, Anna had come home. Three of Aggie's kids, Christine, Danny, and Stephen Gallagher, were trailing her. They were spending their after-school hours with Anna and Maureen while their mother was in the hospital having her ninth baby and were shocked to find their young, pretty aunt sitting in the kitchen, crying in the maple rocking chair with the braided seat cover. The telephone was on the wall behind her, and she was clutching the evening newspaper.

"Anna, Joe's been shot down," Maureen told her sister as tears streamed down her face.

Anna had already seen the newspaper at her sister Mary's, where she'd stopped briefly on her way home. The sisters were so distressed reading about the downing of a *Coral Sea* A-1 pilot that Aggie's two smallest children, who were also there at the time, got scared and ran to hide behind the big wingback chair in the living room.

"No, Maureen, it can't be," Anna said. "How do you know it's Joe? How can you be sure?"

"It's right here on the front page," Maureen said, holding out the newspaper story of the downed pilot. "And I just got off the phone with the Fargo Building . . ."

Then, she paused.

"Anna, do me a favor," she said. "Watch Joe-D' for me for a minute, will you?"

"Sure, Maureen," Anna said, dumbfounded. "Whatever you need."

Maureen quickly got up from the chair and headed upstairs to her bedroom. She had had a sudden impulse to kneel and pray and wanted to be somewhere where it was quiet and she could be alone. Maureen's head felt heavy, and she struggled to organize her thoughts as she made her way up the creaking stairs to the second floor. Maybe a simple prayer would help calm her. She walked over to the side of the bed and carefully knelt down, bringing her hands up near her heart and clasping them together. "Hail, Mary, full of grace, the Lord is with Thee . . ." she began in a barely audible whisper. She stopped then, leaving the prayer unfinished. It was getting dark. The last light of the late winter day crept in through the bedroom's single window, lingering over the figure of a young woman kneeling by a bedside as if to guide a small child through her goodnight prayers. But this woman was alone, her prayer more desperate.

"If he's all right, just let me know," Maureen whispered, her eyes shut tight against the darkening room. "Give me some sort of sign."

The familiar voices of family floated up but sounded as though they were coming from very far away. Maureen grew more relaxed as she knelt there in the dark, her breath slow and rhythmic in the evening stillness. Then, she felt something. She turned around. She couldn't see that well, but she didn't really have to in order to know what was happening.

It was Joe. He was in his green flight suit and moving toward her.

Maureen just stared. She wasn't scared. She knew she wasn't asleep, so she couldn't be dreaming. Then Joe stopped walking. He was speaking but no sound came out. He mouthed the same words over and over again. Maureen kept staring, and then she understood.

"I'm OK," he was saying. "I'm OK." She watched the image for a few more seconds, and then it faded as quickly and quietly as it had come.

Maureen took a deep breath and stood up. She sat on the bed and felt an immense sense of relief. She had no idea if she had really witnessed a sign from God or just a manifestation of her own desire for Joe to be alive, but it didn't matter much. Whatever she saw, it was enough to convince her that Joe had survived whatever had happened in China or Vietnam or wherever he was. That would keep her going at least until she could tell Joe's family and friends and figure out what to do next.

"He's all right," she said, rejoining Anna downstairs.

"What? What do you mean?" Anna asked.

"He just came to me," Maureen said. "He's fine. He told me he's OK."

Years later, Maureen would reflect that any other family, thinking her delusional, probably would have sent her to bed with a cup of tea and a sedative while they called the doctor. But Maureen's brothers and sisters had been raised with a healthy dose of Irish mysticism and superstition. On top of that, they were Catholics steeped in the fantastic tales of the saints and martyrs and all the visions and miracles they had experienced through the ages. So it was no wonder that Maureen's vision was accepted. Consider the story of St. Clare of Assisi, a sickly thirteenth-century Franciscan nun who was said to have received a vision of the Mass while bedridden one Christmas Eve. She became known as the patron saint of broadcasting. Against that backdrop, it didn't seem odd at all that Maureen, caught in a moment of fervent prayer, should see Joe.

Meanwhile, word about the incident was spreading around the world. The Associated Press, whose story Maureen had seen in the paper, and United Press International wire services had moved terse, dramatic accounts earlier in the day. The first UPI report, attributed to unidentified American sources, moved out of Washington at 12:14 P.M. It said that communist China had shot down an unarmed A-1 off Hainan. AP had a similar, early report. Expanded accounts quickly followed.[1]

Anna notified family, making telephone calls as soon as she got home and saw Maureen. Some relatives had already seen the evening paper and were concerned. Maureen's brother Francis quickly conferred with a colleague at the Massachusetts Turnpike Authority whose son worked in the news business in Asia. The son relayed word that junks and sampans frequented the area where Joe's plane reportedly went down.

"That's a good sign," Francis, himself a World War II veteran, told Maureen, surmising that Joe stood a better chance of getting picked up in a populated area. If the Chinese captured him, he would be more valuable to them as a prisoner than dead. And if Joe ended up in the hands of the North Vietnamese, he would be a prisoner of war under the protection of the Geneva Conventions. Either way, he would be alive.

One thing nagged at Maureen. If Joe had been shot down, why had no one from the Navy come to notify her? If the news reports were right, Joe had been shot down almost a full day ago. Even accounting for the time difference, someone certainly should have come by now.

Maureen called CHINFO again.

"Do you have any idea what's going on?" she asked. "This is my husband, and I haven't been notified."

"A casualty officer has been sent, we don't know where he could be," the voice on the other end told Maureen.

"Well, where was he sent?" she asked.

"It looks like he went to 16 Quonset Street," he replied.

"What?" Maureen asked. The address was Joe's old home in Hull, which he kept on record as his permanent address. But Maureen had told Joe's squadron where she was staying. The man sent to tell her that her husband had been shot down had gone to the wrong place.

"Excuse me, in all of the material in his record it said where I was staying," Maureen said, her voice rising as she grew angrier. "You got so excited it was an international incident, you forgot his wife and family!"

Maureen hung up, and the roses arrived soon after. She stared at them, realizing she couldn't put off calling Hennie any longer. She had to get to her before the officer who, she surmised, apparently had been sitting on Quonset Street the entire day, told Henry, who was due home any time. Maureen didn't want Henry to be alone when he heard what had happened.

In Milton, Hennie was fixing dinner when the telephone rang. Maureen heard her sister-in-law's voice and braced herself.

"Hennie, I don't know how to tell you this other than to tell you that Joe has been shot down," Maureen said.

"Oh my God," Hennie gasped. Before she could say much else, Maureen told her to dispatch her brothers to their father's house.

"I'm worried about Grampy," she said. "There's someone out sitting in front of his house."

Hennie hung up and immediately called her brothers. Then she left for Hull to see her father. His grief would be overwhelming. He was so proud of Joe that, when an officer he knew from his years in the Navy yard retired, he bought his old captain's uniform. It was hanging in his closet, waiting for the day Joe got promoted. Later that night, Hennie would stop to see Maureen, who was trying hard not to fall apart.

It wasn't easy. Every time another relative walked into the Randolph house and embraced her, she started to cry all over again. But then she would get busy with a task, like changing Joe-D's diaper or sending her brother James out for more beer, Coke, and chips. Because the Navy still hadn't come to her, she had a lingering hope that it had all been a terrible mix-up.

In the midst of the chaos and grief, the Gallagher kids stood quietly around, unsure of what to do. Maureen was more like a fun older sister to them than an aunt, and it was hard to see her so broken up. The kids could always count on her. When Dan Gallagher got his teeth knocked out in a fight in Everett, Maureen showed up at the local hospital. She told him to put his teeth in his pocket and drove him to world-renowned Massachusetts General Hospital so an oral surgeon could reattach them.

The news of Joe's loss stunned the nieces and nephews almost as much as it had Maureen, who over the course of the next few days would be dazed and overwhelmed thinking of how abruptly her life had changed. One day, she was picking out a light blue dress and coat ensemble to meet Joe's ship. The next thing she knew, she was collapsing in the arms of her sisters and brothers, who struggled to find the words to comfort her.

Finally, at about eight o'clock that night, a Navy officer arrived at the front door in dress blues.

"Mrs. Dunn, I regret to inform you that your husband has been shot down over Hainan Island. He was seen in a fully opened parachute. They are continuing to search for him," he said. "You'll get the telegram tomorrow. We consider him now listed as missing."

It was official. Joe was lost somewhere off the coast of China.

Early on the morning of February 14, 1968, in the Philippines, Joe couldn't have expected much out of the ordinary when he took off from Cubi Point in an unarmed, single-seat A1-H Skyraider that he was ferrying from the base back to his carrier in the Gulf of Tonkin. The aircraft was supposed to have been retrieved two weeks earlier when the carrier originally was scheduled to return to Cubi. But that plan was scrapped when the carrier's time on Yankee Station in the Gulf was extended indefinitely.

Joe was picked for the ferry flight primarily so he could call the Bureau of Naval Personnel from the base, as he'd been waiting on new orders since mid-December and wanted to start making plans for Maureen and Joe-D'. When he reached the bureau, the news was good. He had been assigned to A-7 jets after Vietnam, a good set of orders considering that he had opted against extending his Navy service once his time was up.

The four- to five-hour flight from the Philippines to the Gulf was fairly routine, and on this day Joe was the wingman following the lead plane, an EA-1F, a Skyraider configured with special electronic warfare capabilities that other models lacked.

Even though the long flight wasn't known to be particularly hard or interesting, it was important to pay attention.[2]

To the northwest of Cubi lay Hainan Island, a large tropical island in the South China Sea that belonged to the communist People's Republic of China, which wasn't recognized by the United States. No U.S. president had ever been to China. What little diplomatic contact there was between the nations consisted mostly of sporadic meetings conducted at the ambassadorial level in Warsaw, Poland. And even they hadn't proved particularly productive in advancing the cause of bilateral relations.

China was known to guard zealously against territorial intrusions and its southern outpost of Hainan was armed heavily. So it was imperative that U.S. pilots avoided flying within 12 miles of the island, the boundary where China's territorial claim ended.

To avoid Hainan, pilots had to stay on course. They would skirt around the island, taking care not to cross into Chinese territory, before turning up into the Gulf of Tonkin, which lay between Hainan's west coast and Vietnam. But pilots had few navigational aids to help them once they got out of radio range of Cubi and before they came within range of Yankee Station.[3] The middle of the course was plotted by map, with pilots adjusting for winds as they got fixes on their positions from radar or by checking landmarks—mostly islands, reefs, shoals, and the like between the Philippines and the Gulf of Tonkin—below.[4] By this method of dead reckoning, if a pilot couldn't get a fix, he would have to guess his position simply by comparing the distance he had come against the set course.

It was overcast when Joe's flight, designated Canasta 404 based on the squadron's call signal and the number on the side of the aircraft, took off from Cubi. The flight of the lead plane, which was attached to the *Coral Sea*'s Early Warning Squadron (VAW-13), was designated Robinson 777.

Takeoff was uneventful.[5] Robinson 777, piloted by Lt. Robert B. Stoddert and carrying a navigator and two other crew members, climbed to 8,500 feet. Shortly before 8 A.M., Stoddert spotted Scarborough Shoals about six miles to the south and estimated hitting another landmark, Bombay Reef, in about an hour and a half.[6]

Soon after, with a huge cloud bank on the horizon, Robinson 777 climbed to about 12,500 feet. But the cloud cover was still so thick that the pilot couldn't see another checkpoint along the way, Macclesfield Bank.[7]

Clearing the clouds, Robinson 777 descended to 10,000 feet but couldn't go any lower because of haze. The pilot made out what looked like an elliptical reef off the aircraft's portside wing and reported Bombay Reef to the navigator. The aircraft made a turn.

By then, Robinson 777 and Canasta 404 should have been within radio range of *Coral Sea* or the U.S. military base at Da Nang, South Vietnam. But all the calls put out by Robinson 777 went unanswered. The pilot tried to get fixes on his position by using channels on the aircraft's Tactical Air Navigation radio system but couldn't get any information there either. The aircraft's radar was found later to be functioning marginally, with a maximum range of 40 miles instead of the usual 100 miles.[8]

The pilot then decided to drop down to a lower altitude. He called Canasta 404 to report that he was "going to let down to take advantage of the decreasing winds." Canasta 404 then "joined on my left wing and we let down to 8,500 feet, still above the cloud layer."[9]

When a break in the clouds came shortly before 11 A.M., the Robinson 777 pilot could make out land about eight miles ahead. Almost immediately, Canasta 404 radioed that he had also spotted land. Thinking they were near Cap Mui Ron, North Vietnam, Robinson 777 turned north, paralleling the coast in hopes of spotting a recognizable landmark. But before the turn was completed, the pilot heard a noise on the radio.

When he looked to his left, the pilot saw Canasta 404 about 1,000 yards away, nose down in a 70-degree dive. It was trailing a whitish gray smoke and had no canopy. Above the aircraft, he could make out Joe descending in "an open and filled chute."[10]

Just then, something caught the pilot's eye, and he realized that a Chinese MiG-17 fighter was rolling in on him. He dove into the clouds and lost the MiG, then turned to try to see Joe hit the water. But once he got below the clouds, the MiG came after him again. Robinson 777 evaded the fighter and called out on his radio, broadcasting his estimated position based on his dead reckoning plot. He told them he was "down 360 degrees" 60 miles north of Dong Ha, a provincial capital near the Demilitarized Zone separating North and South Vietnam.[11]

Robinson 777 heard a beeper (presumed to be from Joe's emergency signal device) for two or three minutes. Now flying under the clouds, the pilot made out the base of mountains ahead of him. He estimated a radar position and tried to orient the aircraft toward friendly land.[12]

As Robinson 777 tried to make his way back to South Vietnam, the Navy started looking for Joe. The lead plane's broadcast just after the attack had been picked up by *Deep Sea* 103, an orbiting aircraft that relayed the message to *Coral Sea*. Aircraft, helicopters, and search-and-rescue ships were dispatched immediately to the Gulf of Tonkin off North Vietnam's coast.[13]

Nearly two hours passed with no sign of Joe. His *Coral Sea* shipmates couldn't understand what was happening. If Joe had gone down as Robinson 777 witnessed, why wasn't he turning up?[14]

Despite doubt and confusion, the search went on.

"All units continuing search," read one message sent by a member of the search party at 12:32 P.M., about the same time Robinson 777 was landing at Da Nang.[15] "Intentions continue search. Have considerable doubts about accuracy of datum."[16]

Stoddert, the Robinson 777 pilot, was debriefed immediately upon landing at Da Nang. Meanwhile, U.S. officials were collecting intelligence reports of military activity over Hainan.

"Collateral info indicates ChiCom [Chinese communists] airborne reaction to acft [aircraft] penetrating Hainan airspace off Southeast coast . . . corresponds to time Canasta 404 missing," read one Navy message.[17] When the information reached Vice Admiral William F. Bringle, the commander of the Seventh Fleet, which had responsibility for covering parts of Asia including Vietnam, Bringle apparently broke into ship communications to put the search party on notice.

Your "indications are that there is strong possibility that the aircraft shot down . . . was an A 1 enroute Cubi to *Coral Sea*," read a message sent back to Bringle confirming an earlier message he had sent "by other means" to relay the Hainan reports.[18]

With word of the Hainan activity, and the information gained through the debriefing of the Robinson 777 pilot, the Navy realized what had really happened. The search party couldn't find Joe in the Gulf of Tonkin because he wasn't there. He was off the southeastern coast of Hainan, some 375 miles away in the South China Sea.[19]

The Gulf search quickly was called off. It was now about three hours after the shootdown, and USS *McCard*, a destroyer that was part of the *Coral Sea*'s battle group, was ordered by the Seventh Fleet Commander to head for Hainan. *McCard*, which was en route to Taiwan when it turned around, would take hours to reach the search area, where it was instructed to stay pending further instruction.

"Do not approach closer than 20 miles to Chicom [Chinese communist] territory," the commander ordered.[20]

In the meantime, four F-4 Phantom jets and an A-3 tanker would launch from USS *Kitty Hawk* to conduct an electronic search in hopes of picking up a radio or beeper signal from Joe, who was traveling with two emergency signal devices that could be activated manually or automatically. The jets and tanker would stay 20 miles off the coast of Hainan and see "if radio contact can be made with downed Canasta pilot. Further SAR (search and rescue) dependent results this effort."[21]

Bringle, the Seventh Fleet commander, moved more men and equipment to the search scene, including USS *Kearsarge*, which was ordered to proceed south toward Hainan. But concerned about China's reaction, Bringle also cautioned his forces against any movements that could possibly spark a confrontation. All forces were ordered to stay 25 miles outside of Chinese territory and "avoid provocative action."[22]

Two hours later, *Coral Sea* requested permission to join the search and was approved.[23] By now, *McCard* was in the area and reporting "no visual or electronic contact" with Joe.[24]

Coral Sea was told to proceed "at best speed" toward the scene and to prepare to conduct an electronic search and to provide a rescue air patrol and a protective fighter cap pending instructions from the on-scene commander.[25]

As the carrier made its way toward Hainan, the international implications of the incident didn't escape notice by Joe's shipmates. As individuals, and as military men trained to look out for one another, they were willing to put themselves at risk for a fellow aviator. But they weren't naïve about Cold War realities. It would be easy enough to comb the shores of an ally but this was China, an unfriendly and unpredictable if not downright hostile country with a system of governing antithetical to the United States'. All of that would figure in any search scenario.

Zip Rausa, the pilot who had accompanied Joe on his first day of coastal VC-ing when Joe blew up the lookout tower, went back to his room to reflect on the day's happenings, as was his habit.

"Joe Dunn was in 404 returning to the ship with Robbie, having replaced 404 with another aircraft at Cubi a couple of days ago," he wrote.

"In fact, Joe's flight somehow got north of track and Joe was jumped and shot down by a MiG just on the eastern edge of Hainan Island. This will be a major political event in all likelihood not to mention the personal tragedy. He was reported to have had a good chute."[26]

The inherent tension in wanting to look for Joe without inciting the Chinese was palpable in the ship's briefing room, where Lt. Jay Stone laid out an ambitious scenario before a group of pilots who would launch as soon as the carrier got close enough to the scene.

An intelligence specialist who was the only non-flying member of Joe's squadron, Stone's job was to give pilots a full and accurate picture of conditions, a duty that weighed especially heavy on him since the death of the squadron's previous skipper, Cmdr. Clarence Stoddard, on September 14, 1966.

Stone had briefed Stoddard before his A-1 was hit by a surface-to-air missile off Vinh, North Vietnam. Two months later, another squadron pilot,

Lt. Bruce Marcus, had a close call when a SAM just missed his aircraft before detonating nearby. The incidents underscored the vulnerability of the A-1 to SAMs, prompting restrictions on their use.

That night, as Stone began briefing the pilots who would look for Joe, he saw the skeptical looks as he presented a plan to launch a bunch of A-1s as primary search aircraft, plus helicopters that could perform a sea rescue and half a dozen F-4 Phantom fighters to provide defensive cover against a possible MiG attack.

Stone knew what the pilots were thinking. There was no doubt they wanted to look for Joe. But China already had shot down one American aviator that day. It was one thing to send up a bunch of A-1s, which the Chinese likely would recognize as search-and-rescue aircraft. It was quite another to fill the skies with fighter jets that could be interpreted as a military provocation.

"You gotta be kidding me," one of the pilots said. "If you send a whole bunch of F-4s, they're going to think we're attacking them. They're going to launch a hundred MiGs after us."[27]

As the pilots from *Coral Sea* braced for the search duties ahead, Bringle received word that the *Kitty Hawk* Phantoms had returned from their electronic search and reported hearing a beeper about eight hours after the shootdown. The Phantom pilots estimated a position based on that signal, which faded after about twenty minutes, and relayed it to *McCard*, then about 30 miles southeast of that location.[28]

It was the most hopeful information anyone had received since the Robinson 777 pilot reported seeing a good parachute and hearing a beeper at the time of the attack. Armed with this new information, and with a better idea of Joe's position, Bringle sent out an order to all forces dispatched to the search scene.

"The name of the game is to rescue pilot if it proves to be feasible but doing all possible not to provoke chicoms [Chinese communists] into further overt actions," he said. "To this end [the on-scene commander] keep all aircraft under positive radar control and for the present keep all aircraft twenty miles off shore. Until decision is made by higher authority to proceed inside twelve mile limit should conditions warrant."[29]

Back on *Coral Sea*, Joe's shipmates grew optimistic.

"Hope soared as destroyers and *Coral Sea* turned eastward through the night," Zip wrote. "His beeper had been heard about 1900 H last evening.

A destroyer was within 40 miles of him/or the beeper, at one point. A bold bright moon shone over calm waters."[30]

With two aircraft carriers moving toward the scene and a destroyer on hand, plus the results of the electronic search by the Phantoms, the on-scene commander put together a final search plan that was aimed at maximizing the chances for finding Joe without provoking China.

Four aircraft—three S-2 Tracers and an E1-B Tracer variant—would be launched from *Kearsarge* for an electronic search. Two A-1s would be launched from *Coral Sea* between 3 and 4 A.M. Two helicopters would be airborne, and other rescue, attack, and fighter aircraft would be in ready positions on the carriers for potential launching as needed. Maps of Hainan were put up on bulkheads on *Coral Sea*, and MiG fields were plotted by fighter pilots in the event they were sent up.[31]

There was one obvious problem. Joe was thought to be well within Chinese territory—as close as five miles from shore. But the search party was told to stay fifteen to twenty miles further out than that, at least until searchers were able to pinpoint Joe's location with greater accuracy. Bringle had indicated a willingness to breach Chinese territory once Joe's position could be ascertained with some degree of accuracy. But there were only two ways to zero in on Joe's location. If searchers got lucky and picked up more beeper signals, or made radio contact with Joe, they could narrow down the search field. Without those clues, though, someone would have to spot him from the air or a boat. And that would be virtually impossible from so far out to sea.[32]

Still, after the orders went out, Bringle reported to U.S. Navy Secretary Paul R. Ignatius that he was "optimistic regarding chances of SAR [search-and-rescue] effort if location of pilot can be accurately determined. SAR forces will not proceed inside 12-mile limit unless on scene commander considers pilot has been located with reasonable degree of accuracy."[33]

Bringle's decisions continued to be driven by desires that were, seemingly, at odds with one another. He wanted to approach China prudently while still doing whatever possible to find Joe.

It "is anticipated that success or failure of SAR effort will be determined prior daylight," he wrote. "However, if SAR is still in progress at daylight and existing conditions indicate pickup can be made without provoking chicom [Chinese communist] reaction, SAR attempt will be made. Recovery of pilot is of utmost importance; however, the implications of creating an international incident are appreciated and all decisions will be carefully considered."[34]

As *Coral Sea* and *Kearsarge* sped toward Hainan in the early morning hours of February 15, it was still the day before in Washington, where word of the incident had reached top officials. The U.S. Department of Defense tried to restrict the public's information to the minimum.

"Two unarmed U.S. Navy A-1 propeller-driven aircraft on a ferry flight from Cubi Point in the Philippines to the aircraft carrier USS *Coral Sea* in the Gulf of Tonkin experienced navigational difficulties and inadvertently strayed into airspace approximately five miles off the east coast of Hainan Island," read the first Pentagon statement released about the incident. "One of the planes was shot down by Chinese Communist MiG aircraft. The second departed the area and recovered at Da Nang. Its pilot reports he last saw the other plane in a vertical dive and smoking."[35]

As news organizations picked up the story, two more statements would be released over the next twenty-four hours. The Pentagon stipulated that it was "imperative" that no further information, and no speculation, be provided to the press beyond official statements. Also, personnel connected with Robinson 777 would not be "exposed" to the news media.[36]

At the State Department, press responses also were planned carefully so as not to reveal too much.

Officials decided that reporters asking for confirmation that Chinese communists had shot down a Navy plan would be referred to the Pentagon statement. Those asking if the matter would be raised at the next U.S.–China Warsaw talks would get a vague, anonymous response such as, "I think you may assume that we discuss with the Chinese in Warsaw all matters relating to American citizens who may be detained by the Chinese Communist authorities."

Press officer Robert J. McCloskey followed the directive at his 12:46 P.M. briefing:[37]

> Q: Bob, I understand there is a bulletin just out on the wires that the Communist Chinese have shot down an American plane off Hainan Island, five miles off. Have you gotten anything?
> A: I think Defense is going to handle that for you.
> Q: I see.

Q: Can you confirm it?
A: I'd prefer to let the Defense Department do that.

About two hours after the release of the first Pentagon statement, the first electronic search aircraft were launched from *Kearsarge.*

It was the morning of the day after the attack, and no U.S. force had seen Joe or made contact with him since Robinson 777 reported seeing the open parachute and smoking aircraft right after the MiG attack.[38] No search boat or aircraft had picked up an electronic or radio signal since seven o'clock the night before, when the *Kitty Hawk* Phantoms had heard the beeper for the last time. But that alone hadn't been enough to narrow down the search area to a probable location. And without that, Bringle wasn't going to risk an air war with China by closing in on its territory.

Despite the fact that searchers had come up with little, Bringle decided to move one more piece of equipment to the scene. The submarine USS *Tunny* was ordered to sail "immediately at best speed . . . for possible assistance in recovering downed pilot vic [vicinity] Hainan Island."[39]

Still, with North Vietnam's ongoing siege of the Marine base at Khe Sahn, the recent Tet offensive, and the *Pueblo* hostages still in North Korea, manpower and equipment could be diverted from the war for only so long. Four electronic search aircraft, two rescue aircraft, and *McCard* looked for Joe until daylight, staying well outside Chinese territory. China, probably realizing that U.S. forces weren't looking for a confrontation, just the pilot they had shot down earlier, never reacted except to keep *McCard* and the *Kearsarge* on a radar lock. Just over twenty hours after Joe was shot down, the search for him came to a halt at 7:06 A.M. on February 15.[40]

On *Coral Sea,* Joe's squadron mates were dispirited. But as hard as it was to lose a fellow aviator, the men realized they couldn't dwell on the loss when they had to go out the next day and fly combat missions. Sometimes, when it was certain that a pilot had died, there would be a memorial service. More often, a lost pilot's picture was taken down from the bulletin board, his belongings were packed and shipped home, and his replacement arrived. It was almost as if he had never existed.[41]

"The beeper faded," wrote Zip, who was among those pilots kept on alert status during the search's final hours. "We're heading back to Yankee Station. Because of the political concerns and the dubious regard for territorial waters our part of the search has been terminated. The *Kearsarge* is still in the vicinity. I was alert '30' for a time then, with Dale [Pellot, another squadron pilot], manned aircraft in a chill, gusty wind from 0530 to 0700 on alert '5'. Depressing. Want to go home. Get away from this business."[42]

When Maureen awoke on the morning of February 15 in Randolph, Massachusetts, thousands of miles away from where the search had ended hours ago, she found herself thinking of brown shoes.

The Navy official who had come the night before had worn standard issue black shoes, not the brown traditionally worn by aviators. It was a small thing, but it bothered Maureen. She wanted to speak with a Navy official who knew aviation, not a disinterested emissary from headquarters.

That day, the story spread fast in the Boston area as newspapers and radio stations reported accounts that varied widely in detail.

The morning *Boston Globe* story named Joe and said another pilot had seen him parachute out of a smoking airplane. It cited a Radio Peking broadcast that had been monitored in Tokyo that said Joe's plane was destroyed as a punishment for deliberately violating Chinese airspace. It also said Joe was thought to have been captured by China but didn't say why or offer any substantiating information.[43]

UPI stories published the same day by the *Boston Herald Traveler* and the *Record American,* which ran a big "Red Chinese Down Unarmed U.S. Plane" headline, had some of the same details but didn't name Joe. The *Herald Traveler* specified that the pilot's fate wasn't known. One of the longest accounts was carried by the *Globe*'s evening edition. It featured a headshot of Joe in his Navy uniform and an expanded version of its morning story that contained more details about Joe's background and family and an account of how Maureen had learned about the incident.[44]

As the news spread, those who knew Joe and Maureen felt stricken.

Early that morning at the St. Francis of Assisi convent in Braintree, Sister Mary Prisca, who had known Maureen since her elementary school days, had gathered her community of nuns around her to pray for Joe.

Back when Sister Prisca was teaching at St. Andrew's, Maureen had taken a liking to her. When Sister wrote lessons on the blackboard in her flowing black-and-white habit, Maureen would wave to her from her classroom across the hall. As an adult, Maureen would stop by St. Francis to help Sister Prisca and the other nuns, who didn't drive, with errands and correspondence. She was a familiar figure to students like Pat Barnes, a fifth grader who knew Maureen was married to Joe Dunn, a local Navy pilot who was in Vietnam. Now, as Pat sat at his school desk on the morning of February 15, 1968, in his navy blue pants, white shirt, and red tie, listening to Sister Katrina's special request come over the loudspeaker, he wondered what had happened. Usually, as the school principal, she led them in the Pledge of Allegiance to start the day. But today was different.

"I want everyone to get down on their knees to pray for someone," Sister Katrina said. "I want you to pray for Lieutenant Dunn to come home safely."[45]

The support of friends helped Maureen stay hopeful in those initial days. Even then, it was hard not to get overwhelmed from time to time.

Maureen was emotionally and physically exhausted caring for Joe-D', who was not yet two and very active. She wanted to find a place for them to live so they wouldn't impose on Anna. She had to contend with conflicting and confusing news reports and a military bureaucracy whose performance she found unsatisfactory at best. Worst of all, she felt that in order to survive she had to push away the opinions of those who felt the outlook for Joe's survival was bleak.

A particularly depressing notice came two days after the shootdown in the form of a Western Union telegram from Vice Admiral B. J. Semmes, Jr., the chief of naval personnel.

> It is with the utmost regret I must inform you that a report just received, states the extensive search has failed to locate any trace of your husband, although hope for your husband's survival cannot be encouraged, in the absence of conclusive evidence of death. He will be continued in a missing status pending receipt and review of a full report of the circumstances surrounding his disappearance. My thoughts and prayers are with you in this distressing time.[46]

The morning *Globe* already had reported that the search for Joe had ended and, retreating from its earlier story, said it didn't know if he had died or been taken prisoner.[47] One troubling account, reported by Copley News Service and picked up by the AP, said that the Seventh Fleet commander was ordered by the Pentagon not to get within 12 miles of Hainan to pick up Joe because they didn't want another incident in the area.[48]

Joe's case even came up for discussion that day on WEEI Radio's "Paul Benzaquin Show."

With listeners voicing opinions on how the nation should react to the incident, Maureen felt compelled to call. She was more shocked than angry and trying hard not to lose hope.

"There was one woman that made a statement about, you know, she wished that we could have more love than anger, and I'd like to tell this woman that my husband went over with no anger," Maureen told the show's audience. "With nothing but love for his country and love for the people that he's fighting for and that he just wanted to help everybody. And I just hope that these people that are probably using useless words would change them into a few prayers instead of hopeless, useless sentences.

"And as far as going in after him—the caller that you just had previous on, I agree in one sense," Maureen continued. "If we went in after him, he is only one person. Of course to me he is very important and to his son and to his family, but there are an awful lot of other people and we don't want anything started over it. And I'm just hoping that the Navy can get him out of there and that he can be all right. But I don't want an incident started because my husband is one of many, many millions of people . . . And I hope these people that are calling you and making various statements, predictions, will say a prayer and that's all I ask of them."[49]

Meanwhile, the Copley story prompted the Pentagon to issue a news release detailing the extent of the search effort. Much of the information in the release—including the fact that Joe's beeper had been heard once right after the attack and again eight hours later, before any ships were on the scene—was included in another story published Saturday by the *Globe*.

Maureen wasn't sure what to make of all the accounts. If true, the Copley story didn't quite make sense to her because, even given the obvious concerns about China, she couldn't understand why the Pentagon wouldn't want to rescue one of its own pilots.

As Maureen sifted through the news reports, she found little solace in her Navy contacts.

Still smarting over the initial mix-up over her address on the day Joe was shot down, Maureen found herself, days later, faced with a Navy official who apparently thought it was time for her to face some of the grimmer prospects at hand. She had gone to meet with him to draft a new will, as the Navy had urged as soon as Joe was declared missing.

"You know . . ." the official began, "I was on a medical cruise and I saw a fully open chute and the guy didn't make it out. I've seen more guys with bad chutes make it than with good chutes."

Maureen looked over at his open office window and wondered how it would feel to jump out.

"The Chinese could have his body already and could be using it for fertilizer in a rice paddy," he went on. "They could keep him a prisoner for years and he could end up having children there and staying there . . ."

"Mrs. Dunn?"

Maureen looked up and saw that the young enlistee who had driven her to the downtown office was standing. He looked as stunned as she felt.

"Are you prepared to leave?" he asked.

When Maureen got home and telephoned the Navy to complain, the service, intending to smooth things over, said it would send someone over that night. But when that officer arrived, he was late, had nothing new to report, and smelled like he'd been drinking.

From then on, Maureen decided the only way she was going to learn more about Joe was to take the initiative herself, starting with getting more facts on Hainan. One of the first things she did was to ask her friend Kathy Vena for a ride to Copley Library.

"I want to see where Hainan Island is and read up on it," Maureen said.

"Are you sure?" asked Kathy, an old childhood friend. Kathy's father Luigi Vena, the Boston tenor who sang the Ave Maria at the 1953 wedding of John F. Kennedy and Jacqueline Bouvier, had sung at Joe and Maureen's wedding twelve years later.

"Just get me there," Maureen said.

Maureen also asked the Navy to provide her, in writing, a summary of what they had done to uncover what had become of Joe and what diplomatic channels could be used in the future to gain information.

And she kept track of *Coral Sea,* which had been delayed in Asia indefinitely.

Joe's squadron's commanding officer, Cmdr. Clifford Church, the carrier's Catholic chaplain, and the air wing commander all wrote to Maureen within two weeks of the shootdown. All expressed distress over Joe's loss, praising his friendly demeanor and capabilities as a combat pilot. None of them, though, seemed sure whether to give Maureen hope or prepare her for the eventuality of Joe never coming home.

"I have become very delinquent in writing while hoping for more encouraging news," Church wrote.

"There has been no reason to expect it except that we want it so badly," he said. "Having shared several exciting moments with Joe I have learned to respect his ability. It is very perplexing to have a man, who was more than holding his own in combat exposure, missing on a flight that was supposed to be 'safe'."[50]

Cdr. James B. Linder said the air wing shared her "feeling of shock and disbelief" and offered "prayers for his safe return."

> We in the wing believe Joe has an excellent chance of being alive. There is proof that he was in his chute and had ejected from his aircraft. Though his physical condition was unknown and we could not talk to or see him in the water, his chances of getting in his raft and then being picked up are good.
>
> On the other hand, there is always the possibility that he didn't make it for many reasons. Your future actions are definitely tied to the way you accept or reject this unfortunate situation.[51]

Maureen bided her time and looked forward to the return of Joe's ship. She hoped someone from Joe's squadron or the Robinson 777 crew would have more to tell her. Until then, she wouldn't make any drastic changes. Her days would be spent caring for Joe-D', seeing family, and checking in with the Navy. She would stay with Anna for now, and the belongings she and Joe had accumulated during twenty-two months of marriage would remain in storage until she knew what she wanted to do. It was a holding pattern.

In early March 1968, Maureen learned more about the search for Joe when Church, spurred by press accounts of Joe's case, wrote to her again. This time, he explained how the lead plane had reported incorrectly that the attack occurred off the coast of North Vietnam.

"We wasted three hours searching the wrong area," Church wrote.

Maureen was shocked. The Navy hadn't told her that searchers had looked in the wrong place first, although the Pentagon did make brief mention of it in the news release prompted by the controversial Copley story. But the next day's news stories hadn't picked up on that aspect.

As for Joe's current status, Church told Maureen there was simply no way to assess it. No one knew if he was injured before leaving his aircraft, although if his parachute worked Joe must have been able to extract himself by using a handle that required a twenty- to forty-pound pull. He also had a life vest, life raft, and survival equipment for land and sea.

One more thing perplexed Church. If Joe had survived, why had he never made voice contact despite the fact that he had two radios and a spare battery? As a rescue pilot, Joe would have known that enemy forces often set traps using captured beepers, so he would have waited for an opportunity to talk after using the beeper. Certainly, if he had radioed his call sign, anyone in the squadron would have recognized it.

"Boiling all of the above down we wind up with no reason to believe that he did or did not survive," Church wrote. "Like yourself we can only hope."[52]

Maureen kept hoping, but in May she received two letters that did more than anything that had occurred earlier to make her angry and shake her belief that everything possible was being done to determine Joe's fate.

The first letter, from the Navy, sought to assure Maureen that the State Department had sent letters to China asking about Joe, and would soon be making another inquiry.

But the Navy's letter indicated that the State Department had sent its first letter February 12—two days before the shootdown.

When Maureen called the Navy's Bureau of Personnel, she was told that it was a typographical error and that State definitely had reached out to China twice since Joe went missing. But Maureen wondered if she could trust the information.

"Typographical error?" she asked. "This is a man's life."

A week later, more doubt crept in when the International Committee of the Red Cross (ICRC) in Geneva, responding to an inquiry from Maureen, told her that they had never heard of her husband but would pursue the matter with the Red Cross in Peking.[53]

That was alarming. Maureen knew that the private ICRC had the right under the Geneva Conventions to visit prisoners of war and civilian internees to ensure that their treatment met standards of international humanitarian law. The ICRC also could deliver messages from family and relief packages.

The Navy had told Maureen not to worry about notifying the Red Cross because they would do it. In fact, the American Red Cross had been notified and had sent two cables to its Chinese counterpart. But Maureen didn't know that and, when Geneva said they hadn't been informed, she worried that the correct information hadn't gotten to the right authorities.

The Navy, meanwhile, had concluded that the aircraft had drifted over one hundred miles north of their intended course because of significant winds and navigational errors.[54] A day after the incident, they had found its cause was "inattention to fundamentals of dead reckoning aggravated by limited communications." Officials said the Robinson 777 crew couldn't account adequately for what had happened, indicating an "apparent lack of sound flight planning and mission execution." It suggested that junior pilots be better trained and more closely supervised by their parent squadron.[55]

By the summer of 1968, events had solidified Maureen's resolve to take up Joe's case herself in the quest to find out what had become of him. It seemed the only way she would get anywhere. With a war on, the government could be expected to behave even more circumspectly than usual. If Joe was alive, she couldn't waste time waiting for information that, even if she did get it, might not go beyond the sanitized version approved for public consumption. She did meet with the Robinson 777 pilot, but he offered little that was new. Maureen was grateful that he had come to see her after getting home, but the visit had failed to settle any lingering questions. And there were many.

Why had Joe not made voice contact after his beeper sounded? Did that indicate the time of his capture? If so, how could she find out if he was dead or alive? Was the U.S. government pursuing the case as aggressively as it could? What about the news report that the Pentagon had ordered searchers not to pick Joe up if he was within 12 miles of Hainan?

Impatient, Maureen would begin pushing more aggressively to find out about Joe, not just for herself and their son but for Joe's father and siblings who, as members of a proud Navy family, were more inclined than herself to let the Navy handle the case. Still, anything new that Maureen could turn up might help ease their deep sadness and worry.

Joe's father, Henry, had fallen apart when he'd heard the news, just as Maureen had feared. The only thing he could think to do in those first, awful days was to walk outside his front door in Hull and bury a shillelagh in a pot of sand. The stick would stay there, he vowed, until his son came home.

4

Where Is Lt. Joe Dunn?

Leona Hoey walked over to her sister-in-law Maureen's kitchen counter, picked up the telephone book and flipped to the "Rs." Since Joe's loss, Leona had visited Maureen nearly every day, her young girls in tow. Maureen, frustrated that she still didn't know whether Joe was dead or alive months after the shootdown, was glad for the support.

The more Maureen thought about the mistakes, mishaps, and sheer bad luck that characterized Joe's case, the angrier and more upset she grew. If it weren't for the *Pueblo* incident, Joe would already have been on his way home on Valentine's Day instead of in the cockpit of an old-fashioned propeller aircraft making a long flight over open water in bad weather. If it weren't for unexpected winds and navigational errors, the aircraft never would have strayed into Chinese airspace. If the Navy knew the real location of the attack sooner, searchers might not have squandered precious hours looking in the wrong place.

Maureen didn't know it yet, but the combination of her frustration and concern for Joe were leading her toward a life of activism that she had never envisioned—activism that would soon take her right to heart of U.S. foreign policy-making at the State Department in Washington, D.C. And it all started that day in her kitchen, as she and Leona brainstormed about how to help Joe.

"I'm going to call Sidney Rabb," Leona said suddenly, thumbing through the phone book for the home telephone number of New England's Stop & Shop supermarket chain chairman. The sisters-in-law had come up with the idea of petitioning the government to be more aggressive in seeking information about Joe's fate and, if he was alive, bringing him home. But where would they collect signatures? They needed to plant themselves some-where busy, where lots of people walked by, and figured a bustling super-market was ideal.

"You're out of your mind," Maureen said. "He's never going to be in the phone book!"

But Leona spotted the number and dialed, despite Maureen's protests.

"You're never going to get permission," she said.

"We won't know until we ask," Leona replied, cutting her off.

Maureen and Leona were hardly seasoned activists. They had never taken part in a boycott or protest, much less organized one. But they had good instincts, and they knew petitions were a quick way to show public support for their cause. And without widespread support, it would be difficult to convince the government to help them.

"I will give you my telephone number, I will give you Maureen's tele-phone number," Leona said into the receiver as Maureen, dying to hear Rabb's reaction, looked on. Leona knew men of Rabb's generation were pa-triotic. She didn't want him thinking they would be burning the flag while bewildered shoppers scurried by, clutching their milk and eggs. So Leona spelled it out. They weren't anti-government. They weren't even anti-war. They just wanted information.

"I want you to know that we're legitimate, we're not a bunch of kooks," she said before hanging up and shooting Maureen a triumphant look. Rabb had no objections.

Maureen began drafting petitions. But she also wanted other ideas for publicizing Joe's case. So one night, she asked some of her nephews, sisters, and brothers to come by after Joe-D' had been put to bed. As her family crowded around her long, wooden kitchen table, eating potato chips with onion dip and freshly baked soda bread, Maureen started talking. Her goal was simple. She wanted to find Joe.

"I mean, where is Joe Dunn?" she asked out loud. "Is he missing in China? Is he missing in Vietnam? No one seems to be able to answer any-thing about this guy with a straight answer. Well, it's China, but it's the Vietnam War, but we can't do anything because we don't have diplomatic relations with China . . ."

And then it hit her.

Maureen knew how to get Boston's attention. She would ask everyone the same question she had been asking all along.

"Where is Lt. Joe Dunn?"

Within days, Maureen was on the phone with printing companies, look-ing for the best prices on signs and bumper stickers. Her nephews asked their friends if they would help man petition tables at Stop & Shop, Brock-ton Public Market in Randolph, and Fernande's.

Leona went to beauty shops and five-and-dimes, asking if they wouldn't mind helping a missing U.S. pilot by hanging a sign in their front display window.

Within weeks, drivers cruising down the Southeast Expressway could see bumper stickers in navy blue and orange—colors based on the Navy's blue-and-gold—that featured one question in big, bold print.

"Where Is Lt. Joe Dunn?"

Shoppers saw the cryptic message on vivid blue poster board as they browsed the windows of shoe stores and meat markets. One morning, Jess Cain, the WHDH radio show host, heard from a curious caller.

"Who the hell is Joe Dunn?" the caller asked. And why was his name plastered all over?

As word spread, Maureen knew there would be questions. She drafted a one-page statement that the newly formed Lt. Joseph P. Dunn Committee could type up and distribute to those who wanted more information, using dramatic language to grab people's attention.

"Heroic, patriotic Joe Dunn . . . the man who wanted to make the Navy his career . . . the man who has a wife and young son waiting . . . the man Washington said to forget . . . do you want to forget him? We don't!" she wrote.

We have organized a national campaign to collect signatures to present to Congress and to the president in an effort to have Lieutenant Dunn freed. I do not represent any one church or political organization, nor is this an at-tempt to collect money. It is an honest effort at my own expense to help my husband, Lieutenant Dunn, who is now believed captive in Red China.

There was actually no evidence that China had Joe, but Maureen, as she pursued her campaign, was working on the assumption that Joe had sur-vived the attack and was in captivity.

Three facts cemented her faith: the vision she'd had on the day he was shot down, the good parachute spotted by the Robinson 777 pilot, and the

With the help of family and friends, Maureen started the "Where Is Lt. Joe Dunn?" committee in 1968, one of the first publicly active POW/MIA organizations in the country. Among its activities, the committee printed bumper stickers to draw attention to Joe's case. Later, Joe's name was among thousands inscribed on metal POW/MIA bracelets worn by Americans during and after the Vietnam War. (Photo courtesy of Maureen Dunn)

beeper heard eight hours after the attack. Whatever had transpired on February 14, 1968, Maureen felt sure that Joe hadn't died that day. She knew, intellectually, that he could have succumbed to any number of factors after the attack, as his superiors had suggested to her in their letters. But there was no proof that Joe was dead. And without proof, Maureen had to assume otherwise. He was her husband. As much as they loved each other, if there was a chance that he was alive somewhere in the world, Maureen had to try and find him.

Indeed, during the months since Joe had gone missing, Maureen kept writing to him. She sent newsy accounts and Father's Day cards in care of the Red Cross, hoping he would get to read about the dreary weather in Boston, how well the car was holding up, his brother Paul's summer lease on a deli, and her own prudence in trying to save money.

"I received all the things from the ship that you had bought," Maureen wrote four months after the shootdown. "Freddy set up the tape deck & radio in my room & it's just fabulous. Honey, I love it, the sound is great, with the headphones I feel as though I'm right there with the Boston Pops. I love the pocketbooks & material & tablecloths are just gorgeous. And your new clothes, oh, I can hardly wait to see them on you."

Maureen told Joe about his father, Henry, who came to dinner often, and how Joe-D' enjoyed seeing him. Henry was still anxious and nervous about Joe but had calmed down some since the weeks immediately following the shootdown, when everyone feared he might have a stress-induced heart attack.

"If for no one but him I wish the Chinese officials would just release your condition one way or another," Maureen wrote. "Remember always, sweetheart, that Joe-D' and I love you & think of & pray for you constantly. You're never out of our thoughts. Everyone does. Every morning Joe-D' gets up and kisses your pic and says, 'Daddy Joe' & when he goes to bed he does the same thing. And he loves you so. We know somehow, somewhere, you will be safely returned to us, honey, we've strong faith & hope and just pray that you do."[1]

Joe's loss, it seemed, had ushered in a deeply painful year for the country. When Rev. Martin Luther King, Jr., was assassinated on April 4, 1968, Maureen hoped the civil rights movement wouldn't lose force. While Boston certainly wasn't exempt from racism or poverty, she had grown up in a fairly diverse area and had been shocked by what she had seen in Florida: the houses in poor black neighborhoods patched with newspaper, the time a white neighbor scolded her for eating a sandwich in her kitchen with a black woman she had hired to help with the housekeeping after she had strained her back giving birth to Joe-D'. It was a sad time, and the sorrow only deepened two months later when Robert F. Kennedy, the brother of the slain president, was assassinated after winning the Democratic presidential primary in California. By then, Maureen felt numb. Her life—the entire country—was in upheaval. She tried to focus on what she could control. She would publicize Joe's case and take care of her son, all the while hoping that somewhere, Joe was alive, and that she would find him. Meanwhile, another Navy wife wanted to find Maureen.

Clear across country in southern California, Rose Bucher knew all too well the frustration of having no control over the fate of a husband who'd gone missing in a secretive, communist country.

In January 1968, less than two weeks before Joe was to leave Vietnam,

North Korea had taken Rose's husband, *Pueblo* Cmdr. Lloyd M. "Pete" Bucher, and eighty-two members of his crew hostage. Rose had come to believe that the State Department wasn't being aggressive enough in trying to free the hostages, but when she approached State and Pentagon officials, they seemed unresponsive to her concerns. With no intention of staying silent, Rose and other *Pueblo* families formed the "Remember the *Pueblo*" committee to keep the case in the public eye. She gave speeches and interviews. When the Pentagon refused to give her a *Pueblo* crew list so she could offer support to their families as the commander's wife, in keeping with Navy tradition, she went on *The Mike Douglas Show* and held up a "Remember the *Pueblo*" bumper sticker.[2]

As soon as Rose heard about Joe, she felt a connection to Maureen, even though they had never met. She imagined that Maureen might be as frustrated as she was, and she wanted to contact her. Some months before, a Navy POW official had told Rose he would do whatever he could to help her. She figured it was time to ask the captain to make good on his offer.

"I am requesting the address (and phone number, if possible) of Mrs. Joseph Patrick Dunn," she wrote to Captain E. R. Williams on stationery with red "Remember the *Pueblo*" letterhead. It was November 1968, ten months after the seizure of the *Pueblo*.

"Her husband, Lt. Joseph Dunn, was shot down last February 14, 1968, 5 miles off the coast of Hainan Island and our brilliant State Dept. did not want to 'rock the boat,' so nobody knows what happened to Lt. Dunn. I'm sure you recall this unfortunate incident.

"It is urgent I have her address immediately," she continued. "Do not give me any double talk or State or Defense department jargon. If you do not give me her address, you will make my already heavy burden heavier and I'm sure you don't want to do that. You will recall how long and hard I worked for the addresses of the 82 *Pueblo* next of kin."[3]

While Rose Bucher waited for word from the Navy, Maureen continued making telephone calls, drafting materials, and composing a publicity strategy. She knew Joe wouldn't want her feeling sorry for herself, so she tried not to get discouraged even though she knew it would be exceedingly hard to get information out of China, which so far had refused to provide any help.

American officials had tried to pry information about Joe's case out of China from the start, but their efforts had been futile. China not only had declined to provide details, it was hostile to the inquiries, which typically were made through contacts at the countries' respective embassies in Warsaw.

A few weeks after Joe's shootdown, in early March 1968, a Chinese embassy attaché delivered a letter from China's charge d'affaires in Warsaw, Ch'en Tung, to the American embassy in that city. There was no mistaking China's view on what had taken place on February 14.

"This is a glaring war threat and military provocation against China," the letter stated. "The proofs cannot be denied. You cannot deny them. Chinese territorial airspace is holy and its violation is impermissible. To punish aggressors is a right of self-defense of the Chinese people. The USG (United States government) must cease its war provocations against the Chinese people. Otherwise there will surely be more punishment."[4]

Three months later, Ch'en's counterpart, Walter E. Jenkins, implored China to provide some basic information about Joe.

"I can conceive of no reason why your government would be unable to provide us with a simple statement as to whether Lt. Dunn is alive and to the state of his health, if he is alive," Jenkins wrote, to little avail.[5] China, it seemed, could not be persuaded to cooperate.

Five months later, it sent a terse message: "We have nothing to inform you about the American airman shot down on February 14, 1968."[6]

Despite that response, and despite China's poor record of providing information on such cases, State didn't plan to give up.

Shortly before Christmas 1968, Maureen had a conversation with the Department of State's Paul H. Kreisberg, an expert on East Asian and communist affairs, who reviewed for her State's record of contacts with China on Joe's case. He told her that in recent years, China had only acknowledged two pilots, one alive and one dead, of all those who had been shot down or forced to ditch in Chinese territory over the years. He did not specify how many had been lost in all. But clearly, the odds of getting much in the way of information about Joe weren't promising, if history was any guide.

"I made clear to her [Maureen] that at no point have the Chinese ever indicated that her husband was alive, dead, in their hands, or in any other way that they had information about him," Kreisberg said in a file memorandum about their December 5, 1968, conversation. He assured her that State would bring up Joe's case again in February with Chinese officials, and that she could call him anytime after March 1.[7]

Figuring that the Chinese might want to reserve Joe for use as a bargaining chip at some future point, Maureen dismissed China's resistance for the time being. She put the finishing touches on her petitions and literature, had stacks of copies made, and prepared to hit the streets with the next phase of the "Where Is Lt. Joe Dunn?" campaign.

The campaign would take off soon enough. But first, there were decisions to be made on everything from how to transport folding tables and chairs to petition sites to what committee volunteers would wear.

Maureen, Leona, and Anna, who together formed the committee's core leadership, didn't want to come across as un-American or anti-military, especially not in the working-class communities around Boston, where that wouldn't play well. Wanting to appear wholesome and patriotic, Leona opted to wear red, white, and blue to committee events. Anna, whose younger sisters so envied her beautiful dresses growing up that they would try to sneak them out of her wardrobe, was always the picture of good taste. Maureen, with her perfectly turned-out pageboy, stylish clothes, and adorable young son, seemed the ideal young wife and mother. Even the teenage volunteers, despite their longer hair, were neat and polite, all the better not to scare away the locals.

But even though they carefully constructed their image, the Joe Dunn committee members could never be sure of people's reactions.

Some were happy to sign on when offered a petition. They would grasp a pen and nod sympathetically at the story of how Joe, a hardy, Irish kid like any they had grown up with, had gone missing in a far-away war while his family hoped and prayed back home. Others were wary.

"No, no," one woman protested when presented with a petition. "I don't sign anything against the government."

"I'm not going to do anything against the government," Maureen said. "I love our country and my husband loves our country. That's why he enlisted in the Navy and became a pilot."

As the campaign gained strength, Maureen's feelings of isolation began to dissipate. Word of Joe's case was spreading through the Boston area, and she heard from other Navy wives whose husbands were also missing or prisoners of war. She was especially comforted by the fact that so many *Pueblo* wives were, like her, waiting for some resolution from a communist country over which the United States seemed to have little leverage. She had struck up a particularly friendly correspondence with Rose Bucher, who had succeeded in locating her.

"I enjoy talking with you so much, Maureen," Rose wrote in one letter. "Somehow, I feel better when I do. Hope you and young Joe are fine—as my boys and I are. Time goes by somehow and I thank the Lord for the things we have—our faith, freedom, health and friends. My mother says one is rich beyond expectations when he has those. Keep in touch and keep the faith. Bye now—Always, Rose. P.S. your husband certainly is a handsome Irishman."[8]

As it turned out, Christmas of 1968 was a joyous one for the *Pueblo* families. Exactly eleven months after *Pueblo*'s capture, Bucher and his surviving crew were released on December 23, 1968, after the United States and North Korea struck a deal. Maureen felt that if the *Pueblo* hostages could have a positive outcome after nearly a year of torture and captivity at the hands of the communist North Koreans, then so could Joe. It was one sign of encouragement in a holiday season that otherwise made her sad.

Maureen missed how much Joe loved Christmas, and the fun they used to have going from house to house, arms loaded with brightly wrapped presents for their brothers' and sisters' families. Now she had to make do with digging through the boxes that had arrived from the carrier for the gifts Joe had picked up in Hong Kong. She took out a bright red fire truck and set of Matchbox cars, wrapped them for Joe-D', and put them under the tree strung with tiny white lights. When the lights blinked, they lit up Joe's Navy picture on the table nearby.

A week later, the resolution of the *Pueblo* case brought an unexpected windfall. Maureen received a telegram from sixteen-year-old Antonio Monaco of North Hollywood, California. Active on the campaign to free the *Pueblo* hostages, Monaco wanted to turn his attention to Joe's case and offered to pass petitions out West.

Maureen realized that the Pueblo wives and friends, exhilarated by their recent success, could bring important momentum to Joe's case, so she quickly called Monaco to welcome him as the Dunn committee's West Coast chairman.

The South Shore media picked up on the development. The *Quincy Patriot Ledger* reported in January 1969 that Maureen would get help from citizens who previously had worked on behalf of the *Pueblo*.

With the influx of help, the campaign expanded. Out west, Monaco passed petitions that read, "Return Lieutenant Joseph Dunn. We the under-signed citizens of America request decisive action in the immediate return of Lieutenant Joseph Dunn, United States Navy pilot, from Red China." Within weeks, he had thousands of signatures.

Already, petitions were circulating in the South under the direction of Leona's father, Leo Ely of Jackson, Tennessee, who was trying to muster support for Joe's cause among his fellow World War II veterans. Arguing that a terrific woman needed help in bringing her husband home, the local Veterans of Foreign Wars Post implored its members in a newsletter to sign the Dunn committee petitions. The goal was ten thousand signatures by April 1, 1969.[9]

As other regions picked up on Joe's campaign, publicity also grew back home.

In Randolph, the week of January 20, 1969, was proclaimed "Return Lt. Joseph P. Dunn Week" by the selectmen's board, and parishioners at St. Mary's in Randolph were reminded in the church bulletin to sign peti-tions stacked at the back of the church. In Joe's hometown of Hull, the board of selectmen resolved to urge the State Department to do all it could to secure Joe's release. Copies were forwarded to Massachusetts Senators Edward Kennedy, a Democrat, and Edward Brooke, a Republican, among others.

"We are concerned about Lt. Dunn because he and his family have been long-time residents of Hull, and the mental torture his wife is being forced to suffer because of uncertainty should be ended," William J. Connor, the board's executive secretary, wrote. The selectmen urged that Joe's case be brought up at a scheduled meeting between U.S. and Chinese officials on February 20 in Warsaw.[10]

Maureen began doing TV, radio, and newspaper interviews. Never shy, she answered reporters' questions with characteristic bluntness.

"Now when I see a Navy recruiting sign I think it should say: Join the Navy. The Navy needs you to replace Joe Dunn who we left behind," she told the *Boston Herald Traveler* in a story published in January.[11]

Her steadfast refusal to give up also came through in the stories.

"Maybe I'm an odd ball or a thick Irish mystic but in my heart I know Joe's not dead," she told the newspaper. "At the alter [sic] we said for bet-ter or for worse and these are some of the bad years. Maybe we'll have 25 good years when he comes home."[12]

With Joe's case making news, local groups such as the Rotary and Kiwanis clubs invited Maureen to speak. Realizing she could reach hundreds of people through such appearances, she readily agreed. But when she took the podium on a cold night in January 1969 at Temple Beth Am in Randolph to give her first formal speech about Joe's case, Maureen was caught off guard by a bad case of nerves.

Standing there in her dressy blue suit, looking out at the large assemblage of women, Maureen felt her palms getting sweaty. She hadn't prepared any text, figuring she would just talk about Joe's case the same way she always did when manning petition sites or answering questions from local reporters. But standing there, she realized this was different. It was much more formal, and she hadn't expected such a big crowd.

As she got ready to begin speaking, Maureen's eyes came to rest on three of her older sisters, Anna, Aggie, and Mary, who were clustered up front. While unconditionally kind and supportive, the sisters weren't exactly pillars of calm. Born worriers, at home they would leave the room as soon as Maureen came on a local TV news segment, just in case something went wrong. Thinking about their jitters made Maureen even more nervous, so she looked away and focused on another spot in the room full of nicely dressed women as she collected herself.

"I'm going to say whatever comes into my head," she decided. She was acutely aware that she didn't share faith or ethnicity with her audience of Jewish women that she could draw upon. But they were mothers, wives, sisters, and daughters. If nothing else, they would relate to her consuming desire to reunite her family.

"I feel a strong affinity with you," Maureen began. "My family is not together. The father of the family is not there. And that's always bad to begin with, to not have a mother and father there, but to not know where they are . . ." Maureen's voice trailed off and she looked up. The women were silent and rapt. "I have to thank you," she said, clearing her throat as her tone grew more assured. Maureen was finding her voice. "I have to thank you for helping me to try and find my family."

As more people heard about Joe's case, it wasn't long before some of them began calling on Congress to act on his behalf.

One Dedham woman, wondering if there was any way to prevent incidents like the *Pueblo* and Joe's case, told Democratic Representative James

Burke, Maureen's congressman, that the Navy should review its practices, and that congressional pressure would help. A Somerville woman asked Brooke, the Massachusetts Republican senator, if Joe really had been forgotten and wanted to know the U.S. policy on seeking the return of captive servicemen. A Randolph man went straight to House Speaker John McCormack, a Boston Democrat, asking him to find out about Joe and keep him posted.[13]

Burke and Brooke actually had been active on Joe's case since the beginning, though with little to show for it.

Early on, Burke had contacted Navy Secretary John Chafee on Joe's behalf and, in reaching out to the State Department, relayed a letter from an impassioned constituent in Dedham who wondered with Cold War–era fervor why the United States wasn't more aggressive in fighting North Vietnam—and in taking on North Korea and China, respectively, over the *Pueblo* and Joe. The man insisted that the United States take a tougher stand for the sake of all those Americans who had died in previous wars.[14]

But the United States had no intention of using all-out force against North Vietnam, even though some Americans were impatient for victory. Johnson had always worried about provoking a wider war with Russia or China. As William J. Macomber, State's assistant secretary for congressional relations, wrote in his response to Burke, the United States didn't want Vietnam to escalate into "the thermonuclear exchange which no rational man could want."

Even so, the United States wanted to prevent North Vietnam from taking over South Vietnam. The key question was what it would take to attain that objective.

"United States policy is one of a measured response geared to the activities of the North Vietnamese," wrote Macomber. "We do not intend to use more force than is necessary."[15]

But how much force was necessary? When the military asked for 206,000 more troops in the aftermath of Tet, Johnson asked for an analysis from Defense Secretary Clark Clifford, who took over the office from McNamara on March 1, 1968, two weeks after Joe's shootdown. Clifford found that the nation's top military officials couldn't guarantee victory even with those additional troops. They couldn't say how long the war would last. The only plan they had to win the war was to wear down the North Vietnamese by attrition, and there was no indication that they were anywhere close to achieving that goal. Clifford and other advisers began counseling Johnson not to commit more ground troops and to cut back on the bombing of North Vietnam.[16]

Johnson was stuck. He wanted to win the war but didn't know how much force it would take or for how long. With the war-protest movement gaining strength, and the impressive showing of the 1968 anti-war Democratic presidential candidate, Senator Eugene McCarthy of Wisconsin, in the New Hampshire primary, Johnson was loath to send thousands more troops to fight a war that had no end in sight.

Three days after Burke relayed his angry constituent's letter to State, Johnson addressed the country.

"With America's sons in the fields far away, with America's future under challenge right here at home, with our hopes and the world's hopes for peace in the balance every day, I do not believe that I should devote an hour or a day of my time to any personal partisan causes or to any duties other than the awesome duties of this office—the Presidency of your country," Johnson said on March 31, 1968, in a nationally televised speech. "Accordingly, I shall not seek, and I will not accept, the nomination of my party for another term as your President."[17]

Eight months later, Senator Brooke contacted State concerning Joe's status after speaking with one of Maureen's nephews. He wrote to Secretary of State Dean Rusk in November 1968.

"The lad reflected the concern of his family for Lt. Dunn's safety; significantly, he also voiced the feeling that he didn't feel that our government was taking energetic enough action to effect his uncle's release," Brooke wrote. "As he put it, the family particularly wishes that it might be possible, at the very least, to obtain information confirming that Lt. Dunn is a prisoner of the Chinese.

"Any information you can give me, beyond a mere statement that 'everything is being done' will be appreciated," he wrote. "I would like to know exactly what has been done and what is contemplated."[18]

By early 1969, so many constituents were writing to lawmakers from Massachusetts, California, and elsewhere that letters about Joe were routinely referred to the Navy and State along with requests for information on what was being done to determine Joe's status. In return, members of Congress generally received assurances that China would continue to be pressed about Joe. But they got little new information.

"We share, very deeply, the concern of Lt. Dunn's family with regard to this tragic incident," wrote Macomber in another letter to Burke in January 1969. The response was typical of those sent to members of Congress, including Burke, Brooke, McCormack, Senator Alan Cranston (D-California), Senator Henry "Scoop" Jackson (D-Washington), Representative Bob Wilson, a San Diego Republican, and others who inquired about Joe's case.

"The Department of State has never received any reliable information or intelligence to indicate that Lt. Dunn was rescued and may be held prisoner by the Chinese Communists," Macomber wrote. "We have made repeated efforts to obtain information about Lt. Dunn directly from the Chinese Communists through our Ambassadorial contact in Warsaw. The American Red Cross, with which we are in close touch, has also appealed by cable to the Red Cross Society in Peking for information. I regret to say that none of these efforts has been successful in yielding any information . . . I very much regret that I cannot be more encouraging."[19]

Senator Kennedy took a slightly different approach, suggesting an appeal to the humanity of Chinese officials.

U.S. officials may get little from the usual request for information, he wrote to the new Secretary of State, William Rogers, on February 5, 1969. "If, however, through the exercise of imagination and persistence by our spokesman in Warsaw the Chinese are informed that basic discussions between civilized peoples demand the compassionate consideration of requests for information about men lost at sea, the Chinese may consider these matters more important.

"I urge you, in the name of a courageous young family, to instruct our spokesman at the Warsaw talks to raise this basic issue and to give it the highest priority," he wrote.[20]

State lawmakers also were taking up the cause. As Kennedy composed his letter, the Massachusetts senate passed a resolution urging Congress and the president to "use all reasonable means" to seek Joe's release, arguing that the situation threatened to "heighten the already tense relationship between Red China and this country while [Joe's] family and friends attempt to endure the agonizing wait for information as to his well being."[21] A similar resolution passed the state house.

The high level of official interest in Joe's case helped draw continued media coverage, satisfying one of Maureen's main goals. Throughout early 1969,

Maureen's picture frequently appeared in local newspapers, sometimes holding a "Where Is Lt. Joe Dunn?" bumper sticker. Some out-of-state newspapers such as the *Fort Lauderdale News* and *Sun-Sentinel* that learned of the publicity campaign ran stories. Leona wrote a lengthy appeal that was published in the *Randolph Herald.* The *Boston Herald Traveler* covered a Rotary luncheon at which Maureen spoke. A picture of Joe-D' in the Boston State House, dapper in short, dark pants, dark knee socks, saddle shoes, a white shirt, and a checkered jacket, was published in Boston's *Record American* under the headline "Where Is His Daddy?"

By February 1969, the Joe Dunn committee petitions had drawn tens of thousands of signatures and Maureen made a critical decision. She would spend the first anniversary of Joe's shootdown in Washington, D.C., pleading face to face with congressional, Navy, and State Department officials to be aggressive in trying to find out whether Joe was dead or alive.

The top priority was convincing State to bring up Joe's case at the upcoming U.S.–China talks scheduled to take place in Warsaw on February 20, 1969. Maureen had checked in as frequently as once a week with Asia specialist Kreisberg and others at State since Joe's shootdown. Now she told them that she would be coming by State's headquarters in Washington's Foggy Bottom neighborhood during her upcoming trip and wanted to see someone who could speak to China's actions and intent with regard to Joe. To her satisfaction, U. Alexis Johnson, an undersecretary of state, agreed to meet with her. Maureen wasn't told exactly why, but she figured it had to be unusual for a high-ranking diplomatic official to agree to see an ordinary POW/MIA wife at the height of a war. She had a sense that her persistence was at least partly responsible for the meeting, a suspicion that was confirmed years later by some personal contacts at State. They suggested that, given the publicity generated by Joe's case, officials had decided it was in their best interests to deal with Maureen.

Before she left, Maureen updated the original information sheet she had drafted for the Lt. Joe Dunn Committee. The message was clear. While she had yet to uncover any significant new information, she hoped that more publicity, and public pressure, would make the difference.

> In the past year I have never given up hope. I have written to congressmen, and other government officials; there have been stories in the papers about my son's daddy, and I myself have appeared on TV. Yet, outside of the won-

derful comfort I have received from many thousands of everyday people like my husband and me, nothing else has happened.

Now I realize I'm just one mother and wife but for the sake of my son, for the sake of my husband—for the sake of all the wives, parents, sons and daughters of all our servicemen, something should be done. I know these things take a long time (witness the *Pueblo* crew!) but I also know that the voice of the people still counts for something in this country. I know my husband, Lieutenant Joe Dunn, believes this too.[22]

This was Maureen's hope as she stared out her taxi window at the snow banks on Pennsylvania Avenue that partially obscured the bleachers left over from the recent inaugural parade for the new president, Republican Richard M. Nixon. On the one-year anniversary of Joe's loss—February 14, 1969—she was gambling that federal officials would make Joe's case a priority once they realized how much public interest there was in the case. Not only that, but she hoped her physical presence would give the issue a personal dimension that had been lacking so far. In all the telephone calls and letters that had poured into federal offices, few in Washington had any mental picture of the young wife—now 28—Joe had left behind. Maureen had another hope, too. Maybe the new administration, which wasn't worn down by years of waging a controversial war in Vietnam, would have some fresh ideas for getting China to talk about Joe.

The taxi was taking Maureen to her scheduled meeting at State with Johnson, undersecretary of state for political affairs and a former ambassador to Czechoslovakia, Thailand, and Japan. He was no stranger to the problem of Americans imprisoned in China.

Fourteen years earlier, as the U.S. ambassador in Prague, Johnson had negotiated with China's ambassador in Warsaw over the release of prisoners from the Korean War. It was the first time the United States and China had held ambassadorial talks in Geneva. Ultimately, about twenty Americans were released, and a Chinese scientist working in the United States was allowed to return to China, as he had wanted.[23]

But three U.S. spies captured in 1951 and 1952 were still serving out long prison terms and, since the onset of the conflict in Vietnam, China was thought to be holding at least another ten prisoners, including two airmen.[24] One of them, Air Force Maj. Philip Smith, had been shot down near Hainan after straying into Chinese airspace, like Joe. Smith went down in the Gulf of Tonkin on September 20, 1965. The second, Navy Lt.

Robert Flynn, had been shot down by China on August 21, 1967, while on a mission to bomb a rail yard north of Hanoi.[25]

Johnson, who was briefed on the details of Joe's shootdown and on the Joe Dunn Committee's publicity work, was advised to speak to Maureen only in general terms about the efforts of State and the Red Cross to determine Joe's status. If details were provided, he was told in a briefing memo, Maureen should be instructed not to make them public for fear of dissuading the Chinese from cooperating.

"Thus far all of our efforts to obtain information concerning Lt. Dunn have been to no avail," wrote State's Winthrop G. Brown, a former ambassador to Laos and South Korea, in his memo to Johnson.

"Mrs. Dunn, as well as friends and other interested parties, have been very active in seeking information on whether Lt. Dunn is alive and a prisoner of the Chinese or whether he died following the plane crash," he continued. "There has been considerable Congressional interest in Lt. Dunn's case."[26]

But Maureen, who arrived at State with Burke, Boston lawyer Frank McGee, and a representative from Kennedy's office, hadn't come all the way from Randolph for generalities. And she didn't want to hear how it was best to keep quiet so the Chinese, whose responses to date had been virtually useless, wouldn't be discouraged from responding. She wanted all the details at State's disposal as well as a frank discussion of what could be done to get the Chinese to divulge if Joe was alive.

As the meeting got underway, Maureen and Johnson took seats on two small couches across from one another. A small, low coffee table separated them, and Johnson was glancing through a slim manila folder that obviously contained information about Joe's case.

"Mr. Undersecretary, I just want to know what is happening," Maureen began. "What is being done here to find my husband and get him home? Everyone is either lying to me or passing the buck."

Johnson told Maureen how he had worked on the problem of Americans imprisoned in China fifteen years ago but that such cases presented a real dilemma even for experienced negotiators.

Often, Johnson said, public opinion could be a useful tool in ratcheting up the pressure on another country. But with China, it tended to give the impression that they "have a useful lever and can extract more from us." On the other hand, he said, total silence wasn't advisable. China's logic was difficult to ascertain, and it wasn't clear why the United States had been successful in winning the freedom of some prisoners but not others.

"So there's no apparent logic in their behavior?" Maureen asked.

"They play for whatever advantages they get," Johnson responded. Peking wasn't acting randomly.

"Well, what is the Chinese reaction when asked about prisoners?" Maureen asked. "What is the logic of not informing us if he is dead?"

Johnson said that the United States has tried for years to get information about people whose status was in doubt. The result was that they have always found out about people who were alive, but not those who were dead.

"If the Chinese went to the trouble of shooting Joe down, would they have left him there?" Maureen asked.

"It's not impossible," said Johnson. "Life doesn't mean that much."[27]

Maureen stressed her personal involvement in Joe's case. She talked about the cases of Smith and Flynn, which also would be raised at Warsaw. Maureen had grown familiar with the plight of those airmen, as they also were shot down by China, and she thought she might be able to get some news of Joe in connection with those cases. She started to explain why she believed Joe could still be alive even though China had never indicated as much, when the meeting was suddenly interrupted by one of Johnson's aides. Johnson and Kreisberg excused themselves and stepped out of the room.

Alone on the couch, Maureen found herself staring at the beige file folder on the table in front of her. No one left in the room was going to stop her. And if State really had nothing new to report, what harm could come from looking?

"Oh what the hell," she told herself as she opened the file to reveal a small stack of papers. The top sheet was blank except for a few hand-printed words in bold, black ink. "Do Not Tell Mrs. Dunn," it read.

Maureen felt as if she had been hit by a baseball. She lifted the cover page and glanced at the sheet underneath. It was filled with small, black type arranged in single-spaced paragraphs. The headline, all in capital letters, read, "COMMUNIST CHINA INTERNATIONAL AFFAIRS." Underneath was a date: 15 February 1968.

Maureen heard voices and quickly put the file down as Johnson and the aide returned. She didn't want to challenge them on the spot because, if information had been withheld from her for an entire year, Johnson certainly wasn't going to throw up his hands and give it over to her in the next five minutes. So after the meeting ended, Maureen thanked Johnson and left. Back at the hotel, alone in her room, she telephoned Burke.

"This is not even up for discussion," she said. "I want the file that is in the hands of the State Department in one hour or I'm going to go to every goddamn newspaper there is and say, 'They're lying to me'. I want that report in one hour."

Maureen waited. That afternoon, a congressional aide arrived at the hotel and gave her a manila file. Maureen never knew how Burke had managed it, and she didn't care. She took a seat, opened up the file, and started reading the sheet with the small black type she had glimpsed in Johnson's office. The headline announced the downing of a U.S. Navy plane over Hainan. The story, transmitted in English by a Chinese news service, announced that China's naval air forces had heroically shot down an attack aircraft of the United States' imperialist naval force.

"Oh my God," Maureen whispered. She'd heard for a year that there was no information out of China concerning Joe. Yet here she was, reading English translations of Chinese accounts of his attack.

One commentary in the *People's Daily* newspaper praised the attack on Joe as a victory inspired by the beliefs of Mao Tse-tung for China as well as for North Vietnam in its fight against the United States. It described Joe's airplane as a carrier-borne attack aircraft and said a second airplane was damaged in the attack. Similar propagandizing accounts characterized the attack as a victory of the proletarian revolution over imperialism, heaping praise on those who carried it out.

The next day, an English-language transmission of a story in the *Liberation Army Daily*, the official newspaper of the Chinese military, gave a blow-by-blow account from the time a combat alarm sounded and a red signal flare went up. Immediately, two planes flown by Deputy Group Leader Chen Wu-lu and Airman Wang Shun-I, two naval airmen, took off from Hainan. The story described in overwrought tones how the pilots, feeling as though they were under the command of Mao, whose portrait was in their cabins, sought the enemy aircraft in the clouds. When they spotted them, and reported to their ground commander, he urged them to show no mercy. The pilots approached at full speed but the Americans tried to evade in the clouds. The Chinese gave chase and, coming upon the tails of the U.S. aircraft, fired. One airplane exploded. The other tried to get away with a Chinese airplane in pursuit, firing rounds after it.[28]

Maureen put the file down. Joe's shootdown apparently had been big news in Peking, generating all manner of commentary and propaganda. The pilots who had shot down Joe had been identified by name. The information had been in a State Department file all along. And no one had told her.

5

The League of Families

I n North Vietnam's sweltering climate, the small room with the tin roof grew so hot that Lt. Robert F. Frishman's entire body broke out in heat rash. Mosquitoes feasted on his legs until they swelled up and he passed out. North Vietnamese doctors treated some of his injuries, removing shattered bones from an elbow. But other wounds were left to fester.

Other prisoners had it even worse. They were trussed with ropes, kept in solitary confinement despite serious injuries, burned with cigarettes, and had fingernails torn out. Seaman Douglas B. Hegdahl, who was captured when he fell overboard a Navy ship, was in solitary for over a year.[1]

When Maureen heard the horrifying accounts of the returned prisoners of war (POWs) who were released by North Vietnam in August of 1969 and publicly spoke of their ordeal at the Bethesda Naval Medical Center outside of Washington, D.C., she wasn't surprised.

Word had been trickling out about the torture of American POWs for years. In 1966, Navy Capt. Jeremiah Denton gave the first direct account when he blinked T-O-R-T-U-R-E in Morse code during a televised interview set up by North Vietnam in order to elicit a propaganda statement.[2] That same year, the world watched as crowds attacked American POWs as they were paraded through the North Vietnamese capital in the infamous "Hanoi March."

Maureen, in fact, had heard about POW torture before Joe ever set foot in Vietnam.

Back in Pensacola, Florida, stories had swirled around base of the heroism of Navy Lt. Dieter Dengler, a Skyraider pilot who had crashed in Laos and endured forced marches, beatings, and other torments before managing an astonishing escape through the jungle from a remote communist prison camp.

Now, hearing of the brutalities endured by Frishman and Hegdahl, Maureen considered what could be done for all the war's prisoners and missing in action (MIAs). Realizing that the story of her personal loss resonated with other families throughout the country, she soon would be drawn into a burgeoning POW/MIA advocacy movement. But in late 1969, Maureen was still unsure. She wanted to keep track of Joe's case but she also couldn't deny that progress had come to a virtual standstill. Maybe working with others would give her some fresh ideas.

Just six months before, Maureen had returned from Washington with high hopes. The meetings hadn't resolved anything, but they did bring a personal aspect to Joe's case that had been lacking thus far. Maureen had managed to secure the Chinese news accounts, which wouldn't have happened had she not gone to the State Department. She had delivered petitions with thirty-five thousand signatures. And she had received Undersecretary Johnson's personal assurance that Joe's case would be brought up at the Warsaw talks scheduled to start in a few days.

Her hopes were crushed just one day later when China abruptly pulled out of the talks.

Maureen didn't know the reason. It could have been an internal political decision, or China could have been angered by Nixon's recent statement that he opposed its admission to the United Nations or by the recent defection of one of its diplomats. Whatever the cause, it was clear that U.S. officials had lost a prime opportunity to inquire directly about Joe's whereabouts. There hadn't been any U.S.–China talks in some time, and it was impossible to know when another round would be scheduled. The cancellation set off a flurry of correspondence by members of the Joe Dunn Committee.

One woman, the founder of a Joe Dunn Committee chapter in Rhode Island who had already inquired about Joe to Navy Secretary Chafee, a native of her home state, now complained to U.S. Senator Claiborne Pell, a Rhode Island Democrat on the Foreign Relations Committee, that keeping China out of the U.N. would only aggravate her further. Furthermore, she argued, if the country has a duty to its citizens, why wasn't Joe protected when he needed help, even if he was close to China's shores?[3]

Leona, who sensed her own deeply held confidence in the U.S. government eroding as more time passed with no word of Joe, wrote directly to Secretary of State Rogers. She asked him why Nixon opposed letting China join the U.N. when two years before he had written an article for *Foreign Affairs,* the publication of the influential Council on Foreign Relations, suggesting that the threat posed by China would only intensify if it were excluded indefinitely from the global community.[4]

In its response, the administration argued that there was no contradiction in Nixon's positions. Brown, State's deputy assistant secretary for East Asian and Pacific Affairs who had briefed Johnson for his meeting with Maureen, told Leona that Nixon's earlier statement reflected a long-term view. But that did not mean rushing to recognize Peking as long as it demanded Taiwan's expulsion from the United Nations and refused to promise to abide by the organization's charter.[5]

State, in fact, had already planned to follow up on Joe's case by drafting a letter about imprisoned or missing Americans that specifically asked whether Joe had survived the shootdown.[6] The letter was to be hand delivered by Kreisberg to the Chinese embassy in Warsaw the day after the ambassadorial talks.

In the letter, Rogers tried to preempt China's historic argument that the United States had no right to intervene in the cases of military pilots who intruded into its territory by stating that the United States didn't seek intervention, just information. "There is no plausible explanation for your unwillingness to respond to such a request," he wrote. "My government firmly hopes that you will provide us with whatever information you have as soon as is possible." He tried to entice China with suggestions that their two countries could move into a more "constructive phase" if only the "old and galling" issue of missing and imprisoned Americans could be resolved. By offering to send a representative to Peking, the United Stations had indicated its interest in resolving the present issue, he wrote, and moving U.S.–China relations "out of the deadlocked position it has been in for the last several years."[7]

Still, China's position didn't soften. Even though the talks were cancelled, an American embassy official delivered the letter. The Chinese official responded by stating that China already had made clear its position on Joe. Nevertheless, he said, the letter would be transmitted to Peking. Johnson, the undersecretary who had met Maureen, promised that State would follow up if China didn't respond.[8]

With little progress on the China front, the Joe Dunn Committee kept up the publicity work at home. To help defray paper, printing, and telephone costs, it hosted a Patriot's Day fundraiser. Joe's Hull High School classmates threw a summer dinner dance for the committee's benefit, an effort Maureen found particularly touching.

"I am sure you all know what you are here for tonight, but what you don't know is how much I appreciate it," she told the crowd. Joe, she added, would be "more thrilled" by that event than any other "because it is his own classmates and town that are wondering, 'Where is Lt. Joe Dunn?' and what they can do about it."[9]

Constituents continued to ask members of Congress about Joe, and lawmakers at all levels of government kept at the case.

From outside Massachusetts, Republican Howard Baker of Tennessee and Democrat Richard Russell of Georgia, who as the Senate's temporary presiding officer was third in line to the presidency, made inquiries to State. Massachusetts' state senator James R. McIntyre sent a copy of his chamber's resolution on Joe's case to Nixon and urged "consideration for this worthy family." The Boston City Council adopted a resolution to commend Maureen and support the petition drive.[10]

Maureen's family, too, tried to maintain public awareness.

When news coverage seemed to drop off, one of Maureen's teenage nephews reached out to half a dozen newspapers, asking them to write more stories about Joe's case. James Gallagher, sixteen, told the *Quincy Patriot Ledger,* in one case, that people needed to remember the welfare of an American pilot who was shot down, unarmed, by a foreign government. He even wrote a story for his high school newspaper in which he poignantly described his aunt's plight. She had no reason to think her husband was either dead or alive. What should she do next?[11]

That was the same question haunting Carole Hanson in the spring of 1969.

In El Toro, California, Carole had first read something about Joe's case in a newspaper over a year ago. Hanson's husband, U.S. Marine Capt. Stephen Hanson, had been shot down in a helicopter in Laos on June 3, 1967. For nearly two years, Mrs. Hanson had kept quiet. She wrote to officials around the world but received no news of her husband.

In February of 1969, she broke her silence, blanketing newspapers and churches around the country with appeals for information. A few months later, while speaking with Rose Bucher and some other Californians who knew of Maureen's work, she was reminded of the similarity in their cases.

Both their husbands were missing—and not in Vietnam. Both of them had toddler sons. Thinking they could help each other circulate appeals, Carole obtained Maureen's address.

"I hope you don't mind my writing you, but after reading of your husband once in the paper over a year ago, I have wondered so many times what more had happened, how you were, and if you had had any more information about your husband," she wrote in May of 1969.

Of her own campaign, " I don't know how much good it has done," she said, "but in the last month I have seen more said about the prisoner-of-war situation than I had in all the two years of waiting.

"I know in some ways your situation is more difficult than mine, for we have such poor and limited contacts with Red China, but I pray that with a settlement of the Vietnam war will also come the release of your husband . . . Hopefully, Maureen, we can help each other."[12]

Carole wasn't the only one speaking out. Her letter, which was one of the first direct links Maureen had to other POW/MIA wives, was written just three days after the Nixon administration moved to denounce publicly the mistreatment of American POWs in Southeast Asia.

"Hundreds of American wives, children, and parents continue to live in a tragic state of uncertainty caused by the lack of information concerning the fate of their loved ones," U.S. Defense Secretary Melvin Laird said at a news conference on May 19, 1969. "This needless anxiety is caused by the persistent refusal by North Vietnam to release the names of U.S. prisoners of war.

"I want to reaffirm the continuing hope that Hanoi will provide a list of American prisoners and permit a free flow of mail between U.S. prisoners of war and their families," he said. "We continue to urge the immediate release of sick and wounded prisoners, the neutral inspection of prisoner of war facilities, and the prompt release of all American prisoners."[13]

The statement—a major turn-around in U.S. policy on POWs and MIAs—was vindicating for Maureen, who had spent months trying to get the public and the government to notice Joe's plight.

Until Laird's news conference, U.S. policy was to keep a low profile on POW/MIAs. As part of that, families of the missing and captured routinely were counseled not to speak publicly about the plight of their men, lest the talk antagonize enemy captors. That could spell worse treatment for the POWs and greater difficulties in negotiating for their release and for information about the missing.[14]

But by mid-1969, it was evident, especially to those POW/MIA families who had maintained a frustrating vigil, that the policy of reticence was getting them nowhere.[15]

North Vietnam wasn't abiding by the Geneva Conventions, a series of treaties that set humanitarian standards for the treatment of wounded and sick combatants, prisoners, and civilians in wartime. Among the violations, Hanoi refused to let the International Red Cross inspect its prison camps and declined to release an official list of prisoners, although some unofficial lists had come out.[16]

Although North Vietnam had signed the Geneva Convention governing the treatment of POWs, it had condemned American POWs as "war criminals", a label used to deny them protections.[17] North Vietnam had expressed reservations about the POW Convention, stating that POWs found to be war criminals should not be afforded the same protections as other POWs.[18]

Nixon's goals were simple. Publicity not only might compel North Vietnam to improve the POWs' treatment, and strengthen the U.S. hand in negotiations to begin that summer, it also could generate more public support for his war policies at home. Caught between escalating the war, which the country wouldn't support, and abruptly withdrawing, which might harm the nation's image overseas and alienate Nixon's staunchest supporters, it was decided that the war would be turned over to South Vietnam. But that would take time.

While the process was underway, Nixon appealed to key constituencies, including the POW/MIA families, a group that included a naturally pro-military, anti-communist contingent. Armed with the POW/MIA issue, Nixon could counter critics who sought a quick end to the war with the argument that an abrupt pullout risked leaving American boys in communist prisons. And no one wanted that.[19]

Congress soon picked up on the broader issue. In September of 1969, U.S. Representative William L. Dickinson, an Alabama Republican, reserved a block of time on the House floor for members to speak out about POW/MIAs. He hoped that Congress' voice would reverberate worldwide so "other nations will recognize Hanoi as an uncivilized country, unworthy of a place in the community of nations if she continues to refuse to abide by the Geneva Convention dealing with POWs."[20]

If North Vietnam does not abide by the conventions, he added, "they are without honor, and their word is no good."[21]

Once the White House went public with the plight of the POWs, and Carole Hanson's letter got Maureen thinking about working with other wives in similar situations, more families began coming forward in rapid succession to talk about their own missing or captive men.

In June of 1969, a group of California POWs wives granted interviews to the *San Diego Union,* which served a large Navy community and had already run an editorial praising the administration's new policy of openness. The editors praised Laird's appeal as forthright and predicted it would do more to improve the POWs' treatment than a policy based on fear of angering North Vietnam. "If the Communists read their tea leaves correctly," they added, "they will see emerging a new era in American diplomacy, where concession and vacillation are supplanted by strength and patient resolve."[22]

The story on the wives, headlined "POW Wives Break Lonely Silence," featured head shots of five women. It told of their struggle since their husbands had been captured or presumed captured. They had kept quiet, in some cases for years, worried that anything they said would be used against their husbands. But when word got out that POWs were being mistreated, they decided to come forward.

"Being silent did not help," said Karen Butler, whose husband had been a POW for over four years.[23]

"We tried giving Hanoi the benefit of the doubt," she said. "We did not want to talk if it would mean punishment for our husbands or if it would hurt negotiations. But there are too many discrepancies between what Hanoi tells the world and what they do. The public must be made aware."[24]

Butler and the other wives were part of a local support group, the League of Wives of American Prisoners in Vietnam. It had been organized formally a couple of years earlier by Sybil Stockdale, the wife of a ranking POW, Cmdr. James B. Stockdale, who was captured on September 9, 1965, after his A4 Skyhawk was shot down during a strike mission over North Vietnam.

Shortly after the San Diego story about the Navy wives, the Nixon administration, in a show of solidarity, invited a group of POW/MIA wives to Washington to meet with Laird. Among them was Mrs. Stockdale, who had started bringing members from outside California into her group in an effort to maximize publicity for the POW/MIA cause.[25] The group soon would evolve into a bona fide national POW/MIA advocacy organization with hundreds of original members, including Maureen.

Meanwhile, the drawdown would start in the summer of 1969 with the withdrawal of the first 25,000 U.S. troops. U.S. troop strength in Vietnam had peaked at 543,400 earlier in the year. There were also over 60,000 allied troops, and 600,000 South Vietnamese.

As the American forces slowly began to return, Maureen found herself surprised, and gratified, by how quickly the culture surrounding the POW/MIAs was changing. Back when she was knocking on doors with the Joe Dunn Committee, she got the impression that some folks would have preferred that she just go away. She had even heard once that Speaker McCormack had been complaining that he was tired of hearing about Joe Dunn. Now, less than a year later, even the Pentagon was speaking out. And attention to the cause continued to build.

In October 1969, *Air Force Magazine* ran a cover story, "The Forgotten Americans of the Vietnam War," a lengthy and detailed account of the plight of POWs in North Vietnam. The Air Force had more POWs—nearly half of the 401 known prisoners—than any of the other services. It also claimed over half of the nearly one thousand men who were reported MIA.[26]

There was more news about the POWs as Christmas approached. At the behest of the Nixon administration, which sought to embarrass Hanoi over the POW/MIA issue, wealthy Texas businessman H. Ross Perot tried to fly thirty tons of food, presents, and medicine to the U.S. prisoners in North Vietnam. The cargo never arrived, but the ambitious mission garnered attention around the world, further highlighting the cause. Perot also flew POW wives and children to Paris to appeal to North Vietnam's representatives there and started the organization "United We Stand" to raise POW/MIA awareness. Nearly a quarter century later, the group would serve as the base for a quixotic presidential bid by Perot.[27]

While Perot was planning his Christmas airlift, two California college students looking for a constructive way to get involved with the war found themselves at a Republican political meeting. There they met a few MIA wives and Bob Dornan, a Los Angeles public affairs radio and television host who wore a bracelet he'd gotten from hill tribesmen in Vietnam.[28]

Noticing the bracelet, which Dornan wore as a reminder of the suffering caused by the war, Carol Bates and Kay Hunter thought about going to Vietnam to get more bracelets that people could wear as a reminder of the plight of the POW/MIAs. Realizing the recklessness of that plan, the women, who were members of the student group Voices in Vital America (VIVA), and an adult adviser, Gloria Coppin, came up with another.

A local manufacture agreed to produce plain metal bracelets featuring the name, rank, and date of loss of POWs and MIAs. VIVA would sell them to students for $2.50 and to adults for $3, with proceeds going to buy advertisements, buttons, and bumper stickers to further publicize the POW/MIA cause.

As Maureen prepared for her third Christmas without Joe, she realized her work was undergoing a fundamental change.

So much attention was being paid to the POW/MIAs that it was becoming impossible to focus strictly on Joe's case. Members of Congress and the Cabinet were talking about the issue. POW wives were going to the White House. State and Defense department officials were traveling to metropolitan areas to meet with families.[29] Bracelets were being made. News stories covered all angles, from heart-wrenching stories of bereft mothers to first-hand accounts of torture from returnees such as Frishman and Hegdahl to the POW/MIA issue's impact on war policy.

Maureen had heard from wives like Carole Hanson. Her home telephone rang incessantly as others who heard about Joe's case through news reports or word-of-mouth networking among POW/MIA families sought out Maureen for advice on how to handle the cases of their own missing or imprisoned men. Calls came in from all over the country, as well as from American brides stationed in England and Germany.

Maureen realized then that she was being caught up in an issue that had grown much larger than the fate of any one man. And even though Joe's circumstances as a China MIA were fairly unusual, it didn't seem practical or sensible to isolate his case from the larger debate over the fate of all the war's imprisoned and missing. In any case, Joe was becoming linked inextricably to the larger cause whether Maureen liked it or not. All she had to do was watch the U.S. House address the POW/MIA issue on that night in September 1969 to see that. Representative Jack McDonald, a Michigan Republican, had used the forum as an opportunity to speak out about Joe's case, in which he had developed an interest.

"We are always talking about 'signals' from the other side." McDonald said. "Let Peking release Lieutenant Dunn, if he is indeed a prisoner, as a 'signal' to us of interest in improving relations.

"If Lieutenant Dunn is not a prisoner, and was lost as sea, then at least Mrs. Dunn's long, cruel vigil will be over and she can turn all her energies to the task of rearing her little son, Joe."[30]

In that way, Maureen transformed from a frustrated wife plastering family cars with bumper stickers into one of nearly a thousand POW/MIA relatives who gathered at Washington's Constitution Hall on May 1, 1970, for a congressionally sponsored "appeal for international justice" for the POW/MIAs in Southeast Asia. Congress had commemorated the day as one for urging foreign nations to seek peacefully the fair, humane treatment of the prisoners and missing and their early release. U.S. Senator Robert Dole, a Kansas Republican and decorated World War II veteran who chaired a joint Senate-House "Appeal for International Justice" committee, was master of ceremonies. Nixon declared a national day of prayer for the POW/MIAs' humane treatment and safe return two days later.

"Few—if any—of the evils of war are more cruel than the deliberate withholding of information concerning prisoners," said Nixon in a message to the gathering. "I call upon the leaders of North Vietnam, the Viet Cong, and the Pathet Lao, as fellow human beings, to abide by the basic provisions of the Geneva Convention Relative to the Treatment of Prisoners of War, to which North Vietnam acceded."[31]

The program featured speakers who promoted various ways of trying to secure Hanoi's compliance with the Geneva Convention on POW treatment. One of the hardest-line views came from Perot, who believed Hanoi would respond only to pressure and publicity. He called for riling up Americans with a display of bamboo cages, holes in the ground, cement cellblocks, and people chained to trees in Washington. That way, citizens would be reminded constantly of the POWs' barbarous conditions.

Differences of opinion aside, the evening was an important reminder to the families of how seriously the government was taking the issue.

"We are joined together across the nation and the world in our efforts to make [all people] aware of the desperate plight of our men," said Sybil Stockdale, whose original group of California POW wives had evolved into the National League of Families of American Prisoners and Missing in Southeast Asia, incorporated that month in Washington, D.C. The nonprofit, humanitarian organization had as its sole purpose the return of American POWs, an accounting of the missing, and the repatriation of recoverable remains of those who died in the Vietnam War. It would be financed by private donations, with a voting membership of close relatives of POWs, returned POWs, MIAs, and Killed In Action/Body Not Recovered (KIA/BNR) from the war.[32] Maureen, who had decided to unify her own work on Joe's behalf with the larger, emerging POW/MIA campaign, was among the League's many founding members.

For a year and a half, Maureen had been preoccupied with the work of the Lt. Joe Dunn Committee, the petitions, letters, and speeches that all had helped to raise awareness. But now it was time for new directions.

Having met other POW/MIA families, especially at the recent Washington "international justice" ceremony and the League's first organizational meeting, Maureen turned her attention to helping organize the Massachusetts' relatives. As they got to know one other, they began coming together to write letters to U.S. and foreign officials and to take trips to Navy, Army, and Air Force offices to see the latest POW photographs or propaganda films released by the North Vietnamese.

When the student group VIVA's POW/MIA bracelet campaign took off in late 1970 following a big news conference, Maureen joined in, turning her house into a sort of mailing and packaging center for bracelet orders from the Northeast. VIVA needed the help. At the campaign's peak, it was processing twelve thousand orders a day. In Maureen's home in Randolph, her sister, Aggie, and her friend, Brenda Sullivan, moved into a corner of Joe-D's playroom with tape, pens, envelopes, and little plastic bags of bracelets. Many orders came in for bracelets bearing the names of New England POW/MIAs, including Joe.

Such work consumed time, and gradually the work of the Joe Dunn Committee was subsumed by the League. Maureen's top goal, though, was still finding out about Joe, so as she spent more time on League activities, she fashioned herself as a voice within the organization for Joe and the other six China MIAs. There were so few China POW/MIA cases that she didn't have much competition. Shortly after Joe had gone missing, in fact, she had contacted some of the other China POW/MIA families but found they weren't interested in doing publicity. Now she took it upon herself to make sure the China MIAs weren't forgotten. Whenever someone at the

League would make a speech about Southeast Asia, Maureen would stand and interrupt.[33]

"AND China," she would say. "Don't forget there are men from the Vietnam War missing in China."

When it came to the media, Maureen was just as savvy about using it to advance the League's broader agenda as she had been in promoting Joe's. When a reporter would inquire about developments in Joe's case or up-coming events, Maureen typically would respond, "This is a community effort now. It's a national effort. Joe Dunn is part of it."

Maureen's name grew synonymous with the POW/MIA issue in Mass-achusetts and, as it did, the telephone calls came with increasing frequency. For the next decade, she would be inundated with requests for help on every conceivable Vietnam-related issue, from how an MIA wife could qualify for benefits for her disabled child to whether the U.S. Veterans Ad-ministration could help a war widow with house-cleaning assistance.

Some callers had no particular agenda. There were nights when Maureen's telephone would ring at 3 or 4 A.M. and it would be an American in Burma who had heard something intriguing about Joe's case through a military or a foreign news source and had tracked down Maureen to talk it over.

The work was time consuming but often satisfying. Maureen especially liked helping out those mothers, fathers, and other relatives of missing and imprisoned men who, due to a variety of difficult personal circumstances, couldn't navigate the channels of government and media on their own to seek information.

Some of them, lacking experience with politics or familiarity with how government worked, simply didn't know whom to call. Others were in poor health, or were caring for aging parents, sickly relatives, or a house full of young children. Some were shy and timid by nature. Others were just overwhelmed. So Maureen dug for them, trying to unearth details of a dis-appearance or capture and what, if anything, was being done.

As for Joe's case, aside from keeping the word out, there was little to do but watch and wait.

Maureen monitored the news for reports of visiting Chinese writers, sci-entists, intellectuals, or athletes. She was willing to question just about any-one from China on the subject of American prisoners there. She followed developments on the future of Warsaw meetings between U.S. and Chinese officials. She contacted the State Department whenever she saw a news report on China policy that could possibly have bearing on Joe's case.

But there were no Chinese government officials in the United States to appeal to. There was no embassy to picket. There were no diplomats to corner. And while some wives went to Paris to meet with North Vietnamese representatives, Maureen declined the opportunity. Even though China was an ally of North Vietnam, Maureen believed those meetings should be reserved for wives whose husbands were MIAs or POWs in North Vietnam. She needed Peking, not Hanoi. So she waited and watched China, hoping for a break.

She had last written to Joe at Christmas time, 1969. She sent a photo card of Joe-D' in a straw cowboy hat sitting on a pony with the message "Peace on Earth, Good Will Toward Men."

"Dear Joe," Maureen began. The letter was briefer than usual. She had gotten tired of writing long, newsy letters, only to see them returned unopened, one after the other.

"I'm sending this with the sincerest best wishes that they will allow you to see a pic of your 3 yr. old son," she wrote. "This was taken Sept. 21, 1969 at Milton for a family outing. He looks just like you, right? We all pray that you receive this & that it will be a happy Xmas because of it. Love, Maureen."

That letter, like all the others sent to Joe in care of the Red Cross in Peking, came back. On the envelope, someone had crossed out the address in pen. The word "Refuse" was written out in Chinese characters.[34]

Once Maureen became known as a POW/MIA activist, it wasn't long before the tips started coming in.

Some people would call to say Joe was alive. Others claimed to know where he was. Maureen dismissed most of them as cranks. Once, though, she took an eight-hour bus trip to Montreal after someone called to say that a clue to Joe's whereabouts, or maybe someone with information, could be found in a pew near the back of a church. She went but found nothing.

Then there were offers of help. Some came from traditional, pro-military organizations such as the American Legion, which helped Maureen from the start by passing Joe Dunn Committee petitions and was later very helpful to the League of Families, providing free office space. But Joe's case also resonated with people of varied backgrounds and opinions.

The ultraconservative and stridently anti-communist John Birch Society offered to help Maureen with publicity about Joe's case. Mindful of the

League's status as a tax-exempt, nonprofit, and nonpartisan charity that had to be careful about political affiliations, Maureen declined. She also knew her own credibility, as an individual activist for Joe and as a representative of the League, stemmed in part from her independence.

On the progressive side, Elaine Noble, a state lawmaker who in the early 1970s became the first openly gay politician elected to a state office, offered Maureen her assistance, even directing her to a good photographer should she ever need someone to document a POW/MIA event.

Some offers were more mysterious, but Maureen didn't want to discount any of them in case, by chance, one should lead to Joe.

One day, she answered her home telephone and found herself speaking to a man who wouldn't identify himself. He would only say that he "knew people" who were interested in helping her.

It sounded like something out of an old gangster movie. Maureen's brothers and sisters immediately panicked. They could picture her on the evening news, her youthful face flashing on the television screen as the innocent bystander tragically caught in a gangland shooting.

Maureen wasn't so worried. She figured she had nothing to lose. She came from a big family that knew many politicians, dating back to her brother Francis's work on Democratic campaigns in the 1950s. It was conceivable that some well-known person, not necessarily a criminal, would try to reach out to help her through an intermediary. She agreed to meet the caller at JC Hillary's, a well-known bar in Dedham.

When she arrived, a well-dressed man immediately walked up to her and suggested sitting at the bar. That came as a relief to Maureen, who felt safer sitting out in the open rather than in a secluded booth.

She got the sense that the man really did have underworld connections but she couldn't say why. She didn't recognize him. In her mind, she began turning over all the names and faces of old family friends and neighbors who might have had connections at one time and would want to help her, for old time's sake. Before she could settle on anyone, though, her thoughts were interrupted by her companion's voice.

"We know about your husband's case and we've been told that we can possibly help you with some contacts," he said.

Maureen took a breath. She might as well be direct.

"Are you telling me the mob is willing to get involved in this?" she asked.

"I don't know who you know, Mrs. Dunn," he said carefully. "But I know that the people I know who sent me here want very much want to help you."

"Well, how did this meeting even come to be?" she asked.

"That doesn't matter," he said. "We're trying to figure out ways we can help you. If you need money to finance this issue . . ."

Maureen knew better than to accept. Taking money from a political group would be bad enough. This was quite obviously out of the question.

"The families want to stay independent of any group," she said. "But it was very good of you to offer."

As the meeting wrapped up, the man told Maureen to call if she ever needed anything. He handed her a small white card. She looked down. There was no name. There was no business. Just a single telephone number typed in black ink. Maureen never found out who was behind the meeting. But if her suspicions were right, it wouldn't be last time that someone from Boston's criminal world would try to help her.

While Maureen's rising profile had many benefits, there was a dark side. It came in the form of harassment, public confrontation, and the occasional death threat.

Sometimes people would call her house, threatening with vague language that they were "going to get" her. Some would tell her she was married to a baby killer and hang up. None of them bothered Maureen much. She just dismissed them as frauds, crackpots, or zealots.

Public appearances were more worrisome. Maureen could never be sure how a given crowd would react to her, especially when anti-war protests exploded in early 1970 following Nixon's announcement that he was sending U.S. ground forces into Cambodia and the National Guard's subsequent killing of four students at Ohio's Kent State University. In one show of strength in Boston, anti-war demonstrators turned a May 1970 demonstration at the State House into an impromptu, successful demand that the flag be lowered to half-mast in honor of the slain Kent State students.

With turmoil all around, Maureen found herself feeling out of step with both the war's opponents and its supporters.

She had never agreed with the war protestors. Like many military wives, she couldn't relate to opposing a war in which her husband had fought. Her only gripe with the U.S. government was that it wasn't doing enough, in her view, to help the POWs and figure out what had happened to the missing.

But Maureen also didn't feel in sync with those who supported the war and Nixon's Vietnam policies to such an extent that they refused to acknowledge anything objectionable about them. They saw Maureen as a young trouble-maker, a rabble-rouser who was always complaining about the government.

Caught between opposing camps, Maureen felt like a potential target no matter where she went.

Over the next couple of years, she would see just how ugly things could get.

One of the most frightening experiences would come in the spring of 1972, when Maureen, Joe-D', and other Massachusetts POW/MIA relatives marched in South Boston's famous St. Patrick's Day parade.

It was the first time the state's POW/MIA contingent joined the parade, and it made a dramatic entry. Playing on the popular "Have a Nice Day" smiley-face theme, the group marched behind a black banner with white letters that read, "POW/MIA Families Never Have a Nice Day." A provoca-tive float featured a man crouched in a bamboo cage.

But as they walked through crowded streets, the dignified, supportive applause Maureen expected didn't materialize. People were scowling, and the atmosphere was uneasy.

"They should be shot for bringing this thing here," one woman said within earshot of Maureen and another marcher, a POW mother.

"Thanks, jerk, for ruining my parade," yelled an onlooker to the man depicting the caged prisoner.

"Hey, she's doing all right, she's driving a nice Pontiac," another man said, referring to Maureen's car, which her nephew was driving slowly be-hind the POW/MIA marchers.

Even the children got their share of taunting.

"That's a tough break kid, but you'll get over it," someone yelled out to Joe-D', who was holding a sign that said his father was MIA in China. An-other man turned down a bumper sticker offered by eleven-year-old Joe Lengyel of Peabody, whose father, Air Force Capt. Lauren Lengyel, was a POW in North Vietnam. He said he didn't want bumper stickers clutter-ing his car.

As the jeering got louder, someone hurled an empty beer can. Another was thrown, and then garbage, food, and more cans rained on them from all sides. Maureen, seeing that a near-riot was breaking out, grabbed Joe-D' and a few of the other kids and put them on top of the float and in her car.

The group got away safely. But Maureen was so angry that she wrote a letter to the editor for local newspapers the next day.

"The family members and I will keep fighting for them until we drop, no matter how hard you try to break us," she said. "I am not and never have been a cry baby but this morning I am crying, but not for myself, my son, nor the other families, but for the men and for you, my fellow Americans, because you have lost almost as much as we have by losing your love for your fellow Americans and by losing the nerve to stand up for him by even a simple hand clap to say we are all behind you."

"May I say God help us all," she concluded, "because if this apathy envelopes [sic] us any more, we will not be Americans."[35]

As upsetting as the parade was, it wasn't as bad as the time Joe-D' vanished.

Joe-D' often accompanied his mother on public appearances, including lighting the Christmas tree on Boston Common for several years. If Anna or Aggie or another family member couldn't look after him on site, he would sit, coloring with crayons, by his mother's side or with a nearby security guard.

On the day Maureen spoke at Boston State College, a student who helped to organize the event asked if it would be OK for Joe-D' to sit in the audience with some of the other students. Maureen agreed, but when the speech was over and she approached the student, Joe-D' wasn't with him. Another group of students said they didn't have him either.

"What do you mean, you don't have him?" Maureen asked. After a few frantic minutes, a note was passed up to her from somewhere in the crowd.

"Now you know how it feels to have a child stolen from you, being a baby killer's wife," it read.

"Oh my God," Maureen said. She recalled the signs she had seen on campus denouncing the war and her appearance earlier that day. She had refused to be intimidated, but now she was second-guessing her decision.

"We have to find him," she told the students as panic crept into her voice. "Where is he?"

For half an hour, students, campus police, and Boston police combed the auditorium and nearby classrooms, looking for Joe-D'. Everyone kept telling Maureen to relax and have a cup of coffee, that he would be found. But she couldn't calm down. All she could think of was that she had lost her husband, and now her child was missing. She was telling the police to keep looking, that he couldn't have gotten far, when a commotion erupted down the hall.

"Someone knows something down there," an older man who looked like a teacher told Maureen. She walked down the hallway to where a bunch of students were gathered. One of them opened the door to a janitor's closet. There was Joe-D', smiling and unfazed.

Maureen started to cry. She knelt down and hugged her son, who seemed mystified by all the attention. Maureen knew whomever had stashed him in the closet had only meant to scare her and make a political point. But from then on, she never left Joe-D' with anybody but family.

By early 1970, Maureen had some reason to be discouraged about Joe's fate, but she fought the impulse.

After years of saying next to nothing, China said flat-out in February 1970 that it was holding only two military prisoners, Smith and Flynn. State also believed it was holding four civilians: the three CIA agents apprehended in the 1950s and Bishop James E. Walsh, a Maryknoll missionary.

Kreisberg, the director of the State Department's Office of Asian Communist Affairs who had been in regular touch with Maureen since Joe's disappearance, was given the information about Smith and Flynn when he raised the issue of civilian prisoners during a private conversation with the Chinese interpreter and adviser to the Warsaw meetings. He asked if their statement meant that they were not holding Joe, but the official had no further information.

Kreisberg didn't think this latest exchange boded well for Joe. The Chinese often withheld information but usually didn't lie outright. He telephoned Maureen to relay what he had learned.

"I found the categorical statement that they were holding only Smith and Flynn quite discouraging in terms of the fate of Lt. Dunn," Kreisberg later would write about the conversation. "My own feeling was quite pessimistic . . . I thought the picture looked quite dark."

Maureen asked Kreisberg if he thought China would ever be willing to state plainly that it didn't have Joe. Kreisberg said they would pursue a more definitive statement. At this point, Maureen was prepared for good or bad news. The worst part was not knowing.[36]

After Kreisberg's conversation, the Navy's casualty branch moved to change Joe's status from MIA to Killed in Action.

"Based on the circumstances of the loss of Lt. Dunn's aircraft off Hainan

Island, it was considered highly improbable that Lt. Dunn had survived. In view of this information that only (Smith and Flynn) are being held, it is believed that a change in the status of Lt. Dunn is strongly indicated," said Laverne D. Miller, head of the casualty branch.[37]

Maureen fought the change, believing there still wasn't any conclusive evidence that Joe was dead. After Frank McGee, her lawyer, sent a letter opposing the change in status, Maureen didn't hear anymore about it.

That wasn't the end of the disappointments, though.

China released Bishop Walsh on July 9, 1970, after eleven years of captivity. But he was unable to provide information on other Americans being held there.[38] The next month, George Watt, a native of Ireland who was arrested and imprisoned while working for a British firm in China, was released. Watt, shown photographs during his debriefing, was able to identify Smith and said he thought three or four Americans were held in the same Peking jail where he was imprisoned. But he could not identify anyone other than Smith.[39]

Finally, Maureen had heard something about prisoners in China. The problem was, the news wasn't good.

January 1971 was "Prisoner of War Month" in Massachusetts. Maureen, who was serving as the League's state publicity chairman, marked the occasion by manning tables with other POW/MIA wives in Boston City Hall to tell people how to write to officials in North Vietnam.

The American Red Cross and the League had teamed up on a campaign to flood Hanoi with letters. As always, the goal was to convince the North Vietnamese that they would benefit, in the eyes of the world, by observing the Geneva Convention for humane treatment of POWs.[40]

In Massachusetts, home to some thirty-three of the roughly sixteen hundred POWs and MIAs, cities and towns were urged to adopt proclamations in support of the campaign. Churches were asked to pray for the POWs and MIAs, and schools and civic groups were encouraged to invite a POW/MIA family to speak. Local Red Cross chapters and veterans groups were prepared to help, flyers about the letter campaign were included with January's New England Telephone Company bills, and post offices expanded their hours to accommodate extra mailings.

Many were happy to comply.

Boston Mayor Kevin White wrote to Hanoi in mid-January, asking offi-

At a post office in Massachusetts, Maureen and Joe-D' take part in a campaign to send letters to Hanoi, part of a movement to pressure North Vietnam into treating the American POWs humanely in accord with the Geneva Conventions. Some anti-war activists opposed the campaign, believing it detracted from what should be the main goal of bringing the war to an end. (Photo courtesy of the U.S. Postal Service)

cials to, "in the name of humanity, publish a list of all prisoners of war and those known to be dead, release the sick and seriously wounded, and permit a free flow of mail. Such action on the part of your government, I believe, would be a major step toward achieving world peace."[41]

Boston's Catholic newspapers published a letter from Archbishop Humberto S. Medeiros urging participation that was read to 1.8 million parishioners in over four hundred churches. High school students in Wellesley were shown slides and asked to write, and students in Milton, Quincy, Easton and Abington took part, as did fourteen thousand postal workers from the Greater Boston area.[42]

One of the biggest drives, which Maureen helped organize, took part in Needham, home to the parents of Air Force Maj. Charles E. Greene, a POW.

The *Needham Times* ran editorials urging citizens to join the campaign, which also received coverage in its news columns. A newspaper ad placed by the Needham Rotary Club included an envelope mock-up with the Hanoi address and a reminder to use a 25-cent air mail stamp.[43] When thousands showed up at the local post office to mail letters, Greene's parents were there to greet and thank them.[44]

But not everyone thought the campaign was a good idea.

Peace activists worried that the U.S. government would use it to detract attention from the fact that it hadn't repudiated its goal of a military victory in Vietnam. They wanted to end the war. And they believed that ending the war was the best way to get the POWs home.

Russell Johnson of the Quaker-founded peace and social justice group American Friends Service Committee (AFSC) called the letter-writing campaign counterproductive. North Vietnam already had said it would discuss releasing the POWs once the United States halted the air war and set a date for withdrawing its troops, he said. But the letter campaign, by emphasizing North Vietnam's ill treatment of the POWs, could be used by Americans to justify more fighting.[45]

The AFSC and other groups, including Clergy and Laymen Against the War and the Massachusetts Political Action for Peace (Mass PAX), also went after the telephone company. They argued that by including a leaflet promoting the letter campaign, the company was endorsing a political message. They wanted equal time, and asked that a flyer on their views be included with the next month's billings.[46]

Some elected officials, too, saw the campaign as one-sided.

Brookline Selectman Eleanor Myerson refused to sign her town's proclamation because the campaign would do nothing, in her view, to end the war. It addressed North Vietnam's failure to abide by the Geneva Conventions, she said, but said nothing about the United States' "indiscriminate bombing, napalming, defoliation, the massacre at My Lai and the prisoners in tiger cages at Con Son," a notorious South Vietnamese prison camp.[47]

"By such a proclamation we are encouraging the expansion of the war and the continued suffering of servicemen and their families on both sides— whether in prison or in combat," Myerson said.[48]

The League of Families didn't see its advocacy in political terms. To Maureen and other members, it was reasonable to demand that North Vietnam reveal which men it was holding and treat them humanely regardless of anyone's position on the morality of the war itself.

"We're trying to get across to the public that we are not backed by any government association," Maureen said. "We're just concerned family members of prisoners of war. We are not financially backed by the government. We are nonpolitical and nonprofit."[49]

Charles Greene, Sr., the father of POW Greene, said critics were investing a humanitarian effort with too much political importance.[50]

In the end, millions of people wrote letters and signed petitions. At the end of January, a small group led by Joe McCain, the son of Adm. John McCain, Jr., commander of the Pacific Fleet, and brother of Navy Lt. Cmdr. John McCain, a POW, stacked six tons of mail on a Paris sidewalk in front of North Vietnam's delegation office. The intent was to show that so many Americans cared about their POW/MIAs that their letters filled a space five feet high and thirty feet long.[51]

The League's impact was now being felt nationwide. Beyond Massachusetts, local and state chapters engaged in all sorts of fundraising and publicity drives, from an Alabama rummage sale that raised $1,000, to a Dallas mailing of a hundred thousand letters, to an effort in Fort Walton Beach, Florida, to raise $12,000 so that eight League members could travel to Laos.

Despite its success, there was some concern that the families of POWs held outside North Vietnam and those of the missing not feel "left out" because so much attention had focused on the North Vietnam POWs, about whom more was known. With some information having come out about their conditions, and North Vietnamese leaders and events such as the U.S.

raid on Son Tay prison outside Hanoi making news, the POWs in the North naturally drew notice. By contrast, virtually nothing was known about prisoners in China, Laos, Cambodia, or South Vietnam, nor about any of the missing.[52]

Wanting to avoid a split, the League's leaders committed to working to "stimulate more interest in and more publicity about those who are imprisoned or missing in other places than Hanoi" and to find ways to publicize the plight of those men.[53]

"All of the prisoners and missing will get our undivided attention," they said.[54]

Maureen, who already was committed to bringing attention to the China MIA cases, made sure Massachusetts did its part. Of all the states that participated in sending letters to Hanoi, Massachusetts was the first to include letters to communist forces outside North Vietnam.

Still, she wasn't hopeful for a resolution anytime soon, despite Nixon's October 1970 proposal for an "immediate and unconditional release of all prisoners of war held by both sides." The speech came in the mail to Maureen's house, together with a note from the White House.

"I continue to hope and pray that we can make progress on the prisoner issue, and I hope that this new initiative may speed the way toward relief for their plight," Nixon wrote.[55]

Around the same time, Maureen received another letter from Admiral E. R. Zumwalt, Jr., chief of naval operations, who promised to support increased benefits for POW/MIA families, as some Navy families had proposed recently. Those included improved home loan eligibility, moving expenses, and convertibility of G.I. bill benefits for wives and children.[56]

It all sounded good, but Maureen had had too many frustrations and disappointments to put stock in encouraging words or promises. Joe had been missing for nearly three years, and she still didn't know what had happened to him. A magazine article came out portraying POW/MIA wives as drinkers and adulterers, upsetting Maureen even though the women had been painted as courageous and steadfast in many other stories. The war's end was nowhere in sight.[57]

As she told one reporter, when years went by and you didn't know if your husband was dead or alive, your existence became a kind of living death. Still, you had to keep going.[58]

Christmas would be festive. Maureen decorated lavishly with pine garlands, velvet bows, and a big, fresh tree adorned with sparkly ornaments and lights. She loved to make the house beautiful, even though Christmas was sad without Joe and she managed to get sick every year around the holiday. This year, she would be busier than usual because she and Joe-D', now four and a half, were moving into a new house.

Scraping together a down payment, Maureen had bought a $30,000, brown-shingled Cape Cod on Grove Street in Randolph. She and Joe had seen the house going up while they were dating. They had both loved it.

More than anything, Maureen tried to do what Joe would have wanted. Be strong. Don't give up hope. Don't worry about what other people think. Do what you think is right.

She thought of what a Pentagon official, Brigadier Gen. Daniel James, Jr., had said around the time that the League was formed.

Defense Secretary Laird, he said, felt a responsibility to the men who were prisoners and missing. When they came home, he wanted to be able to "look them in the eye" and tell them that they had done everything they could think of to help them.[59]

That's what Maureen wanted, too. If and when she saw Joe again, she wanted him to know that she had done everything possible to find him and bring him home.

*** **6** ***

Peace

With the war dragging on in the spring of 1971, Maureen worried that people were growing apathetic about the POWs and MIAs. Ambitious, vocal, and active in the League, she recently had been chosen as northeast regional coordinator responsible for activities in fifteen states. Her goal was to come up with an innovative way to remind the public that American men were still suffering in communist prisons while others were missing, their families unsure if they were alive or dead.

Maureen thought about what drew people together: jobs and neighborhoods, schools and churches, economic status and ethnic background, Brigham's ice cream and the Boston Red Sox. She remembered long, lazy summer days growing up in Forest Hills, when Maureen would tag along with neighborhood kids as they went up the Jamaica Way to Longwood and then to Fenway Park. If a kid didn't have the buck and a half he needed for a ticket, he'd duck under the turnstile while someone else distracted the ticket-taker and a third acted as lookout.

When the Red Sox played at night, you could hear the transistor radios blaring from front porches as neighbors sat on their steps, sipping from cans of Schlitz or glasses of lemonade, hoping Ted Williams would reach the right field seats. Since the Red Sox last won the World Series in 1918, they had been back only twice. But everybody still rooted for them. And that made Maureen think. If she could support a team for all those years, win or lose, maybe they would support her.

That was how Maureen ended up taking the field at Fenway on a beautiful summer day in 1971 to throw out the first pitch.

When she had approached the Red Sox about doing something for the

POW/MIA families, they had responded by declaring July 6 "Salute to Families of POW's Day" at Fenway. The team hosted about eighty families for a buffet lunch. The First Naval District Band played on the field and the district chaplain introduced Maureen, who got a round of applause. Characteristically, Maureen implored the crowd to write to Hanoi and other communist governments that were holding U.S. prisoners. By now, over sixteen hundred Americans were missing or imprisoned in North Vietnam, South Vietnam, Cambodia, Laos, and China. Maureen stressed that people could help the men even if they didn't support the war.

"I don't care how you feel about the war, whether you're for or against it. That's not important," she told the crowd. "The important thing is that the prisoners of war are human beings and they're being treated like animals. If you care for human beings, you've got to help these men. But people have to be pressured.

"Maybe if the Congress and the President get enough letters, they'll do something to make sure the prisoners get humane treatment, at least," she continued. "We put these men where they are. Now we've got to get them out."[1]

As the POW/MIA issue gained prominence through the early 1970s, the League of Families clung to its mandate of pursuing a strictly humanitarian goal. It stressed that this goal—getting a prisoner list and making sure the prisoners were treated humanely and could receive mail—was separate from the larger issue of whether the war was right or wrong. But as the war grew more controversial, it became harder to isolate the POW/MIA goal from broader questions. The League began drawing fire from those who didn't see it the way it saw itself. Meanwhile, Maureen's own profile in the organization was rising. Her views mirrored the League's overall philosophy, and as she took part in demonstrations, meetings, letter-writing campaigns, and other activities, she became known for her commitment, sense of humor, energy, and outspoken manner. In another year, she would realize how far she had come. Roiled by internal dissension over the direction Nixon was taking in Vietnam, the League would pick three representatives to bring its concerns to the White House. Maureen would be one of them.

But first, there was more work. The League had to keep the POW/MIA cause in the public eye while stemming criticism that it was overly supportive of the military, Nixon, and the war itself.

There were those in the anti-war movement who had never seen the League in nonpolitical terms.

War protestors already had come out against the "Letters to Hanoi" campaign. Then, in March 1971, peace activist Cora Weiss argued before a House Foreign Affairs subcommittee that it was both political and inhumane to separate concern for the POWs from the rest of the war. Such a position, she said, fed into the public perception of a vicious enemy, playing into the hands of those who opposed an immediate end to the war. The effect was to prolong the war, extending the suffering of the POWs and all the war's victims.[2]

Such views, however, didn't mean that the relationship between the POW/MIA families and the war's opponents always was defined easily.

Mrs. Weiss, while she was against the very policy that the League was pursuing of distilling the POW issue from the overall war, also helped POW mail get in and out of North Vietnam. She co-chaired the Committee of Liaison with Families of Servicemen Detained in North Vietnam, formed in January 1970, which traveled to Hanoi and facilitated the exchange of letters and packages between POWs in North Vietnam and their families. She also accompanied some released POWs home and had sympathy for the families despite her opposition to the war.

Families, meanwhile, had mixed feelings about the committee. Some refused to have any dealings with it. Maureen, who didn't stand to gain much from the group anyway with Joe missing in China, believed that the committee was unfairly manipulating the emotions of families in hopes of getting them to oppose the war, and that it was being used as a propaganda tool by North Vietnam. She told one newspaper reporter that Joe would kill her if she associated herself with the group. But others, especially those with reason to think their husbands, brothers, or sons were alive in captivity in North Vietnam, accepted assistance.

"I have mixed emotions about the Committee of Liaison, but you get so you don't care where the help comes from," said Mrs. Lengyel of Peabody, a mother of four whose husband was shot down in 1967.[3] For two and a half years, she heard nothing. Then she contacted the committee and received a letter in the spring of 1970.

"Ho Chi Minh himself could bring the letters and it wouldn't matter now," she said. "Just seeing my husband's writing—I can't describe the joy."[4]

And when the Committee of Liaison turned up with a letter from

Michael O'Connor, the brother of a dear friend who was feared dead, even Maureen had to give it credit. She may not have liked its tactics, but she couldn't deny the joy and relief on her friend Kathleen's face when she heard that her beloved brother was alive.

It wasn't only anti-war groups who saw the League as having a political agenda. Members of Congress also had concerns about how it was coming across. During a meeting of the League's board of directors in early 1971, it was revealed that a dozen U.S. senators had told one of the organization's regional coordinators that they had the impression the League was "pro-war, and that this impression should be corrected."[5]

In fact, even as League leaders outwardly denied a political agenda, an internal debate had begun over whether the organization should take a harder political approach to the upcoming 1972 elections. The war would be a major issue in the presidential election—the third since the war's longest-held POW, Army Special Forces Capt. Floyd "Jim" Thompson, was captured by the Viet Cong in March of 1964 after his L-19 observation plane crashed in South Vietnam. The League, some believed, might benefit more by campaigning and raising money for supportive candidates, rather than by just sticking to its issue advocacy.

In the Northeast, Maureen had heard from families who wanted to be more politically active and those who wanted to stay strictly humanitarian. The regional group, on the whole, was very active within the League, going to many Washington events in part because of proximity. Also, families from states like Massachusetts and New York with strong political cultures were comfortable dealing with government and the political process. At the national meeting in May 1971, Maureen laid out the case presented by her more politically minded members. Still, the consensus that emerged, and with which she agreed, was that the League had to stay nonpartisan in order to maximize its influence. If it didn't want to alienate anyone who might rise to power, it couldn't take sides now.[6]

With the political question settled, League members redoubled their awareness efforts. That included ensuring that Americans carried in their minds and hearts a sympathetic portrait of long-suffering POWs that stimulated their compassion and concern. But now another challenge arose. While the families were painting one picture of the U.S. military in Vietnam, a harsher, more disturbing one was emerging in stark contrast.

Since the beginning of their activism, the POW/MIA families had wanted the world to see their men as they saw them: courageous souls who had freely answered their country's call to duty only to be left to languish for years in filthy, desperate conditions. But after years of war, stories were getting out about how American troops had committed unspeakable acts of cruelty against Vietnamese that went far beyond the scope of what ordinarily was accepted in warfare.

Among the most shocking accounts was Seymour Hersh's 1969 Pulitzer Prize–winning story of how U.S. soldiers had massacred over three hundred unarmed civilians, mostly women, children, and the elderly, the year before in the South Vietnamese hamlet of My Lai.

Twenty-six military men eventually were charged in connection with the massacre, but just one, Lt. William Calley, was convicted of premeditated murder and sentenced to life in prison. After appeals, his sentence was reduced. He would be freed in 1975 after serving three and a half years under house arrest.

And it wasn't just journalists with disturbing tales to tell.

In January and February of 1971, Vietnam Veterans Against the War, an organization formed four years earlier after half a dozen Vietnam veterans took part in a peace demonstration in New York City, held hearings in Detroit.[7]

Over one hundred veterans testified in the so-called "Winter Soldier Investigation." They told of crimes that, as one VVAW member, Lt. John F. Kerry of Waltham, Massachusetts, would summarize a few months later for the Senate Foreign Relations Committee, were committed on a "day-to-day basis with the full awareness of officers at all levels of command." The veterans had described committing or witnessing rapes, decapitations, and torture, the killing of civilians, poisoning of food supplies, razing of villages, shooting of animals, and more.[8]

Kerry told the senators that the country had created a "monster in the form of millions of men who have been taught to deal and to trade in violence, and who are given the chance to die for the biggest nothing in history." Returning veterans, he said, were full of anger and betrayal at having been "used in the worst fashion by the administration of this country."[9]

VVAW, whose membership eventually would grow to over thirty thousand, supported the immediate withdrawal of U.S. forces from Vietnam, as did other opponents of the war.[10] Having witnessed the horrors visited by the war on Vietnam and the Americans fighting there, the group wanted it to stop, and soon. As for the POWs, Kerry, who had met with both sides in Paris, told the committee there was little need to keep U.S. troops in Vietnam because, "if the United States were to set a date for withdrawal the prisoners of war would be returned."[11]

If League families had been annoyed with anti-war groups for opposing their "letters to Hanoi" campaign, that was nothing compared to the outrage over Kerry's testimony.

Many families, including Maureen, disagreed with those war opponents who argued that the POWs would be returned quickly once the United States halted the air war and set a date for troop withdrawal. Peace activist Weiss, for instance, had told the House Foreign Affairs subcommittee on national security policy in March that, "No amount of pressure, no amount of petitions, no amount of holiday packages, no amount of speeches at the U.N., no amount of radio spots, of ads, of letter campaigns, of money, or of threats to mine Haiphong harbor can bring the prisoners back . . . All that is necessary, as the other side has made perfectly clear, is to set the date."[12] But Maureen and others in the League thought it naïve to assume that North Vietnam would comply readily; they wanted to keep U.S. troops in Vietnam as leverage until every American was either out or accounted for.

But even that wasn't what angered families the most. Even those sympathetic to the enormous suffering of Vietnamese civilians couldn't fathom how veterans like Kerry could make blanket statements of U.S. atrocities when American military personnel were still in enemy hands. North Vietnam had long argued that captured Americans were no better than war criminals, and had tried to get POWs to admit as much under torture. Now, in some families' view, American veterans essentially had given the enemy what it had sought.

Maureen, who had met Kerry once at a Dedham High School forum on the war, couldn't accept such accusations. She was saddened by the slaughter of innocent Vietnamese but also believed in the fight for the humane treatment of men who, rightly or wrongly, went to fight communism because their country asked them to. As she told the *Boston Herald Traveler* in the summer of 1971, Joe was doing a job he believed in when he was shot down. That was the American way, as she saw it, and nothing to be ashamed of. "If anything, I have found that I have become more patriotic than I ever thought possible," she said.[13]

Though the League and the VVAW would never see the war in the same way, Maureen would learn to put aside her differences with Kerry when necessary. He would go on to represent Massachusetts in the U.S. Senate and run for president, and he and Maureen would find themselves working on the same POW/MIA and veterans' issues for years to come.

The fact that the League's positions had inspired opposition was an indicator that, a year after its official formation, it was having an impact on the national debate over Vietnam.

Since coming together in May 1970, POW/MIA family members not only had drawn personal strength from one another but had generated much more publicity than would have been possible had they stayed on their own. The League was commanding attention from domestic and foreign leaders; since January, Sybil Stockdale and other wives had been meeting every other month with Nixon's National Security Adviser, Henry Kissinger, who was negotiating terms to end the war with the North Vietnamese. Members traveled to Budapest, Hungary, for a World Peace Council meeting where representatives of the North Vietnamese, Pathet Lao, and National Liberation Front communist forces were expected. They met with the International Committee of the Red Cross and the United Nations High Commissioner for Refugees in Geneva and went to the site of the Paris peace talks.

Most significantly, the POWs in North Vietnam saw their conditions improve dramatically in late 1969, after the death of Ho Chi Minh on September 3, 1969, and around the time the League was first coming together. There was more food, less torture, and overall better living conditions.[14] It was impossible to say how much of the improvement stemmed from the publicity and how much from Ho's death, but the publicity certainly didn't hurt and probably helped.

The work didn't come free. By May 1971, one year after its incorporation, the League was spending $10,000 to $12,000 per month and bringing in about $4,000 per month in private contributions. Aided by the White House and other supporters, the League looked to other nonprofits for help, getting advice and services from the Ad Council, which develops public service announcements, and obtaining free office space from the American Legion, a courtesy that would be extended for many years. It received royalties from the sale of wristwatches featuring a caricature of Vice-President Spiro Agnew and was allowed free flights on military aircraft.[15]

The League's main goal of getting the POWs out remained elusive. And any accounting of the MIAs was certainly far off. But after one year, the League was being taken seriously as, within the organization, Maureen continued to establish herself as an active and outspoken presence who took part in virtually every campaign the group devised, sometimes in a leadership role. Beyond that, she had Joe's case to keep sight of.

One breakthrough seemed possible in late 1971, when China announced that it would be releasing two prisoners. Even though China previously had said it had only two military prisoners, Smith and Flynn, Joe's family and friends were excited, especially when word spread that one of the prisoners had been captured back in 1968. Maureen tried to be realistic. When Joe-D' heard on television that prisoners were getting out of China and ran to his mother yelling, "My father's coming home! My father's coming home!" she patiently explained that his father, if he was a prisoner in China, wasn't the only one.

The release didn't turn out as many had expected. China freed the CIA's Richard Fecteau, one of the three agents captured in the 1950s. Neither Smith nor Flynn was released. Instead, China freed a young woman, a California student whom U.S. authorities assumed had died in a sailing accident off China's coast in April 1968. In truth, she had been detained on spying charges.[16]

Maureen, understandably disappointed, sought a meeting with Fecteau but it never materialized. It didn't matter, though, because her attention soon was drawn to an even more promising scenario.

For some time, the Nixon administration had been making tentative overtures to China.[17] Now, Nixon planned to be the first U.S. president to visit the country. A trip was planned for February 1972.

Maureen told the *Patriot Ledger* that the trip was the most promising event related to China in nearly four years.[18] Then, as she read that year's White House Christmas message, in which Nixon pledged to secure the POWs' release and resolve the status of the missing, she had an idea.[19] She would ask to go to China with the president.

Already, Joe's supporters were on the case, reminding the White House to bring up the matter in Peking. Burke, who was still Maureen's congressman, said her situation was the most tragic one he had ever encountered while in Congress. He sent a poignant letter to Nixon that told of the years Maureen had spent careening "from hope to despair on a day-to-day basis, pursuing rumors and unconfirmed reports, not wanting to give up hope, yet not wanting to encourage false hopes." Despite countless inquiries, no one has been able to answer the central question. "What happened to her husband on his fateful flight over the China Sea, February 14, 1968?" Burke asked.[20]

Despite such passionate arguments, the White House wasn't inclined to let Maureen go.

The State Department, in drafting a response for Burke, said his concerns had been brought to the attention of the president, who would try to get information about the missing in China and get the prisoners out. "We are aware of the anxiety of the Dunn family," it wrote.[21] Even so, the White House was concerned that the presence of an MIA wife in China could have a negative impact on the talks. Maureen, who had heard from a presidential aide, thought she understood, until she read in the papers that hundreds of people were expected to make up Nixon's entourage. In that case, she couldn't see how one wife more or less would make a difference. She asked again on Valentine's Day of 1972, the fourth anniversary of Joe's loss. Again, she was denied.[22]

In the end, Nixon's historic visit received tremendous press coverage, much of it positive. Americans were riveted by the sight of an American president at majestic sites such as the Great Wall that had been largely hidden from Western view since the communists had assumed power in 1949. But there was no new information about Joe to be had.

Maureen took heart in the fact that the channels of communication with China were now more open than they had ever been since Joe's loss. So much improved was the climate that Nixon and Chinese Premier Chou En-lai agreed to continue their contacts through their respective ambassadors in Paris.[23] Ronald Ziegler, the White House press secretary, insisted that the location was chosen for convenience and was unrelated to the fact that Paris was the site of the Vietnam peace talks.[24] Maybe so, but Maureen still hoped that the juxtaposition boded well for eventually finding out something more about Joe.

With Nixon's visit behind her, Maureen turned her attention to the United Nations, where she was part of an eleven-person League delegation that met in March 1972 with Secretary General Kurt Waldheim, an Austrian veteran of World War II who later was accused of being a Nazi sympathizer and ally.

Hoping Waldheim would intervene with North Vietnam in order to get accurate information on the American POW/MIAs, the representatives updated him on the League's activities, made a case that North Vietnam wasn't revealing all it knew about missing Americans, and presented petitions asking him to act.[25]

Waldheim, a former Austrian foreign minister, was familiar with the problem of POWs. Austria at one time had approached embassies in Budapest and Moscow to try to get information from North Vietnam on behalf of a visiting American delegation that was seeking details on three missing pilots.[26]

But although Maureen found Waldheim to be a sympathetic listener, he clearly favored quiet diplomacy over the power of public opinion. He told the League representatives that "the more publicity given, the less likely that North Vietnam would be forthcoming." Above all, he did not believe North Vietnam should be chastised publicly as not forthcoming on the issue of captured Americans.

In any case, North Vietnam did not belong to the U.N., and Waldheim said he could not "produce miracles."[27] But he promised to explore possible humanitarian grounds for intervening, to ask Moscow to reach out to North Vietnam, and to speak with the Chinese ambassador about Joe.

It was as much as could realistically be hoped for. Waldheim was at least open to what might be done for the American POW/MIA cause from an international standpoint. Yet Maureen found herself growing impatient with talk. Nixon talked to the Chinese. Waldheim would talk to the Chinese, the Soviets, and maybe others. But would any of the discourse produce results?

Maureen was ready for some action. The opportunity arrived the very next month in the unlikely form of ping-pong.

When Chinese ping-pong players came to New York City in April of 1972—one move in the "ping-pong diplomacy" that had begun a year earlier when a U.S. team made a surprise stop in China—Maureen decided it was the best opportunity she had had to date to present Joe's case. The fact that the visitors were athletes, not diplomats, didn't faze her. So few Chinese had come to the United States in two decades that, as she would say later, she would have approached butchers, street sweepers, acrobats, or anyone else from China, just for the sake of it.

Determined to see someone in the ping-pong delegation, Maureen showed up at New York's Roosevelt Hotel, where they were staying. She figured out the floor they were on by riding the elevators and then thought of how she might get past the few security guards that a chambermaid had told her were posted at doorways and exits.

The next day, Maureen put on a plain white blouse and a dark skirt and headed for the sixteenth floor. When the door opened, she peered out and immediately spotted what she needed. Darting out of the elevator and looking around, Maureen grabbed a cleaning cart loaded with disinfectant, cleaning cloths, and small soaps and began pushing it down the corridor.

Maureen could see a Chinese man posted outside one room and she made a beeline for it. He smiled at her as she knocked. When the door opened and another man saw her standing there, a woman with an armful of fresh towels, he stepped aside to let her in.

Hoping to buy time to consider her next move, Maureen went into the bathroom and began tidying up. She wasn't sure what she thought she would accomplish. All the conversation in the next room was, of course, in Chinese.

After a few minutes, Maureen walked out of the bathroom and into the main hotel room, where she took a seat. Several Chinese were gathered around and a few of them turned to look at her quizzically, as if to ask why she wasn't making the beds.

"My name is Maureen Dunn," she began. "My husband is missing in China."

Maureen tried to explain the case further as the Chinese, obviously confused and unsure of what was happening, got one in their party to interpret. When they realized what she wanted, their conversation grew more animated and one of them made a telephone call. Maureen knew that, even if there were party officials among them, they certainly weren't authorized to deal with the American wife of a downed airman.

In broken English, one of the Chinese men tried to address her as a knock came at the door.

"We can't help you, we can't help you," he said. A man from hotel security arrived, and Maureen was escorted out.

But that wasn't the end of their interaction.

The next day, wearing a streaked blonde wig and carrying a bunch of New York newspapers, Maureen showed up again. Once again, she was allowed in, but when a woman in the room recognized her she was quickly but politely escorted out by the same security guard, who by then knew a little about Joe's case.

The next day, Maureen found herself in the elevator with a young man and a room service cart.

"What floor are you going to?" she asked, about to push the button for her own floor.

"Sixteenth," he said.

Maureen paused just for a brief moment.

"I have friends on that floor," she said.

"I don't think these are your friends," the man replied. "These are the Chinese people here for that ping-pong thing."

"Oh good," she said. "You know, I have a story to tell you."

By the time they had reached the sixteenth floor, Maureen had convinced the young man to let her carry a teapot into the room.

"If anyone asks you what happened, I'll just say it looked like the pot was about to fall off the cart and I helped you," she said. "You didn't know a thing."

Once again, she was greeted by the smiling guard and made it inside. But this time, she was recognized at once. One woman threw up her hands, muttering in Chinese as she picked up the telephone to summon security yet again.

By then, Maureen was ready to give up. She was satisfied that she had done all she could to make her point. And she didn't feel that she was coming away empty-handed. She now had a fresh story about Joe's case to share with reporters back in Boston.

Within the League, Maureen turned her focus to politics. With the upcoming presidential election, she decided to devote the rest of the year to ensuring that voters and candidates kept the POW/MIA issue at the top of their political agendas, even though the League couldn't make any endorsements.

It was tricky work. The war had grown so politicized, and was such a major election issue, that it was virtually impossible for the League to push a relatively narrow POW/MIA agenda without appearing to take sides of the larger question of Vietnam, which it would not do.

It was a sign of just how polarized the country had become that Maureen was tagged a communist after addressing Rhode Island's state senate in the spring of 1972.

The speech was not out of the ordinary. Maureen praised the lawmakers for moving to create a scholarship program for POW/MIA dependents, complained that public apathy was hurting the issue and told of her harsh reception two weeks before at the St. Patrick's Day parade in South Boston. As she tried to leave, state senator Erich A. O'D. Taylor, apparently taken aback by her candor and under the mistaken impression that Maureen wanted the United States to acquiesce to North Vietnam's demands in order to get the POWs out, told her she was like a communist.

A shocked Maureen made the most of it, telling members of the state house, where she next spoke, all about it and grabbing a headline in the state's leading newspaper the next day. But the confrontation between two such mainstream figures as a state senator and a military wife showed just how touchy the politics of the war had become.[28]

Undeterred, Maureen tried to stick to the League's narrow agenda. She developed questionnaires for members of Congress to discern their positions on the war as they related to the POW/MIA issue.[29] Delegates to the national political conventions were asked about their and their candidates' views on peace, the POW/MIAs, and their respective party platforms.

"Has your candidate stated a definite plan to achieve peace and to secure the release of Prisoners of War and to obtain an accounting of those Missing in Action in Southeast Asia?" read a question from one delegate questionnaire. "If not, will you urge him to make a definite statement of his plans?"

Democrats vying for their party's presidential nomination to challenge Republican Nixon in November were put on notice that the League wanted each of them to explain his or her plan for securing the POWs' release and an accounting of the missing.

"Our mission will not be to argue ideologies or events of the past but to elicit a plan for the future," Maureen wrote to former Vice-President Hubert Humphrey, the Minnesota Democrat who lost to Nixon in 1968 and wanted a rematch. In January, Humphrey had called for an immediate end to the war when he announced his candidacy for the nomination.[30]

"We would appreciate receiving a clear statement as to what you intend to do—a position on which you will be willing to be judged at the polls," wrote Maureen, who planned to attend that summer's Democratic National Convention in Miami Beach with other League wives.

Maureen told Humphrey that the POW/MIA issue should take precedence over all personal and political ambitions, and that she hoped he would consider meeting individually with POW/MIA families on his campaign appearances in the various states.[31]

The public, too, was pressed into service. Friends of POW/MIA families, students, and women's organizations were urged to question their home state delegates to the national conventions, and to quiz the presidential candidates on campaign stops.

To guide people, Maureen, who by now was also heading up a nonpartisan state political action committee, composed a flyer that showed a picture of two beleaguered POWs under the headline, "POWS*MIAS: Dying to vote in '72."

She drafted questions for people to ask candidates on Vietnam-related issues, including how they planned to achieve peace, the POWs' release, and the MIAs' accounting and how they believed the future of all of Indochina—Vietnam, Cambodia, and Laos—should be determined.

There were now about seventeen hundred Americans considered missing or imprisoned in Southeast Asia.

"Unless we have overwhelming concern for these men we fear they will be abandoned!" Maureen wrote in her flyer. "Make sure you know every candidates [sic] answer before you vote!"

While the League had concerns that Democrats such as Humphrey and George McGovern, the South Dakota senator who eventually would win the presidential nomination, would do too little to guarantee the freedom of the POW/MIAs, there was also growing unrest over Nixon's policies.

For the most part, the League had backed Nixon on the war since he took office in 1969. But three years later, with POW/MIAs still captive and unaccounted for, families were getting impatient.

At a national meeting in Washington, D.C., in May 1972, the League adopted a resolution that expressed "extreme distress" at the failure of the administration to secure the POWs' release. The resolution said that Nixon's policy of turning the war over to South Vietnam hadn't produced any resolution of the POW/MIA problem. It called upon the administration to set a policy whose goal would be to get the POWs out and the MIAs accounted for, not just to withdraw U.S. combat troops.[32]

Carole Hanson, who was now the League's board chairman, said the statement resulted from a sense of mounting frustration in an election year.[33] Others said that the families were outright disgusted.

Louise Mulligan, the wife of Capt. James A. Mulligan of Lawrence, Massachusetts, who had been missing in North Vietnam since March 20, 1966, said most wives had concluded that if they couldn't compel Nixon to negotiate an end to the war, they would find someone who would.[34]

The angriest families didn't stop there. About fifty of them, concerned that the April 1972 resumption of the bombing of North Vietnam after three and a half years meant that the U.S. war effort wasn't being ratcheted down, went to the White House to demand a meeting with Nixon. When they got there, they were shown to a basement door, where they dropped off a letter in the White House mailroom.[35]

The matter might have been forgotten right there. But a meeting was granted a week later.

By this time, Maureen was not only a well-known member of the League but one who embodied the particular concerns of those families who knew virtually nothing about their men's fates. Unlike the relatives of some of the North Vietnam POWs, the families of the missing and those presumed captive in Cambodia, China, Laos, or South Vietnam had little to cling to. They had gotten no information, and they worried that their concerns wouldn't be addressed in any agreement to end the war. So when the League picked three representatives to meet with Nixon, Maureen was among them. The others were both wives of North Vietnam POWs: Sybil Stockdale, the League's originator, and Phyllis Galanti, whose husband Paul Galanti, a Navy jet pilot, had been shot down in 1966.

The day of the meeting, May 15, 1972, dawned hectic at Maureen's house in Randolph. Maureen and her brother Freddy, who had offered to go with her, had planned to fly out first thing from Logan. But by the time Maureen woke Joe-D', helped him dress, fixed breakfast, and got him to her sister's, they had missed the 7 A.M. flight.

"Jesus, Maureen, I can't believe this," said Freddy, who was methodical and a worrier by nature, when they arrived at the airport gate to find that the flight had gone. "You're going to go to the White House and you miss the flight. The meeting is at ten!"

"Calm down, we'll catch the next one," Maureen said. She wasn't nervous, just determined. Plus, she recognized some of the attendants from

other Boston-to-Washington flights. When she told them she was headed
to see the president, they assured her that she would get two seats on the
next flight.

They were seated, as promised, and when they landed there was just
enough time to grab a taxi and get to the White House, where they were
led inside after a quick security check. Freddy was shown to a waiting area,
and Maureen was taken down a hallway where Sybil and Phyllis were gathered. The women greeted one another and went over their plan. There was
nothing formal, but it was understood that Sybil, as the wife of the senior
naval officer in captivity and the League's initiator, would take the lead. As
they waited, an aide chatted on about their historic surroundings, pointing
out such novelties as the colonial-style pewter ashtrays sitting on a table in
the Cabinet meeting room.

Before long, another aide announced that the president was ready for
them. The women were taken into another room, where two men were already waiting. Maureen immediately recognized Kissinger. The other man
was Brent Scowcroft, Nixon's military assistant. The president was shown
in and, after a round of greetings, the six took their seats in a horseshoe
formation. Nixon sat next to Sybil in two chairs at the top. Maureen and
Scowcroft sat on a small couch to one side of the chairs, and Phyllis and
Kissinger sat across from them on another couch.

While familiar with politics, Maureen had never worked this high on
the national level before. But she had developed confidence since that cold
winter night over three years ago when she had delivered that first, shaky
speech to the temple women's group. Now, sitting in the White House in
her tailored blue dress, she felt calm and resolved. No matter what, she was
bringing up the unique plight of the MIA families, who she felt were
counting on her.

Nixon, who had courted the support of the POW/MIA families actively
while trying to disengage from Vietnam, didn't want to lose their trust
now. He stressed that the mining of Haiphong Harbor one week before
would serve as leverage for getting the POW/MIAs out. Amidst speculation that the mines might be removed before Nixon's upcoming trip to the
Soviet Union, the president said the mines would stay in place to guarantee the Americans' release.[36] Given Maureen's presence, Nixon added that
he had brought up the POW/MIA issue during his February trip to China.
About twenty minutes passed that way, and as Nixon tried to bring the dis-

To Mrs. Maureen Dunn
With best wishes,

Richard Nixon

On May 15, 1972, Maureen Dunn and two other POW/MIA wives tell President Richard Nixon and advisers that members of the National League of Families of American Prisoners and Missing in Southeast Asia are worried that the war is dragging on too long. Maureen stressed that any final settlement should address the problem of the missing as well as the POWs' return. Seated left to right are Brent Scowcroft, Maureen, Sybil Stockdale, Nixon, Phyllis Galanti, and Henry Kissinger. (Photo courtesy of the Nixon Presidential Materials Staff, National Archives and Records Administration)

cussion to a close, he asked if there were any other concerns. This was Maureen's chance.

"I'd like to say something," she began. She explained that relatives like herself, whose loved ones were missing or presumed captive outside of North Vietnam, wanted reassurance that their men wouldn't be forgotten in any settlement to end the war. Nixon said he would be happy to address that issue and then asked if anyone would like to have coffee.

"Do you have any Diet Pepsi?" asked Maureen, who was known in the League for finding humor in unorthodox circumstances. The comment injected some light-heartedness into the otherwise serious discussion. Maureen got her drink, and Nixon continued the meeting, offering assurances that the fate of all POW/MIAs would be considered as the United States sought to bring its long military involvement in Vietnam to an end. When the meeting broke up after about forty-five minutes, the president asked again if there was anything he could do for the women.

"To tell you the truth, I collect antique pewter and I'd love one of those ashtrays that have been lying around for two hundred years," Maureen said, referring to the large plates she had seen earlier in the Cabinet room. She didn't really expect to get an ashtray, so it was with some shock that she opened a box that arrived at her house not long after the White House meeting and pulled out an ashtray and a nice note from Scowcroft. Nixon apparently had directed him to send the wives a memento.

The women, who held a news conference at the White House directly following the meeting, were pleased with the outcome of their visit. It was impossible to say precisely how the POW/MIA issue would be resolved, but they believed Nixon had taken their concerns to heart.

"The president reassured us that the prisoners and missing are uppermost in his mind, and I believe that his action which he has taken demonstrates his concern," said Sybil. "I personally feel very reassured."

In particular, the women had been persuaded by Nixon's argument that the mining of North Vietnam's waterways would provide important leverage for the POW/MIAs. "This could be very, very instrumental in what we want," said Phyllis, who said she had been "very, very critical of the administration in recent months . . . This mining has given me that assurance, and the meeting today has given me that assurance. I hope that the other families in our organization will be heartened by this also."

Maureen felt confident because Nixon had been willing to address the concerns of various League factions. Mostly, she didn't want other MIA wives to worry.

"I am the only MIA wife here," she told the gathered reporters. "Please be reassured that the President is encompassing all aspects of Southeast Asia, all prisoners and missing in actions in Southeast Asia. This includes Laos, South Vietnam, and Cambodia. Please be reassured . . . I was very reassured, and I think that now we should all unify behind him."[37]

Despite the media interest, the meeting didn't capture the kind of news coverage that Maureen had hoped for. While some families were happy simply that Nixon had consented to see them, Maureen believed it was crucial to their cause to get solid play on the evening news and in the next day's papers. In fact, the meeting did get coverage but was knocked off many front pages by even bigger news. That same day, segregationist Alabama Governor George Wallace was shot and paralyzed in an assassination attempt in Maryland, where he was campaigning for president.[38]

Privately, Maureen had concerns about the war that she hadn't aired at the White House, where her focus was on getting assurances for the other MIA families. While satisfied that the missing wouldn't be discounted, she worried that the war would go on indefinitely. Nixon seemed hell-bent on ensuring that South Vietnam was fortified against a communist takeover, something she wasn't sure was even possible. Meanwhile, the deep divisions at home and loss of faith in elected leaders were disheartening. Like others in the League, Maureen was against a unilateral troop withdrawal, but she had come to believe that the United States could call a ceasefire and set a date for the withdrawal without compromising the POW/MIAs, as long as all the American troops didn't leave before the Americans were released and accounted for.[39]

That was another worry. Just how would the government be able to ensure an accounting of the missing? It hardly seemed likely that the U.S. military would be able to sweep through remote, communist-held areas of Vietnam, Laos, and Cambodia, not to mention China, seeking lost men. Yet no one wanted a repeat of the confusion and controversy surrounding the repatriation of American POWs from the Korean War.[40]

Despite two prisoner exchanges in 1953, questions persisted as to whether any living American POWs had been left behind in North Korea.[41]

After the war, U.S. and United Nations Command officials tried to sort out the issue but were met with resistance from the communist side. On September 9, 1953, a little over a month after the armistice was signed, the UNC provided the communists with a list of over 3,400 men who were unaccounted for, including 944 Americans. That number was later whittled down to 389, including both missing men and those who possibly could have been captured.[42] While the meaning of that number would be distorted over the years to imply that all the listed men had at one time been in communist captivity, the point for Vietnam-era families was that they didn't want to spend years wondering who had survived.

With the election approaching, Maureen wanted to raise the stakes. Under her guidance, the League's Massachusetts chapter took out an ad in the *Boston Sunday Globe* in October 1972 for POW/MIA bracelets entitled "Don't Leave Us Behind!!" The ad stated that the United States should never again cease hostilities without first demanding a full accounting of men and called for neutral international inspection and identification of all POWs in Southeast Asia.[43] As Maureen told the *Quincy Patriot Ledger,* the families planned to keep up the pressure so the men wouldn't be written off.[44]

Nixon raised the stakes too. A few weeks before the election, he made an appearance at a national League meeting. Kissinger was supposed to address the group, but Nixon went in person to thank the families for supporting the renewed bombing of North Vietnam and the harbor mining. He asked for continued backing.

"I am speaking of support for a cause bigger than an election, a cause of an honorable peace," Nixon said. Negotiations were ongoing in Paris, and there were two conditions for an agreement, he said. The first was that a communist government would not be forced upon South Vietnam. The second was that, "We shall, under no circumstances, abandon our POWs and MIAs, wherever they are."[45]

Ten days later, a deal was announced. North Vietnam and the United States had come to a broad agreement on terms to end the war. Although details still had to be worked out, and South Vietnam was opposed to any scheme that allowed Hanoi to keep troops in the South, Kissinger held a televised news conference on October 26, 1972, and told the world, "We believe that peace is at hand."[46]

Maureen worked the issue well into the campaign's last weeks. She accepted a sorority's invitation to speak and sell bracelets at Suffolk University in Boston as part of a "POW Week" program, where she lashed out at Weiss of the Committee of Liaison for participating in what she saw as North Vietnam's well-timed propaganda release of three U.S. POWs.[47] In turn, anti-war students accused her of being unfeeling about the damage inflicted on Southeast Asia and too supportive of Nixon's policies. One member of VVAW who was present argued that, if she wanted to get the POWs home, she should work to end the war.

Maureen stuck to her view to the end. She told the young man it was none of his business whom she voted for, and his vote was none of hers. She said she was interested in one thing and one thing only. And that was bringing the prisoners home.[48]

Weeks later, Nixon won a landslide victory over McGovern. But while his "peace is at hand" model had bought him some time, the POW and MIA families soon would grow restless once again.

With the elections over, Maureen turned her attention back to Boston and Joe.

In mid-November 1972, she and Joe-D' planted what would be the first of many "freedom trees" around the country on the Boston Common. A thick, white program featured a simple black sketch of a tree, above which read the inscription, "Lt. Joseph P. Dunn—February 14, 1968," and explained that the tree's growth was intended to symbolize the growth of freedom around the world.[49]

Christmas approached, and the Massachusetts POW/MIA families gathered together at a party organized by supporters at the Boston Yacht Club. The families were grateful for the chance to give their children some holiday fun, although they weren't sure what to expect out of Vietnam. The peace supposedly at hand hadn't yet materialized.

Charlotte MacPhail of Chelmsford, whose husband Don had been missing in South Vietnam since February 8, 1969, told one newspaper that she was still in a wait-and-see mode, although she felt more encouraged than she had in a long time.[50] Meanwhile, the families would do what they could to get through Christmas, one of the hardest times of the year.[51]

Maureen, while encouraged about the POWs, still felt edgy about the MIAs. As she told one reporter, there were now about 1,355 MIAs in Southeast Asia, and if anyone thought North Vietnam would be allowed to "kiss them off, they've got another thing coming."[52]

Christmas 1972 proved even more emotional than usual. Peace talks had stalled, and Nixon ordered more bombing of the North to force negotiators back to the table. All over the country, POW/MIA relatives felt exasperated and frustrated, as Maureen heard over and over again. She hung onto the hope that Kissinger, as he tried to close the deal with the North Vietnamese, would demand that independent inspectors comb Indochina after the war. In any case, she gave Nixon a deadline. If the League didn't hear anything more definite on the POW/MIAs by his January 10, 1973, inaugural, it would get more vocal.[53]

Peace was announced on January 23, 1973, a day after former President Johnson, who sent the first combat troops into Vietnam, died of a heart attack. Kissinger and North Vietnam's Le Duc Tho would be awarded the Nobel Peace Prize for their efforts (Le Duc Tho declined it).

In a radio and television broadcast, Nixon said the historic accord would be signed by the United States and North Vietnam four days later in Paris, when a ceasefire would take effect.[54]

Within sixty days of the signing, "all Americans held prisoners of war through Indochina will be released," Nixon said. "There will be the fullest possible accounting for all of those who are missing in action."[55]

Nixon singled out the POW/MIA families for special praise, calling them "some of the bravest people I have ever met.

"When others called on us to settle on any terms, you had the courage to stand for the right kind of peace so that those who died and those who suffered would not have died and suffered in vain," he said. "Nothing means more to me at this moment than the fact that your long vigil is coming to an end."[56]

The end finally seemed to be in sight. Still, families were cautious. Delia Alvarez, the sister of Navy Lt. Cmdr. Everett Alvarez, who had been held for eight and a half years in North Vietnam, making him the longest-held POW in the North, told the St. Paul Dispatch that her family wouldn't celebrate until they heard her brother's voice on the telephone.[57] Boston native Maureen, borrowing a phrase made famous by a patriot during the American Revolution's Battle of Bunker Hill, told reporters she wouldn't believe the POWs were really free until she saw the "whites of their eyes."

Kissinger elaborated the next day. The POWs would be released in roughly equal installments at regular intervals of every two weeks or fifteen days. There were no American POWs reportedly being held in Cambodia. Those held in Laos and North Vietnam would be turned over to U.S. medical evacuation teams in Hanoi and flown out on American airplanes. Prisoners in South Vietnam would be released to American authorities at designated locations.[58]

All parties were obligated to help each other obtain information about prisoners, the missing, and gravesites of military personnel. An international commission had the right to visit the last place where prisoners were held and from where they were released.[59]

Still, it was difficult to know just who would be coming home. Those families who had received letters from their captive men had a reasonable expectation that the men would be freed, though it was always possible that a loved one had died in captivity since they had heard from them last. But the families of the missing, of POWs whose letters hadn't gotten out, and of those believed captive in Laos, Cambodia, South Vietnam, or China had no idea what to expect.

Maureen, for her part, wondered if North Vietnam, having achieved peace with the United States, would compel its ally, China, to turn over prisoners captured during the war. She recalled what Waldheim, the U.N. secretary general, had said when they had gone to see him. As a U.N. member— Peking assumed China's seat in 1971—China would have to account for its own prisoners. And Maureen didn't even know if Joe was a prisoner. When China had said that it was holding only two military men, Smith and Flynn, she had told herself that the official who had spoken simply might not have known enough about Joe to say anything. But now the day of reckoning was here. Maureen tried to keep herself calm by thinking of Joe's return as an extra-special present. If she got it, it would be spectacular. If she didn't, she wouldn't be crushed because, deep down, she hadn't truly been expecting it in the first place.

As officials gathered in Paris to sign the peace agreement, Maureen and other POW/MIA families nervously gathered in Washington. They were to get the official list of prisoners released by North Vietnam before it hit the news wires.

Maureen's plan, once she checked on Joe's status, was to scan the list for Capt. Donald G. Cook of Vermont, who was captured by the Viet Cong while working as an adviser to the South Vietnamese on December 31, 1964. Depending on what she found out, she was going to telephone his wife and her friend, Laurette Cook.

But before she got word, a Navy casualty officer pulled her aside.

"Maureen, we want to talk to you for a minute," he said. "We have a list from China, and Joe's on it. It's Smith, Flynn, and Dunn."

A jolt of hope hit Maureen before she took a deep breath and a step back. She didn't want to let her guard down at this late hour after all the disappointments of the past.

She thought back to last summer, when House Majority Leader Hale Boggs (D-Louisiana), and Minority Leader Gerald Ford, (R-Michigan), returned from a trip to China. Writing to a Florida woman interested in

Joe's case, Boggs said he had discussed Joe's case "in the highest quarters when I was in the People's Republic of China. While I was unable to obtain any information about his release, I was assured that he was in good health and that the matter was being actively considered by the government."[60] The Navy consulted with a Boggs aide who was on the trip and concluded that Boggs had confused the name Dunn with Flynn, a known China detainee.[61] If Maureen had had any doubts, she never got the chance to ask Boggs. In October 1972, months after returning from China, Boggs was presumed dead along with two other passengers and a pilot when the airplane they were traveling in disappeared in Alaska.[62]

Maureen snapped back to the present when officials brought word that the list was out. There were Massachusetts names, including Lauren Lengyel, Charles Greene, Don MacPhail, and others whose families had worked closely with Maureen. Paul Galanti and Jim Stockdale would be coming home too. Phyllis Galanti, who received word while having dinner with the League's board of directors at the Army-Navy Club, was ecstatic. There were wonderful surprises for some family members such as Jim Sehorn, who learned his son would be freed even though there had been no word of him, not so much as a picture or postcard, since his 1967 loss over North Vietnam. But such joy was tempered with sadness for the many families of the missing who had to face the fact that their men weren't listed as prisoners.[63] Charles Bifolchi of Massachusetts, whose mother had said the rosary twice a day for his safe return, wasn't on the list. Donald Cook was, but with a notation indicating that he had died in captivity. Maureen decided not to call Laurette after all. She knew the Marines would send someone and, anyway, it wasn't the kind of thing to tell someone over the telephone.

A man's voice interrupted Maureen's thoughts.

"Maureen, it's an erroneous report," he said.

Maureen looked up. "What?" she asked. It was the same Navy officer who'd approached her about the China list.

"It's an erroneous report," he said. "Joe's name is not on the list."

Maureen stood up, all the anger and frustration of five years welling up inside her.

"OK, that's it!" she said. "You people have got to do something! It just can't always be me doing stuff for the Navy guy. I'm not accepting that anymore . . . I want you people to go to the State Department and tell them that I want a visa. If the president is so friendly with China that he can go, then I want to go too."

When she got back from Washington, Maureen fell into a deep depression. After so many years of fighting, it was hard to believe that she and Joe-D' wouldn't be able to celebrate a homecoming along with all those families they had gotten to know who would be jubilantly greeting husbands, sons, brothers, and fathers. She would always have hope until she learned for sure that Joe had died. Until then, there was still a chance he would be found alive in some remote corner of China. But she also knew that life might never go back to the way it was before Valentine's Day, 1968.

The first POWs were released in February 1973, and by then Maureen had begun to regroup. She couldn't pull herself away from the televised coverage of the men's return. Having gotten to know so many families, and recognizing so many names, she was mesmerized by the sight of frail but obviously happy men emerging from airplanes to kiss the ground or embrace gleeful wives and children.

Now six and a half, Joe-D' was transfixed as well. Having been immersed in the POW/MIA movement his entire young life, he understood that the men he was watching had been lost in the war just like his father. Now that the fighting was over, the men were coming home.

"Maybe they made a mistake," he said, turning toward his mother. "Maybe Daddy will come out. Maybe he will surprise us."

Maureen looked at her son. It was one of the hardest moments she had had since Joe was shot down.

"No darling, he's not going to surprise us, he's not on that plane," she said, swallowing hard. There was still a chance that they would celebrate his father's homecoming another day. But not that day.

$\star\star\star$ 7 $\star\star\star$

The Missing

It was a dreary late winter day when the doorbell rang at Maureen's house. She pulled the door open and found herself face to face with a skinny man whose skin was tinged an odd yellow. He wasn't entirely unfamiliar, yet she couldn't place him.

"I hear that I have to thank you for bringing me home," he said.

Maureen stared for another moment before it clicked. It was George Wanat, a former POW who had returned to Massachusetts just a day or two before.

An Army captain who served as a senior adviser to South Vietnam during the U.S. troop drawdown, Wanat was captured at Loc Ninh near the Cambodian border during an April 1972 communist offensive. Separated from his Vietnamese allies, he evaded enemy forces for a month, hiding out in remote hamlets and subsisting on green bananas and rice supplied by friendly Montagnards, the tribal people of Vietnam's Central Highlands. Weakened by malaria, he was sitting under a bush one day when he was captured. After being taken to a POW camp inside Cambodia, he spent the next ten months in chains.

George looked frail and unhealthy, and Maureen wasn't sure how to respond. She had grown friendly with his wife, Gretchen, who shared her birthday. While quieter and more laid back than Maureen, Gretchen obviously had been telling George about Maureen's work in keeping the POW/MIA issue alive. Since the POWs began returning, Maureen's emotions had swung wildly between feelings of joy and satisfaction and utter despondency over the fact that she and Joe-D' would not have the same happy reunion with their husband and father that so many other families were having. She looked at George again. Then she stepped forward and embraced him.

"If I can't do it to Joe, I'll do it to you," she said. In that moment, all the effort Maureen had expended since the first days of the Lt. Joe Dunn committee became worth it. Joe hadn't returned, but if George Wanat could show up at her house days after coming home, then Maureen knew that all she and other families had done for the POW/MIAs had mattered, and not just in terms of policy. It had mattered to the men themselves.

Maureen felt her depression lifting. Cheered by George's visit, and with families and hometowns all over the country basking in the POWs' return, and talk of giving them parties, cars, trips, and new wardrobes, it was hard not to get caught up in the celebratory spirit. "Even though it wasn't Joe Dunn, it did help me," she told the Associated Press regarding the homecoming hoopla. "No one will ever tell me that, with the pressure we've put on, we didn't help stop this war."[1]

In all, 591 American POWs, including 566 servicemen from the Army, Navy, Air Force, and Marines, and 25 civilians who worked for U.S. government agencies, returned home in "Operation Homecoming" in early 1973. With the prisoners back, the POW/MIA advocates would shift their efforts to those who hadn't returned. Maureen, who had long tried to look after the interests of the missing, would soon take the helm of a refocused movement as it pressed for an MIA accounting in the face of new obstacles and challenges.

When the POWs first arrived home, there was an adjustment period for the men, their families, and the MIA families who had work to carry on even as the journey of friends whose men had returned was coming to an end. Maureen, whose rise within the League had continued and who by now had a seat on the fifteen-member board of directors, tried to hold a middle ground on the POWs. She didn't want to attend every welcoming event she was invited to for fear of putting a damper on the festivities by reminding everyone of the men who were still missing. But she also didn't want to come across as bitter by turning everyone down. Above all, she thought everyone should give the POWs some space, a position taken publicly by her friend and prominent local veteran, Jerry Canaan, who commanded the South Weymouth naval station and wore Joe's MIA bracelet.

A Navy pilot, Canaan was shot down in down in 1951 and held in North

Korean prison camps for twenty-two months. He began speaking to civic and community groups in late 1972 in order to help ease the Vietnam POWs' transition. He recalled how he had ended up in the hospital after just four days of home leave following his release, so overwhelming were the demands on him to give speeches, join area clubs, march in parades, and more.[2]

Canaan warned that Korean returnees suffered from high rates of alcoholism and divorce. The Vietnam POWs would have to readjust not only to changed families but to profound cultural and societal shifts that had come about while they were gone.[3] Military psychiatrists warned that the hunger, isolation, and sleep deprivation endured by the POWs could produce behavioral changes. Men might experience fatigue, anxiety, impatience, memory lapses, emotional instability, and other problems.[4]

Aware that the military had warned families about the difficulties that might arise after the men came home, Maureen regularly checked in with friends like Gretchen to see if they and their husbands were adjusting OK and if she could do anything to help.[5] With others, she again walked a fine line. She felt guilty if she didn't get in touch but also didn't want to seem intrusive. And she sensed that some of her friends, too, had guilt. Because even if they had hard days, they also had a husband or son or brother who had come home, something Maureen didn't have.

That reality was inescapable. After five years, she still didn't know what had happened to Joe. So once the celebratory spirit surrounding the POWs' return died down, Maureen regrouped to focus on the challenge ahead. The POWs were back, but the search for the missing was just getting started.

Right from the start, the search for those missing and killed in the war was riddled with problems.

The United States and North Vietnam had agreed to cooperate on the matter, by helping find graves to speed the exhumation and repatriation of returns and by taking "any such measures as may be required to get information about the those still considered missing in action."[6]

At first, U.S. officials were hopeful. By the end of March of 1973, prisoner exchanges were wrapping up. Brigadier General Russell G. Ogan, who was directing POW/MIA matters, said at a news conference at Clark Air Base in the Philippines that the North Vietnamese were prepared to facilitate the U.S. search for the missing and the recovery of bodies.[7]

About 1,330 American military personnel and civilians were missing in action in North and South Vietnam, Laos, Cambodia, and China and had not been accounted for. Additionally, about 1,100 bodies of U.S. military personnel killed in action had not been recovered.[8]

North Vietnam said it was not hiding any prisoners and would hand over any bodies or remains in its possession, including those of men who had died in captivity. A Joint Casualty Recovery Center was established in northeastern Thailand, and U.S. search units planned to work with other governments and the International Committee of the Red Cross for three to five years to search battlefields and crash sites for bodies.[9]

But progress proved slow. By July, search teams had conducted just six investigations. One was at the site of the crash of a passenger plane that had no Americans aboard and that Vietnamese civil authorities had already investigated.[10]

Brigadier General Robert C. Kingston, who was in charge of MIA search operations, said communist officials were not cooperating. North Vietnam hadn't released a list of men missing in Laos. Continued fighting in Cambodia and other areas, and difficulties in forming a new government in Laos, hampered search efforts. The vast majority of crash and grave sites to be investigated were in communist-held or disputed territory, and Kingston refused to take investigators into places where armed conflicts were ongoing. In one case, U.S. officials wanted to send a team into a disputed northern coastal area of South Vietnam near Da Nang to look for remains, but the Viet Cong warned them to stay out.[11]

Part of the problem was that, while the war was over for the United States, North Vietnam was still fighting. Its preoccupation with achieving a military victory over the South lessened its capacity for cooperation on the POW/MIA issue.[12]

And the peace agreement itself technically applied only to Vietnam. While the North Vietnamese had assured Kissinger that they would account for POWs and MIAs throughout Indochina, no Cambodian or Laotian negotiators were present at the peace talks and there were essentially no procedures in place to make sure that accounting was done. It was telling that none of the POWs who came home in 1973 had been held in Laos for any significant length of time. Those who had been captured in Laos actually had been transferred earlier to Hanoi and held there.[13]

Finally, just as the POW/MIA families had feared, the United States had little leverage once its troops were withdrawn. Even in the best of circumstances, it would take time to get an accounting of the missing. If progress was slow, North Vietnam knew that the United States had few options to speed it along. It was politically impossible for Nixon to recommit troops to a highly divisive war for the sake of enforcing the peace accord's MIA provisions. Congress had moved to cut off funds for combat activities in Indochina after August 15, 1973, and was not inclined to approve the $3.25 billion in reconstruction aid that North Vietnam wanted and Nixon had promised. Moreover, the president himself had become increasingly distracted and weakened by the emerging Watergate scandal.[14]

Maureen's hope for a full accounting dimmed as soon as lists of prisoners were exchanged on the day the peace accord was signed and, in the case of Laos, four days later.

Families and Pentagon officials were dismayed that the lists didn't include the names of more live Americans even though an earlier list of 368 names, released in December 1970 to Senator Kennedy, also had appeared incomplete.[15] Families, incredibly frustrated, wondered when they would ever get a full accounting of prisoners, and Maureen lashed out at North Vietnam as soon as she returned home. Gathering Massachusetts POW/MIA relatives around her, she held a nighttime news conference at the local Holiday Inn at which she brandished a pamphlet featuring fourteen men who hadn't been listed even though the Pentagon believed they had been captured alive. She denounced North Vietnam as inhuman for failing to release a thorough list and end the families' suffering once and for all.[16] She didn't blame the United States for the gaps. From the interactions she and other League members had had with members of the Nixon administration, including regular meetings with Kissinger throughout late 1972 and early 1973, Maureen believed the country would find a way to hold North Vietnam accountable.

Meanwhile, POW/MIA families and supporters kept up the publicity.

Days after the Holiday Inn news conference, Maureen and Joe-D' appeared at a New York event run by VIVA, the student group that had started the POW/MIA bracelet campaign during the war. Activists there implored Congress not to approve any aid to rebuild North Vietnam until a full accounting was made.[17] Americans were asked, over and over, to keep wearing their POW/MIA bracelets. An ad placed in the *Boston Globe,* and financed by the League, VIVA, and others, told of problems with North Vietnam's prisoner list and said it would take more than a few inspectors to enforce the peace pact's terms on the missing. Featured was a photograph of Navy Lt. Ronald W. Dodge, who would emerge as a poster boy for North Vietnam's poor accounting. Dodge didn't return at the war's end even though a photograph of him in captivity had run in a 1967 edition of *Paris Match*.[18]

"Don't Take Off Your Bracelet!" the ad implored. "There Is More You Must Do!"[19]

In the end, Maureen and the other Massachusetts families wanted, if nothing else, an "honorable end" for their men. In a statement released at the Randolph news conference, they urged Americans to support a thorough accounting so that the world would know what had become of each and every one of the missing. "If dead, let us know now," they said, "and if possible remove their bodies home and let us bury them on free soil in a country they loved."[20]

While there was no word of Joe, Maureen held out a small hope that news of his fate would emerge through the larger quest for the missing. But that wasn't all that kept her going. She thought, just as she had when joining the League, that her outspoken nature and understanding of government and the media could be put to good use. She knew families who weren't sure what to do about their missing men. They didn't have the know-how, or the support of a large family with political connections—Maureen's brother Francis, with whom she had worked on Democratic campaigns as a kid, was campaign manager for state representative John Costello and worked on the 1964 Democratic gubernatorial campaign of Francis X. Bellotti—or the benefit of living in a state with a vibrant political culture where citizens regularly availed themselves of the right to petition their elected officials. Maureen had all that and she had been working the issue for five years. Plus, as she told the AP, she believed she and the others deserved to see their men again, if only to lay them to rest.[21]

There was also Joe-D' to consider. Nearly seven, he sent his father Valentine's Day, Christmas, and birthday cards every year, despite the fact that he didn't remember Joe and all the cards came back, rejected as having an incomplete address or unknown addressee.[22] Maureen worried that he would be badly affected if the first thing he really wanted and worked for in his life—the return of his father—didn't come to pass.[23] Yet she didn't feel right telling him that Joe had died if she wasn't sure. All she could do was keep digging and tell him that if his father was alive, he was in China, and if he wasn't, he was with God.[24] Either way, they had to know.

The next month, there was discouraging news. China released its last known U.S. prisoners, and Joe was not among them. On March 15, 1973, China freed the Air Force and Navy pilots, Smith and Flynn, who also had been shot down during the war. John T. Downey, the last of the three U.S. spies captured in the 1950s, had been freed three days before. Fecteau had come out in 1971, and the third spy, Hugh Redmond, had died in captivity. But when the returnees were debriefed, none could provide any information indicating that other Americans were still imprisoned in China.[25]

"There is no evidence that the PRC is holding any others," Marshall Wright, State's acting assistant secretary for congressional relations, wrote to Senator Alan Cranston, a Democrat from California.[26] Maureen decided to keep after any information about the seven Navy men still listed as missing, including Joe.[27] Later in the year, China would tell Kissinger, on a return visit to Peking as Secretary of State, that they had conducted searches and investigations into the missing personnel based on information provided by the United States. Nothing had turned up but they would keep looking.[28]

Joe had been gone for five years. Back home, another "Lt. Commander Joseph P. Dunn Week" was proclaimed in Randolph from February 11 to 17, 1973. The selectmen took out an ad in a local newspaper that called on citizens to keep writing to Nixon, Representative Burke, and senators Kennedy and Brooke. No U.S. money should be spent on North Vietnam, they said, until it accounts for Joe and the others whose fates remained a mystery.[29]

That week, Maureen put on a hat and warm coat and took Joe-D' to Mass at St. Mary's Church in Randolph to observe the five-year mark. It was a muted observance. Some of Maureen's family attended the service, and after they would go back to Maureen's house for sandwiches and tea.

As Maureen slid into the pew, knelt, and made the sign of the Cross, staring at the crucifix hanging behind the altar and the statue of the Blessed Mother to one side, she couldn't believe how much time had passed since that first grief-stricken night in February 1968, when she had prayed alone in the darkness of her bedroom and had received the vision of Joe. It was a bittersweet time. She was grateful to the people she had come to know through years of Washington meetings, petitioning, and demonstrating, both her fellow families and supporters and those in positions of power. Kissinger himself had offered to deliver letters for her personally to a Chinese delegation in Washington and to Premier Chou En Lai, if she thought it would help. But she no longer believed she would definitely see Joe again. Her love for him was strong as ever, and she didn't want him to slip into anonymity, with everyone forever unsure of his fate. But her conviction that he would one day return had begun to fade as soon as she heard he wasn't on any enemy prisoner lists. Now she just wanted to know what happened. She had been in limbo too long.

Other families were getting restless as well, but in different ways. Some, eager to move on, wanted the government to change their men's status from missing to deceased even when the available information didn't justify such a change. Others wanted a moratorium on all status changes until, in the words of a Pentagon official, "Southeast Asia can be swept for grave sites and combat locations where men were lost."[30]

By law, the secretaries of the military services had the authority to change the casualty classifications of personnel and, by the late spring of 1973, after the last of the American POWs had returned, about seventy men already had been reclassified as killed (KIA). Another dozen cases were under review. But even while changes were underway, at least one high-ranking Defense Department official was worried.

William Clement, deputy secretary of defense, wanted the procedure for making status changes to proceed case by case, but was concerned that the intense emotions of family members would overtake the process. In July 1973, he composed a memo to Nixon, writing that it was unjustifiable, legally or morally, either to rush or to stop all status changes. Instead, the process should continue as always, so that the cases of missing men could continue to undergo review despite a dearth of new information out of Southeast Asia.[31]

By law, the case of every missing man was supposed to be reviewed within a year of his being declared missing. If information showed he had died, or was such that he couldn't reasonably be presumed to be alive, then a report or finding of death would be made. A man also could be reclassified from missing to captured if the facts of the case warranted such a change.[32]

The status determination process "should be allowed to function as prescribed if we are to maintain fairness, credibility, and consistency," Clement told Nixon. "It is not our intent to write off our missing men prematurely, but at the same time we cannot condone building undue hope for the family members without justification."[33]

Essentially, Clement thought there was enough information to show that most, it not all, of the missing probably were dead. He had indicated as much three months earlier in a discussion with another Defense Department official, Roger Shields, the head of the department's POW/MIA task force, who was in Clements' office to talk about POW/MIA policy. When Clements indicated that he didn't think any Americans were still alive in Indochina, Shields had contradicted him.

"I don't believe that you could say that," he said.

"You didn't hear what I said," Clements shot back.

Shields thought he might be fired.[34] Clements, for his part, was putting faith in what the POWs had said after their return. They had confirmed the deaths of fewer than one hundred unaccounted-for personnel. And they said none of the other missing had been taken prisoner. Knowing that the POWs had devised ways to communicate with and account for one another, Clements figured that they surely would know if any of the missing had been captured. Then there were the other side's repeated statements that no missing Americans were still being held prisoner. Given this information, and the fact that many of the missing were thought in the first place to have had only the slimmest chances of survival, Clement believed it was time to declare the men dead, except in those cases where true reasonable doubt existed. In any case, as he wrote to Nixon, the status changes shouldn't be "unalterably tied to the inspection of combat sites, the recovery of remains, or the personal desires of family members."[35]

Not surprisingly, while some family members were more than ready to proceed, others found that approach threatening. They didn't want any status changes until more information was forthcoming from North Vietnam, which still hadn't granted much in the way of authority for inspecting crash sites or recovering bodies.[36] And they worried that too much weight was being given to what North Vietnam said in the absence of supporting data.[37]

Other questions also were surfacing. Some families were concerned that servicemen such as Lt. Dodge, who at one point was known to be alive in captivity, would be written off hastily as dead. Bodies that did come back could be hard to identify and, in some cases, relatives feared that the wrong bodies had come home.[38] Through the League, Maureen had met Jerry Dennis, an Ohio fireman who obtained a court order to get his brother's status changed from killed to missing, pending a hearing, after trying unsuccessfully to convince the Navy that the body identified as his brother's really belonged to someone else.[39] Frustration was mounting and, two days after Clements wrote his memo to Nixon, five relatives of the missing filed a class action lawsuit in a U.S. District Court in New York to prohibit changes in the status of unaccounted for personnel. The suit argued that the law governing such changes was unconstitutional because it violated the Fifth Amendment guarantee of due process.[40]

Maureen, who worked behind the scenes in support of the lawsuit, thought the existing process for making status changes was secretive and arbitrary, and that families should have a chance to comment before their relatives were declared dead. The issue had financial as well as emotional ramifications, because next of kin collected a man's pay as long as he was considered missing. Once he was declared dead, the payments stopped.

With litigation underway, and status reviews temporarily halted by a court injunction, Maureen focused on making sure people didn't forget about the missing with the war over and the POWs home.

As Christmas approached, she organized a "tree unlighting" ceremony on the Boston Common to highlight the issues at stake in the lawsuit. A tree planted in Joe's memory had been strung with Christmas lights, seven of which Joe-D' unscrewed to demonstrate how easy it was under the current system to end a life legally. Maureen watched the little colored lights go out one by one and considered that while all the MIAs couldn't be alive, some probably were. She didn't want them to be written off easily.[41]

The most dramatic ceremony in the winter of 1973 took place at twilight on a cold November night at the State House. Dressed in a camel-hair suit, Maureen solemnly stood with George Wanat as Beacon Hill's golden dome glowed behind them against the darkening indigo sky. George opened the ceremony by walking over to Lt. Gov. Donald Dwight and handing him a folded black-and-white POW/MIA flag. Created two years before as the movement's symbol, the flag strikingly depicted the bowed, silhouetted head of a prisoner against a distant watchtower. The flag was raised, a Catholic priest gave a benediction, and a procession began as Maureen and George carried a lit lantern down the State House steps and over to the Common, the first stop on Boston's "Freedom Trail" commemorating famous places and events of the American Revolution. There, George's wife Gretchen and a state lawmaker joined in, taking the lantern and walking along with George and Maureen to the next stop. At each stop on the trail, the lantern was handed off to a different set of MIA relatives, returned POWs, and state lawmakers, all of whom joined the procession to its conclusion at the Old North Church. The lone lantern burned in the dark the entire way, lighting a path for the missing.

Another event, held right after the holidays, was designed to contrast the joy of the families of returned POWs with the lonely plight of those still waiting for word on the missing.

It was January 27, 1974, the first anniversary of the peace accord, and Massachusetts POW/MIA families took their spots at two trees in Boston.[42] Army Green Beret Sgt. Donald MacPhail of Chelmsford, who spent over four years as a POW, stood before a festively decorated tree on the State House lawn to symbolize the returnees' joy. At Joe's unadorned "freedom tree" on the Common, meanwhile, Barbara Cleary of Marblehead stood silently with her children. Barbara's husband Peter, an Air Force fighter pilot, went missing over North Vietnam during the last minutes of his tour's last flight. Like Maureen, she wanted Americans to realize that many men were still missing.[43]

Maureen had helped plan the tree demonstration but couldn't go. She recently had been named the League's acting national coordinator, filling in temporarily when the regular coordinator stepped down, and was headed to Washington to testify before the Senate Foreign Relations Committee, which had been flooded with hundreds of postcards and letters from families who wanted it to look into the MIA issue.[44]

Since "Operation Homecoming," virtually no progress had been made on accounting for the roughly thirteen hundred missing and others who, due to incomplete information, were still listed as POWs. Maureen worried the issue was losing steam, not only because Americans wanted to forget Vietnam but because other international issues were emerging that threatened to push it out of the spotlight.[45]

Walking into the formal Senate hearing room in January 1974, Maureen was determined to grab the senators' attention by making as strong and succinct a case for the MIAs as possible. She glanced around to take stock of the room, which was filling up. Men and a few women chatted in the area designated for the public as they waited for the hearing to start. Up on the dais, a few senators had taken their seats and were listening to youthful aides who crouched beside them, speaking in hushed, earnest tones as they clutched clipboards and stacks of papers. Others came in and out of the side doors that led to the committee's private offices.

Maureen sat behind the witness table and tried to clear her head of any preconceived notions about her audience, as she always did before speaking in public. She didn't want to come across as jaded, so she tried to erase anything she had heard about the committee members' personality quirks or bad habits or what they already had said about the war. But she did take note of who was there. When she answered questions, she wanted to be able to adjust her tone depending on whether she was addressing a brash young man, a courtly older southerner, or an East Coast aristocrat.

Maureen also wasn't inclined to cut anybody much slack. She didn't like speaking to empty seats and, in past appearances before law-making bodies, had been known to stop partway through a statement if members didn't seem attentive or if a key lawmaker had been distracted one too many times. "I'm going to stop right now to give you a chance to give your messages to your aides because I know it's important," she would say. She knew what word some used to describe her and she accepted it because, deep down, she believed that the lawmakers were there to serve her and the other taxpayers who funded their salaries. And while she knew they were busy with issues beyond the MIAs, she was busy, too. Just to come to Washington for one committee appearance, she had to find and pay for transportation, pack, write testimony, and arrange for a relative to care for Joe-D', all without the help of a paid staff or secretary. So when she spoke, she wanted people to listen.

Maureen also made it a point to look like a woman with a job to do. She had learned early that she would not get respect by playing the demure wife who missed her husband. So she always dressed professionally. Ever since the days of wanting her baseball cap to match her T-shirt, Maureen had been conscious of fashion. When she represented the League and Joe's case in winter, she typically would wear a tweed suit with matching shoes and handbag. Outside, she would add a wool coat, beret, and matching gloves. In warmer months, she often would don a dress-and-coat ensem-

ble. Those in her party who ignored her dictate to "dress right" did so at
their own peril. George Wanat knew it. Even though he favored blue jeans,
he invested in a couple of pairs of European-tailored trousers specifically
for his POW/MIA appearances with Maureen.

That day in the Senate hearing room, Maureen could feel her energy rising as the gavel fell and the hearing came to order. When it was her turn to
testify and she was recognized, she opened with a description of Joe's case.
Despite its unique characteristics, she said, it mirrored those of others
whose fates remained a mystery.

"Next month marks the sixth anniversary of my husband's disappearance and the ninth and tenth anniversaries of others. Must we be obliged
to be good Americans and suffer six years or ten years more? I sincerely
hope not. Not just for myself and other POW/MIA families, but for the
honor and dignity of all the men still over there who deserve more from
their country than complete and absolute oblivion," Maureen said. Government efforts to get an accounting have been ineffective, she continued,
and once a senator had even told her that, since the Senate hadn't ratified
the peace accord, it wasn't the Senate's problem to see that its MIA provisions be upheld.

"As I go from school to school, service clubs, shopping malls, etcetera to
speak, questions inevitably arise about what our senators and congressmen
are doing about the situation," she continued. "For years I have answered
that they are trying . . . that they are doing everything in their immediate
power to rectify this injustice. But of late, I feel I am not answering with
strong conviction that I feel you in the Congress are doing everything in
your power to clear up this issue. I am beginning to feel, as do most family members, and many concerned citizens in your respective states, that
our problem has been Watergated, Agnewed, Richardsoned, Energy Cri-
sised, and Mid-Easted practically out of existence."

To secure a full accounting, and get the bodies of the dead returned,
Maureen urged members of Congress, the Cabinet, and the president to
demand with one voice that North Vietnam live up to the promises of the
peace accord on the POW/MIAs.

"I'm sorry, but you gentlemen, as elected officials of this country, must
assume the responsibility for these men," she said.[46]

E. C. Mills of Bakersfield, California, an MIA father and League board
member who also testified, concurred, calling for a worldwide awareness

campaign and no liberalized trade with the Soviet Union, an ally of North Vietnam, until it helped secure an accounting.[47]

State and Defense officials agreed that virtually no progress had been made on either accounting for the missing or returning the remains of those killed since the United States' withdrawal from Vietnam, and that the issue had slipped in the national consciousness. But they stressed that U.S. officials, far from being apathetic, were consistently at work on the issue. They had made no progress because they had been met with intransigence and stalling on the other side.[48] "We are deeply conscious of the plight of our missing men, of North Vietnam's refusal to provide information, and of our present inability to satisfactorily resolve the cases of those still missing in Indochina," Frank Sieverts, special assistant to the deputy secretary of state for POW/MIA matters, told the senators.[49] Privately though, U.S. officials believed that almost all the missing men were dead, even as they backed a full accounting. Asked by one senator to estimate how many of the missing men might still be alive, Sieverts declined. Even if just one man had survived, he said, the point was to account for all of them.[50]

The lack of progress on the MIAs also was having ramifications within the League. In early 1973, with the war ending and the POW/MIA issue constantly in the news, the League had more than three thousand members. One year later, membership was down by nearly half.[51]

Some of the decline could be expected as a natural outgrowth of the POWs' return. As husbands and sons came home, some wives and mothers, but not all, became inactive once their personal stake in the issue was gone.[52] Others left after getting information from returning men that indicated that their missing men had, in fact, been killed.

Steve Hanson, whose helicopter crashed in Laos in 1967, was still missing after the ceasefire when his wife, Carole, had the chance to speak with a returning crewman. She concluded after their conversation that Steve could not have survived the firefight that broke out after the crash. Carole, who had reached out to Maureen back in 1969, had spoken out early about the POW/MIA issue. She treasured the emotional support she had received from other wives and served as one of the League's first national coordinators and later as board chairman. Yet while the League had played a major role for her during the war, she knew when she accepted the likelihood of Steve's death that it was time for her to close that chapter of her life.[53]

What worried Scott Albright, the league's executive director, wasn't natural attrition. It was the hundreds of others who had dropped out of the League due to a sense of overwhelming sorrow or hopelessness that nothing had been done or would ever be done to resolve the question of the missing. Only the diehard fighters remained.[54]

Maureen could be counted among that hardcore group for reasons that went beyond Joe's case. Increasingly, she wanted the League to try to set a precedent for future military families, so that if the country ever got embroiled in another war, relatives wouldn't have to spend years wondering or waiting for remains, except maybe in very unusual cases. The League had even begun to make an impact overseas.

In April 1973, an official of the Pakistan Council for Repatriation of Prisoners of War in Rawalpindi had written to the League, asking it to lobby Congress to help free an estimated ninety-two thousand Pakistani soldiers and civilians who were languishing in tense, squalid POW camps in India even though the last war between the countries had ended sixteen months earlier.[55] Later, when Maureen and other League members met with a group of Pakistani women representing the council in Washington, Maureen found herself deeply affected. At first, she was merely sympathetic and captivated by the women's warmth and exoticism. But as she listened to them speaking in their flowing salwar kameez, asking for advice on how to free their POWs and keep the issue alive, Maureen felt a distinct pride. Because of the League's work in elevating the POW/MIA issue in the public eye, women of vastly different heritage from half a world away were reaching out to them as sisters in loss. They had come a long way.

Beyond those reasons, Maureen's commitment was enforced by a deep-rooted belief that all soldiers, dead or alive, should go back to their native lands. She could still remember sitting in her small wooden and metal desk in her plaid uniform in grade school, opening a faded English text at Sister's instruction to "In Flanders Fields," the great World War I poem written by Lt. Col. John McCrae, a doctor in the Royal Canadian Army Medical Corps. Silently, she'd read the sorrowful words:

> In Flanders fields the poppies blow
> Between the crosses, row on row,
> That mark our place; and in the sky

The larks, still bravely singing, fly
Scarce heard amid the guns below.

We are the Dead. Short days ago
We lived, felt dawn, saw sunset glow,
Loved, and were loved, and now we lie
In Flanders fields.

Take up our quarrel with the foe:
To you from failing hands we throw
The torch; be yours to hold it high.
If ye break faith with us who die
We shall not sleep, though poppies grow
In Flanders fields.

Maureen read the poem twice but still couldn't understand why the Dead were still there. They had been felled in the northern part of Belgium known as Flanders, but why hadn't they been sent back to their own countries to be buried? She still felt that way. If Joe turned up alive tomorrow, she would work to bring home the others who had died.

A day before the sixth anniversary of Joe's shootdown in 1974, the MIA families scored a legal victory. A three-judge panel of the U.S. District Court for the Southern District of New York ruled that the law governing status changes was unconstitutional because it permitted men to be declared dead without notifying their next of kin and giving them a chance to be heard.[56]

The judges said next of kin who stood to lose financially if a man was reclassified as dead should have a "reasonable opportunity" to attend a status review hearing with a lawyer, if they chose. They should be given "reasonable access" to the information used as a basis for the review and be allowed to present other information they considered relevant.[57]

The decision gratified some families. Although status reviews would proceed, the process would be more transparent and families who didn't want any change in their men's status could state their case. But others were more single-minded. That summer, hundreds of relatives of unaccounted-for men argued at the League's annual meeting in Omaha, Nebraska, that all status reviews should be halted until more information was forthcoming from North Vietnam. They wanted pressure brought to bear on communist forces thought to have information on the missing, and they wanted the League headed by someone who would make that case forcefully to the U.S. government and public. Maureen was elected as the new chairman of the board.[58]

State Department officials thought that MIA militants had taken over the League.[59] But Maureen thought it was time that the organization became more vocal and assertive, and she was ready to steer it in that direction. After the POWs' homecoming, she had devoted much of her time over the past year to benefits issues, successfully prompting the military to extend medical care for the returnees and to ensure that men had wills and powers of attorney in order before they left for war. But that work was done. Now, as she told the *Omaha World-Herald* during the four-day League convention in 1974, MIA families were irritated that their long-time ally, Kissinger, was trying to solve problems around the world while failing to follow up firmly on the MIA accounting issue. Tired of waiting and making polite requests, the families would start making demands, never getting off the Pentagon's back until the missing were accounted for.[60]

North Vietnam, though, wasn't any more willing to cooperate. In a diatribe against the United States published in August 1974, officials argued that the United States was sabotaging the peace accord by supporting South Vietnam in the ongoing conflict. If other parts of the accord weren't being followed, they argued, they would not abide by the section requiring an accounting of the missing.[61] A similar message was conveyed to a St. Paul, Minnesota, youth group that traveled around the world that summer to increase awareness of the MIA problem. In Laos, a communist official told the group that no progress would be made on any accounting until all foreign troops left Indochina and peace was firmly established.

As Maureen prepared for her new role as the head of the League's board, she took consolation in the fact that people were still thinking of Joe even though no progress had been made in resolving his case. One day, out of nowhere, she received a letter from an Alabama man who had been a twenty-four-year-old aviation electronics technician aboard *Coral Sea*. He had been prompted to write after reading a story, picked up in the local newspaper, about how Joe-D' still sent birthday and Christmas cards to his father. The man told Maureen that, for years after Joe's loss, he had worried that maybe he had made some mistake that caused the aircraft to malfunction. Later, he prayed that Joe would be among those released at the war's end. He still prayed that someday Joe would be reunited with his family. In all these years, he had never forgotten.[62]

Even within the White House, Joe was remembered. When Joe-D' made his First Communion in 1974, he received a fourteen-carat gold four-leaf clover from Nixon, along with a personal note of congratulations from press secretary Ron Ziegler, who also wrote to Maureen. He told her that he still remembered the day a couple of years before that she had given him Joe's MIA bracelet. "I still have it," he wrote. "I haven't forgotten."[63]

That summer, few people were focused on the MIA problem. The nation was riveted by the plummeting fortunes of Nixon, who under the pressures of the Watergate scandal resigned from office on August 8, 1974. Maureen was saddened. While she understood that Nixon had had his own political motives for cultivating close ties with the families, she also believed that his concern for the men's well-being was sincere. Even so, Maureen already was working to connect with the new president, Gerald Ford, a veteran of the Navy and Congress, whom she had met numerous times beginning with her early trips to Washington with the Joe Dunn Committee and League when he was the House Republican leader. Maureen and other League officials also had reviewed POW/MIA issues with Ford when he was vice-president. Now, Maureen contacted White House aides to ensure that the League's views were considered in the drafting of an amnesty proposal reportedly in the works. But Ford moved fast. Eleven days after taking office, Ford shocked the audience at the national Veterans of Foreign Wars convention in Chicago by announcing that, contrary to Nixon, he favored leniency for the fifty thousand or more men who had evaded the draft or deserted.[64]

Nixon had taken a hard line against amnesty, which generally was opposed by traditional veterans groups such as the V.F.W. and those in the League who didn't want deserters ever allowed back into the country.[65] But others, including some in the military who were disillusioned by the war, favored a complete amnesty that didn't punish resisters or deserters. They thought it was wrong to penalize men who had been right about Vietnam all along. Maureen didn't mind amnesty for men who had resisted the draft out of genuine opposition to violence or the war, but she wanted harsher

treatment for deserters. She thought the latter had abandoned their country while men like Joe paid the price.[66] Above all, she was adamant that the
issue be put on hold until more had been done for the MIAs.

Regardless of what anyone thought, Ford forged ahead, hopeful that the
painful divisions sown in the country by Vietnam would begin to heal. The
next month, he announced a plan through which draft evaders and resisters
who hadn't yet been convicted or punished could perform twenty-four
months of alternate service. Those already convicted by a military or civilian court could have their cases reviewed by a clemency board.[67] In signing an amnesty proclamation and executive orders, Ford said he hoped to
restore the "essential unity of Americans within which honest differences
of opinion do not descend to angry discord and mutual problems are not
polarized by excessive passion."[68]

But passion was just what the League wanted. Maureen was growing increasingly angry and frustrated. No matter how many speeches or news
stories were devoted to the topic of the missing, it was virtually impossible,
she thought, to drum up much concern. The entire country seemed tired
of the issue. At the same time, during the national debate over the justice or
injustice of granting amnesty to deserters, she couldn't help but notice that
those who didn't serve in Vietnam often received sympathy, while those
who went were characterized as misguided, or worse.

"Can anyone believe they were right and the men who served their country were the dishonorable ones? The hell they were. They were the back-
bone of America," Maureen wrote in a newspaper editorial published in
September 1974. "They didn't ask why, right or wrong, when they were
called. They just did their duty. It was a job that every American military
man has had to do for almost two hundred years. And no one will ever convince me that they were not honorable men who loved their country and
served when called."[69]

But there was little to be done, except agitate further. In November, wanting Kissinger to raise the issue of the MIAs to world leaders, Maureen and
other League members gathered outside the White House on a cold afternoon and tossed thirteen hundred red carnations over the fence. Congress
devoted a joint session to the issue in March 1975 that was followed by a
steak dinner courtesy of House Speaker Thomas P. "Tip" O'Neill, Jr., the
powerhouse Boston Democrat. Meanwhile, Democrat Ray Flynn and other

state lawmakers backed a statewide "Adopt an MIA Day" to raise awareness. Maureen appreciated the efforts, though none of them compelled action on the part of North Vietnam, which by April 1975 was closing in on Saigon.

As Maureen watched footage of panicked South Vietnamese trying to board helicopters that were evacuating personnel from the roof of the U.S. embassy, she couldn't help but feel that the war's original goal of stopping the spread of communism was just, despite the serious mistakes that were made along the way. She felt a certain empathy with South Vietnam. Once, a visiting South Vietnamese delegation to Washington had presented her, a League representative, with a beautiful lacquered box as a gesture of the thanks for the service of the League's men in the war. The top featured a delicate gold painting of feathery water grasses and goldfish, a traditional Asian good luck symbol. Inside, a silver tab was inscribed, "from President Nguyen Van Thieu, Republic of Vietnam."

Now, Maureen could only hope that peace, even at the hands of a communist victory, finally would bring progress on the MIAs. She didn't expect much anymore from China, which hadn't approved her request for a visa. By the year's end, it also would wrap up its own investigation of the cases of U.S. personnel who were missing or killed in its vicinity. Nothing new had been uncovered about Joe.

"On February 14, 1968, two U.S. military planes intruded into China's airspace over Hainan Island," read a memo presented to President Ford on December 4, 1975, in Peking. "One was shot down into the sea, and the other was hit and damaged. The Chinese side has no information on the pilot about whom the U.S. side has made inquiries."[70]

While Maureen waited for movement from North Vietnam, she began thinking about taking her life in some new directions and enrolled in a one-year course in floral design. She thought she might like to own a flower shop someday, and she would later study interior design and work in that field. Joe-D', a tall and muscular nine year old, played baseball, joined a drum and bugle corps, and worked on model airplanes. Mindful that his dad wasn't around to help his mom, he took out the trash, shoveled snow, and, when something broke around the house, pulled out the hammer and pliers.[71] When reporters asked him what he wanted to be when he grew up, he said he wanted to be a pilot.

In late 1975, Kissinger telephoned Maureen. He was just back from the

China trip with Ford and wanted to speak with her. Even though Maureen had grown frustrated with Kissinger for moving on to other issues, she still respected his intellect and put faith in his views. Now, he told her that Chinese officials, if they did know more about Joe than they had let on, would probably take decades to divulge it. Maureen basically had gotten all she was going to get. And even if she did get any more, it wouldn't necessarily mean that Joe was alive.

"I don't think you will ever see Joe Dunn walk through that door again," Kissinger said. "But I do feel they know what happened to him." Maureen thanked him for his time, hung up the phone, and went to her bedroom where it was quiet, just as she'd done on the night she first had heard that Joe was shot down.

Maureen knew that the chances of finding Joe alive were getting slimmer with each passing year. But for someone of Kissinger's stature to imply that Joe was dead made it suddenly seem real. She heard footsteps and looked up. Weepy and feeling sick to her stomach, she saw her sister Aggie and Brenda Sullivan, her old friend who had worked on the bracelet campaign, in the doorway. They were in the house when the call came in.

"Maureen, what is it?" Aggie asked. Twelve years older than Maureen, Aggie was protective of her, especially since the death of their mother.

"I don't know if I can even repeat it," Maureen said. "It was Kissinger. He told me that he didn't think I'd ever see Joe come through the door again."

The women didn't know what to say. So they did the only thing they could think of. They walked over to Maureen and took seats on the bed on either side of her. There, the three of them sat in silence, knowing they had to start facing the one thing that none of them had ever wanted to face. Joe was gone for good.

✳✳✳ **8** ✳✳✳

Acceptance

It was the middle of a weekday, but Maureen was lying in bed, her head on a clean, white pillowcase, a cool, blue washcloth folded neatly over her closed eyes. She had had frequent headaches and upset stomachs ever since Kissinger's call the previous week and could barely drag herself out of bed in the mornings to pour some cereal with milk for Joe-D' before he headed off to the fourth grade at the neighborhood Belcher School. Weekends were spent mindlessly performing tasks or lying on the couch, half-reading magazines and half-staring into space. Joe-D' would often play with his cousins, a support for which Maureen was grateful.

A few weeks passed in a fog. Slowly, Maureen's natural resilience took over. She didn't cry as much. Her appetite improved. She slept more soundly and had more energy. She laughed at her nieces' and nephews' silly jokes. Without realizing it, she was trying to live up to the lesson that Helen had taught her, and that she had tried to impress upon her own son: Don't waste time feeling sorry for yourself.

The nation celebrated its bicentennial in 1976, and Maureen wanted the MIAs to be a part of it. She knew she could count on the Massachusetts POW/MIA families; they had gone back to Southie after that first bad experience in the St. Patrick's Day parade and, after getting a better reception, had returned every year since.

Maureen, Leona, and others built an enormous wooden A-frame float for the approaching bicentennial events. Weekends were spent sawing, hammering, and painting. The float was so large, they had to get permission to store it in an industrial hangar south of the city. Whenever they went down to work on it, they brought bags of carrots and apples so their kids could feed the huge Clydesdale horses in a nearby stable.

With the float, Maureen wanted to convey the message that the country wasn't complete without its MIAs. One side of the A-frame featured a sketch of a cracked Liberty Bell and read, "The Longer We Forget, The Wider the Crack Gets." The other was emblazoned with slogans such as "We are not whole" and "Who has forgotten the missing men?" Still, there wasn't much progress, a message that Maureen, who was wrapping up her tenure as League board chairman, conveyed to President Ford when he made a bicentennial visit to Boston.

It was an election year and Maureen, who still retained a seat on the board, where she would serve for a decade, felt comfortable when she met Ford at the Colonnade Hotel. She had dealt with him on POW/MIAs and amnesty during his service as a congressman, vice-president, and president. Now she told him that, if he wanted to make any progress on getting an MIA accounting, the time was now. The political climate was far different than it had been four years ago, when the war was an all-encompassing issue in the presidential race.

In 1976, political candidates didn't seem to be talking much about the Vietnam MIAs. Certainly, Maureen had heard nothing to indicate the issue was a top priority, and she didn't know what would happen if Ford lost in November. While the families couldn't reasonably expect to always have the same high level of access afforded them by Nixon's Republican White House during the war, Ford at least offered some continuity. By contrast, Maureen worried that a Democrat with drastically different priorities would shut the families out.

"This whole issue is going to be erased," she told Ford. "If you lose, you need to leave a legacy of helping us." Ford seemed skeptical that he could get anything out of Vietnam over the next six months and, as it turned out, that was all the time he had. He lost in November to Democrat Jimmy Carter, the Georgia governor. Carter, a naval academy graduate who had criticized Ford's performance on MIA accounting during the campaign, took a new tack, reaching out to Vietnam. If criticism hadn't brought about an accounting, maybe better relations would.

Meanwhile, a congressional investigation into the MIA issue was wrapping up. After fifteen months, the House Select Committee on Missing Persons in Southeast Asia, chaired by U.S. Representative G. "Sonny" Montgomery, a Mississippi Democrat, concluded in December of 1976 that "no Americans are still being held alive as prisoners in Indochina, or elsewhere, as a result of war in Indochina." It recommended that the military service secretaries resume reviewing MIA cases for possible status changes. It further concluded that a total accounting is "not possible and should not be expected" because of the "nature and circumstance" of combat losses. However, a partial accounting is possible, and State should engage the Indochina governments in direct talks in order to bring that about.[1]

Some families took the findings hard, accusing the committee of playing God. Maureen, who had testified before the panel about problems with the status review law and about the State Department's failure to act aggressively to get her a visa for China, complained that the report's release ruined Christmas. But similar conclusions were reached the next year by a presidential commission appointed by Carter soon after taking office. The commission, whose purpose was to lay the groundwork for potentially normalizing relations by seeking MIA information from the governments of Vietnam and Laos and listening to their concerns about such issues as foreign aid, traveled to Southeast Asia. It received the remains of twelve U.S. airmen in Vietnam, and, like the House committee, concluded that there was "no evidence to indicate that any American POWs from the Indochina conflict remain alive." It also said that, even though Vietnam had provided assurances that it would seek further MIA information, it probably would be impossible to account for most of the missing because of time, weather, terrain, and the circumstances of loss.[2]

In 1977, the military services resumed status review hearings under new rules, written in wake of the families' successful lawsuit, which sought to give the missing men's next of kin a greater role in the process. On October 19, 1977, the Navy notified Maureen that Joe's hearing would take place in December.

Maureen, thinking the hearing premature because she hadn't had a chance to review all the relevant U.S. government records in Joe's case, immediately took action. She began seeking documents. She asked the Navy, the State and Defense departments, various offices within the Pentagon, and the National Security Council to give her material from Joe's case files. In the meantime, the Navy obliged Maureen by canceling the December 8 hearing. For the next four years, Maureen would collect records, file Freedom of Information requests, and seek postponements as she tried to build a case for why Joe shouldn't yet be declared dead.

Records weren't the only reason to get the Navy hearing delayed. Maureen still hadn't gotten the full story about Joe from China, which formally established diplomatic relations with the United States in 1979. She had no visa. But when China opened its embassy in Washington, she saw an opportunity. For the first time, she could take her case directly to the Chinese government without leaving her own country. But she had to work fast.

Maureen believed China wouldn't feel compelled to deal with her if Joe's own government thought he was dead. But they might want to provide information, in the interest of maintaining good relations, on a pilot who was still listed as missing after eleven years. Maureen had bought herself some time with the Navy hearing postponement, but she knew the hearing wouldn't be put off forever. She devised a strategy. She would first get a meeting with Chai Zemin, China's first ambassador to the United States. She would then convince Chai to act as her intermediary with officials on the mainland in order to gain permission to go to China and meet the pilots who had shot down Joe. After more than a decade, one question was still haunting Maureen. She knew the pilot of Joe's escort plane had spotted an open parachute. But she had never heard what, if anything, the Chinese pilots had seen. She wondered if the man who had shot down Joe had seen him parachuting toward the open sea.

"For eleven years this has been my one desire to face him and discuss my husband," Maureen wrote to Chai in March 1979. "I would be willing to travel to China to carry out this mission if I have to. I sincerely hope that after our meeting you would be gracious enough to assist in securing such a meeting." She further pleaded with the ambassador to help give her and Joe-D' peace of mind, so they wouldn't have to keep going "through life wondering if we did everything we could do to justifiably resolve my husband's fate in a way that was honorable."[3]

By October of 1979, having received no reply to two letters, Maureen telephoned the embassy. A spokesman acknowledged, somewhat surprisingly, that they had gotten the letters and apologized for the lack of response. Then Wang Hongbao, secretary to Chai, got on the line. She quickly displayed familiarity with the case, interrupting to mention Hainan as soon as Maureen mentioned Joe's name. Maureen thought then that they must have read her letters carefully. If that was true, they couldn't have dismissed her concerns and request summarily. She made another pitch to meet the ambassador. Ms. Wang said he was away. But she didn't forget about Maureen. Two months later, she called to give Maureen additional details about Joe's case, including the name of the province (Guangdong) closest to where Joe was shot down and the water levels at the time. Maureen didn't really care about water levels, but there was more. Ms. Wang said she was contacting the mainland in an effort to locate the pilot who had shot down Joe. She said she also was trying to arrange a meeting for Maureen with Chai in January of 1980.[4]

The Navy, meanwhile, kept trying to schedule Joe's status review hearing. Maureen kept trying to put them off. After twelve years, she had managed to enter into a semi-productive dialogue with China and didn't want her painstaking efforts at personal diplomacy destroyed by a hearing that just as easily could take place after she met the ambassador. Maureen knew she probably couldn't stop the Navy, ultimately, from declaring Joe dead in the absence of evidence that he was alive. But she could try to keep him alive in the eyes of the U.S. government until she met with Chai and then, she hoped, with the pilots. In March 1980, seeking another postponement, Maureen sent a letter to a naval official involved with Joe's hearing in which she stressed that Ms. Wang had been extremely interested to learn that Joe hadn't been declared dead. "I feel that if he had been PKIA [presumed killed in action] at this time, our discussion would have ended long ago. I feel his active status is the leverage needed for the meetings," she wrote.[5] After an intercession by the House Speaker O'Neill, the hearing was pushed off until August 1, 1980. Maureen still had a chance to pursue her case with China.

But there was no Navy hearing in August either. Again it was postponed after Maureen's plans to meet with Chai fell through. Now, though, it seemed the Chinese were finally ready. A meeting between Maureen and the ambassador had been slated for early August 1980 and, so far, was still on schedule. Two nights before, as Maureen packed a small bag for herself and Joe-D' with pajamas, toothbrushes, and a change of clothes, she thought back to the first time she had gone to the embassy.

It was early 1979. The embassy had opened recently. Maureen had decided, since she would be in Washington anyway on separate League business, to deliver a manila envelope containing details of Joe's case and a petition for information. But when other POW/MIA families heard what she had planned, they wanted to go too. So many joined in, the trek turned into a sort of pilgrimage up Connecticut Avenue. When police saw the crowd of some one hundred people, they cordoned off the area immediately surrounding the embassy. Maureen, because she had gotten a permit for a public demonstration in advance to make sure she could get near the building, was the only one, plus Joe-D' and one MIA mother, allowed to cross the police line. But even then, the police warned her. "Mrs. Dunn, you have to keep moving in front of the embassy," they said. "You can't stop at any time or you'll have to leave."

Maureen made her way to the front of the building and knocked on the door, but no one answered. She wasn't ready to leave, so heeding the police officer's advice, she began walking up and down in front of the building. Occasionally, she would go up to the front door, knock, pace back and forth, and then return to the street when no one answered. Supporters in the very front of the police line would yell out whenever they saw someone peeking out from behind an embassy window shade or curtains. "Hey Maureen," they'd call out. "They're in there. Someone's looking out on the second floor."

While Maureen was working the front of the building, George Wanat and some other supporters were sneaking up to the back where they conducted a renegade publicity campaign, plastering Joe Dunn and POW/MIA bumper stickers on a number of embassy windows, parked cars, and trees before alarmed embassy personnel called the police.

Back out front, Maureen kept up a pace, walking and knocking, until finally, the door opened slightly. Maureen immediately jammed her foot in the crack and thrust the envelope through the doorway. She had barely gotten a glimpse of the young woman on the other side but called out anyway.

"You are in America, and I'm an American. If you're here, you have to accept this," she said loudly, having no idea if the woman would actually buy such off-the-cuff logic. She didn't have much time to find out. A police officer quickly appeared by her side.

"Mrs. Dunn, you're going to have to leave, now you're really pushing it," he said. But as Maureen was led away, and the door slammed behind her, she had no regrets. She had gotten the envelope inside.

Early the next year, after Maureen already had established contact with the embassy through her letters and telephone calls, she made another attempt to get in. This time, she had greater success.

In Washington again for League business, Maureen found herself with some unexpected free time and grabbed a cab. When the taxi pulled up in front of the embassy, it looked deserted. The streets were quiet. There were no guards. There were no men in dark glasses sitting in parked cars, scanning the street for possible threats, at least not any that Maureen could see. She simply strode up to the front door and rang the bell. When a young man answered, she said, "Hello, my name is Maureen Dunn. Would you please tell Mrs. Wang I'm here to see her?"

When the man opened the door wide and gestured to Maureen to come in, she could hardly contain her surprise. She stepped over the threshold and looked around. She had spent years thinking about China in terms of war and death, dogfights in the sky and diplomacy on the ground. But now, on Chinese territory at last, all she could think of was the furniture.

The place didn't look anything like the severe, modern outpost of communism that Maureen had long envisioned. Instead, its over-stuffed chairs and damask fabrics evoked the feel of an old British trading company, circa 1920s Shanghai. Maureen's reverie was interrupted when embassy staff brought her in to have tea with Ms. Wang, whom she knew from their telephone exchanges. Ms. Wang had little new to report, as she was still trying to secure a meeting for Maureen with Chai. But as Maureen sipped her tea, she was pleased with the outcome of her spontaneous visit. Just as she had during her first trip to Washington in 1969, she had managed to put a face to Joe's case.

Maureen did considerably more planning for her third and next visit to the embassy on August 6, 1980, the date of her long-awaited meeting with Ambassador Chai. Maureen flew down with Joe-D' and her brother, Freddy, who wasn't very political but went along anyway, just as he had eight years before to the White House. He didn't want Maureen to have to make the trip alone with her son.

Such support was typical of Maureen's family and close friends. They had been fixtures in her public life since the early days of the Joe Dunn Committee.

When it came time for a Washington demonstration, or a meeting, or a protest, or a congressional event, Maureen would get a bus, often donated, and aunts, uncles, and cousins would pile in for the weekend trip. They would cram into a few motel rooms to save money, and Anna would always pack a cooler with drinks and sandwiches. In 1978, a bunch of them went down to tie yellow ribbons around the White House fence in a show of support for the MIAs. The youngest niece of the bunch, Freddy's daughter Erin Hoey, could be counted on for entertainment even though she was just a toddler. Once, on a ride back to Boston from Washington that seemed particularly interminable, she obliged with endless versions of the Mickey Mouse Club theme song. Other kids would recite poems or tell jokes. The younger kids didn't truly know what the trips were all about, but it didn't matter. Whatever was happening, they were together. Others who didn't take part early on became active as adults. When Maureen needed help manning POW/MIA petition tables at the Bayside Expo Center and at air shows in later years, Hennie and Fran's adult son, Jimmy Kelly, would volunteer, even bringing his own kids along.

On the day of the embassy visit, Maureen could tell as soon as she walked in with Joe-D' and Freddy that China was taking the meeting seriously.

The three were greeted formally by staff and ushered into a room. Maureen saw the same English-style furniture she had seen on her previous visit and her thoughts turned to James Bond. She wondered as she sat in her armchair what sort of intrigue was unfolding out of earshot. But when Chai entered, his manner didn't reveal anything secretive or tense. He was relaxed, though formal, and greeted the visitors warmly. Later, he would say that he had agreed to meet with Maureen because, from what he'd heard about her, he didn't think she would ever give up.[6] Maureen, excited finally to be speaking to a high-ranking Chinese official, said through her interpreter that she wanted very much to meet with the pilots who had shot down Joe. She didn't blame them, as she knew they were doing their jobs just as Joe was doing his. It was just that, as far as she knew, they were the last people on earth to have seen him alive.

Chai, just as Maureen suspected, told her in response that he was "extremely impressed" that Joe had continued "to go up" after the incident. Maureen had no idea what he was talking about. One of the interpreters, seeing the quizzical look on her face, explained that the ambassador was referring to the fact that Joe had been promoted to the rank of commander after he was shot down, and that he was still carried as "live military" by the U.S. government.[7]

Maureen felt a smug satisfaction; she had been right all along that China would be more willing to deal with her if Joe wasn't officially considered dead. In the end, Chai promised to do what he could to arrange for the all-important meeting with the pilots. Then, as they stood to leave, he did something that left Maureen speechless. He walked up to Joe-D' and embraced him. No matter what happened from then on, it was clear that China's position had evolved considerably since the days of refusing to say anything about the American "criminal" who had invaded its airspace. It gave Maureen hope.

While Maureen pursued China, and tried to put off the Navy, she also grew more concerned with conditions in her own community. As Joe-D' got older, she naturally had taken more notice of schools and other local affairs. As a result, she had grown worried that too much development was destroying the quiet, residential quality of towns close to Boston, including Randolph. But as evidenced by her work in the POW/MIA movement, Maureen didn't believe in complaining without acting. She decided to try to make history. She would run for a seat on the Randolph board of selectmen, which in the town's 191-year history had never had a woman member.

The first time Maureen ran, in February 1979, she didn't win. But she came close, losing by less than a hundred votes in a field of eight candidates. The next year, she tried again, using her record as an activist to convince voters that she would work hard to improve senior citizen services and manage growth and development, using the same persistence she had shown on the POW/MIA issue. She went to bingo nights and coffee klatches to convey the personal touch she would bring to voters' problems.

The colorful race saw Maureen pitted against one other challenger and a six-term octogenarian best known for his swing vote five years earlier that had allowed Randolph's first fast-food restaurant to open.

After weeks of campaigning, Maureen sat nervously in the Knights of Columbus hall on the night of March 10, 1980, waiting for the returns to come in. One hour dragged into the next until Maureen's brother James called just before the 11 P.M. news. His father-in-law in Tennessee had just heard on television that Maureen had defeated the nation's oldest candidate for public office. Shortly after, with the results confirmed, Maureen joyfully embraced Joe-D'. She would take office as Randolph's first woman selectman, a job she would hold for nine years. But even as Maureen enjoyed her town duties, she declined repeated efforts by Democratic Party officials to get her to run for a state office or Congress. There were numerous reasons, but mostly Maureen didn't want to assume the more extensive responsibilities of a state or federal office while still tackling the MIA issue, which remained her top priority.

As Maureen mastered the details of local governance, she was acutely aware that the years were passing without any significant movement on achieving a full MIA accounting.

While the remains of more than forty American were repatriated in 1977 and 1978, the Carter administration had obtained no information from Laos, and its efforts to court Vietnam had fallen apart after Vietnam's invasion of Cambodia, which had been decimated under the genocidal Khmer Rouge. Furthermore, virtually all of the MIAs had been declared dead as the military services resumed status review hearings on a case-by-case basis. The League was angry.

"The government had written off the possibility of anyone being alive, and our missing family members were being presumptively declared dead," it said.[8] Adding to the frustration were reports of reputed "live sightings" of Americans in Southeast Asia that began pouring into the Defense Intelligence Agency (DIA) in the late 1970s as refugees streamed out of the region. By the time Republican Ronald Reagan, the former actor and California governor who defeated Carter in 1980, took office, the DIA had received literally hundreds of reports. Some were hearsay, but the League didn't want them ignored.

"Now there is new data in the possession of the Defense Intelligence Agency . . . that Americans are currently in prison in both Vietnam and Laos," Maureen wrote on January 26, 1981, in a mailgram to President Reagan. "I feel it is incumbent upon a Reagan administration to take immediate action to secure the return of the prisoners and obtain an accounting for those who died while serving our country."[9]

Maureen sent the message in late January—a time when she and other League members usually would have been in Washington, marking the anniversary of the Paris peace treaty with a candlelight vigil or other ceremony. But less than a week earlier, Iran had freed fifty-two Americans who had been held hostage for over a year. The POW/MIA families didn't want to detract from the celebratory spirit surrounding their release, so they stayed home. Maureen had flashbacks of the Vietnam POWs' homecoming as she sat watching the televised coverage of the weary hostages' return to freedom. She felt the same mixed emotions she had back in 1973. This time, though, she couldn't help but wonder if some of the war missing might not also have come home had the U.S. government been more aggressive, ceaselessly pressuring the Southeast Asian governments on their behalf.

The next month, Maureen received a response to her mailgram, signaling that the Reagan administration, as part of an effort to reinvigorate POW/MIA policy, would try to be responsive to the families' concerns. A Pentagon official, Rear Admiral Donald S. Jones, wrote that all live sighting reports, both firsthand and hearsay, were being evaluated to see if there was any truth to them. He said the government would continue to work for an MIA accounting even though it continued to meet with resistance and other obstacles in working with the Southeast Asian governments. "We believe the Indochina governments can and ought to do more and we are determined to continue pressing them," he said.[31]

Maureen, though pleased with the quick response, was distracted by her dealings with the Navy, which in January 1981 said it would delay the scheduling of any new status review hearing on Joe's case in light of the progress Maureen had made in establishing formal contact with China. Months passed. Then, on May 19, 1981, both Navy and Chinese officials composed letters to Maureen. The Navy told her that enough time had passed, and a new hearing had been scheduled for August 1981. Chinese officials, meanwhile, advised Maureen to get in touch with the China International Travel Service in Beijing to make arrangements to go to China and see the pilots. She could come by the embassy to pick up her visa.[11]

Incredulous and elated, Maureen immediately lobbied the Navy to delay the hearing until October so she could go to China in September.[12] But the Navy, which by now had declared almost all of its missing men from the Vietnam War dead, had run out of patience. The best it could do was to push back the hearing a few weeks, to September 11, 1981.[13]

On the day of the hearing, Maureen, Joe-D', her lawyer, Frank McGee, and a nephew, Joseph Gallagher, walked into a bland, Spartan hearing room at the Arlington Navy Annex in Washington to face Navy Capt. John G. Colgan, the hearing officer.

Already upset that she hadn't managed to delay the hearing long enough to make it to China, Maureen also was put off by Colgan's presence. Previous dealings had caused her to think he was predisposed to declaring Joe dead, so she asked McGee to object to his presiding at the hearing. Colgan denied the request, insisting that he could be objective and would conduct the proceeding just as he had been assigned to. McGee asked for another postponement, until Maureen could go to China. Again, he was denied. He asked to keep the hearing record open so Maureen could submit information she might get from the Chinese pilots. That too was refused, although McGee later appealed to the Navy secretary, who said he would consider ordering another hearing if "significant new information" emerged from Maureen's trip.[14]

As far as Maureen was concerned, the hearing was off to a bad start. And it wouldn't get any better. Although Maureen had accumulated a tremendous amount of information, she hadn't found anything new in the government files to indicate that Joe was alive. And the Navy, in fact, always had presumed that Joe had survived the initial hit to his aircraft, as Maureen would learn later. That is why Navy officials didn't think it necessary to wait until Maureen spoke with the Chinese pilots before conducting a status review hearing; they didn't think the pilots would tell them anything they didn't already know.[15] It was essentially over.

After both sides reviewed the case history and the hearing ended, Colgan drew his conclusions. He found that Joe had landed in water off the coast of China and had died there. He figured that Joe was able to get out of his aircraft and use his emergency survival radio, but that he may have been hurt in the initial attack because he never used the "voice mode" of his emergency radio, which as a search-and-rescue pilot he would have known to do. Colgan believed that China had never found any part of Joe or his aircraft. As for the emergency beeper signal heard by searchers hours after the shootdown that faded after twenty minutes, Colgan surmised that the batteries probably wore out.[16]

"It is my opinion that CDR Dunn was not recovered by the Chinese and died in the water sometime after his successful extraction from the aircraft," he wrote in his September 11, 1981, memo to the Status Review Board. "It is my recommendation that his status be changed to presumed killed in action."[17]

Two months later, Joseph Gallagher walked into the main office at St. Sebastian's School and asked to see his cousin, Joe Dunn. When Joe-D' got word in class that he was wanted in the office, he figured he was in trouble. But when he saw his cousin, who looked upset, he knew. The Navy had declared his father dead, just as he had expected. He didn't feel particularly emotional. The decision wasn't surprising. But he was worried about his mother.

Earlier that day, when the telephone rang and Maureen heard the Navy official's voice on the other end, she knew right away what had happened. Usually, a letter went out to next of kin, informing them that a change in a man's status had been made. Maureen had insisted on a telephone call. "I don't want that," she'd told one Navy commander about the prospect of getting a letter. "I don't want it to be like a memorandum that you're late for a bill. This should be done for everybody."

"I don't know why you feel these people are so special," the commander, obviously annoyed, had responded.

"They weren't special," Maureen shot back. "We made them special."

The next call she made was to St. Sebastian's, then to Joseph Gallagher. "They're going to release Joe-D'," she told him. "I want you to bring him home." When Joe-D' walked into his house, he went right up to his mother, who was brewing tea and laying out soda bread and snacks for the relatives who would be coming by to make sure she was OK. He kissed her on the cheek.

"I'm so sorry, Mum," he said. Maureen looked at him, a little startled. She realized then that all Joe-D' really knew of his father had come through the prism of other people's recollections, mostly hers. It was as if the loss belonged entirely to her, and not at all to him.

When all was said and done, in November 1981, thirteen and a half years after being shot down by China, Joseph P. Dunn was the last Navy man missing as a result of the Vietnam War to be declared dead.

"It is with deep regret that I write to inform you I have decided to change your husband's status to presumed killed in action," Navy Secretary John Lehman wrote to Maureen. He said the decision was mostly based on the fact that so much time had passed without any new information suggesting Joe had survived. "I trust that the strength you have demonstrated throughout this long ordeal will continue to sustain you and your son in the future, and that you both will find comfort in your husband's faith in his country, his willingness to serve it, and his sacrifice for it," he said.[18]

Later, the official date of death was moved by a couple of weeks. Maureen's congressman, Democrat Brian Donnelly, intervened so she could receive an increase in the lump sum payment to widows that was taking effect December 1, 1981.

About two weeks after Lehman wrote his letter, a light snow fell in Boston as Maureen got out of her car in front of St. Thomas Aquinas Church in Jamaica Plain, where hundreds gathered for a "Mass for Peace" for Joe. Family, friends, and supporters, including people who had never met Joe but had worn his POW/MIA bracelet, packed the church, filling its pews and standing in its outer aisles. Maureen looked around and, seeing her nephew Paul Gallagher standing a short distance away, walked over and grabbed his arm. She had one more thing to do for Joe, and he could help.

"Paul, I've got a case of Schlitz in the car," she said.

"What?"

"I've got beer in the car," she said. "You've got to get it and hide it in the church. Don't tell me where. Just let me go in there and know that it's there."

"OK, Maureen," Paul said. "Whatever you want."

Paul would find out later that Maureen was acting on Joe's instructions. He had told her once, half-joking, about the kind of funeral he wanted. "If I get killed and they can open the casket, open it, I'm a handsome son of a bitch," he had said. "If not, have a nice picture of me and a case of Schlitz beside me. I'll want to take it with me."

Joe actually had wanted to be buried in Pensacola, where he had trained as an aviator. He wanted to be far away from Boston, or even from Arlington National Cemetery, so Maureen wouldn't be tempted to weep over his grave. He had told Maureen that, should something happen to him, he wanted her to get on with her life and marry again. "Have other kids, Maureen, have a good life," he had said. "That's the best way you could honor me."

In the past couple of years, Maureen actually had gone on a few dates. But she had concluded that it was too late for a second romance. It had nothing to do with age or even parenthood. It was just that, by the time she had started dating again, Maureen was so firmly associated with the POW/MIA movement that it was nearly impossible for any man to get to know her as just Maureen, a single mother raised in Jamaica Plain who loved politics and decorating. Anytime she went out to dinner, she would have to remind her date not to introduce her to friends by first and last name. Because inevitably, once someone heard her name, they would ask, "Are you THAT Maureen Dunn?" The entire night would then unfold under Joe's shadow and that of the POW/MIA movement. It was a tough way to start a relationship, and Maureen eventually gave up. She cultivated her friendships and family relationships, went to Joe-D's school, sports, and drum corps events, carried on with her activism and her official town duties. She got on with life. Just not in the way that Joe had envisioned.

As Maureen entered St. Thomas Aquinas with her son, she felt as if she were floating through space above the huge crowd. She could see Joe's father and brothers, Hennie and Fran and their kids, her own sisters and brothers who had helped sustain her during the long years since Joe's loss. It all seemed unreal. Maureen stood in the back of the church, listening to a singer perform her and Joe's wedding song, "Moon River," and then "Born Free," which Maureen thought captured Joe's spirit. Then she listened as the prelude concluded with "The First Time Ever I Saw Your Face," one of Maureen's favorite songs. It captured how she had always felt about Joe. How she still felt.

She watched as one of her nephews walked to the front of the church to deliver brief, welcoming remarks. Then the procession began. Maureen walked in slowly behind the color bearer, Navy cadet Seamus Flatley, who was dating and would later marry her niece, Christine Gallagher. Where Maureen once had walked down the aisle in a brilliant white dress with Joe in her sights, waiting at the altar in his crisp white uniform, she now made the same walk in a deep blue suit to honor him at his memorial. She didn't cry. She just couldn't believe that a life that had begun in such happiness had ended up like this.

The service was beautiful and moving and, at the end, Maureen walked up to the front of the church to deliver a few words of thanks. As she returned to her pew and sat back down, Joe-D', now fifteen, leaned over. Placing his hand lightly on his mother's arm, he whispered, "Mum, I want to say something."

Maureen was surprised but didn't want to discourage him. While her son had begun talking to reporters a few years back, making comments here and there about the POW/MIA situation or his mother's political career, he hadn't indicated any desire to speak at the Mass.

"Are you sure, Joe?" his mother asked. Looking at him, she knew the answer before he could respond. He'd inherited his father's single-mindedness.

Once he decided that it would be a good idea to say a few words at his father's service, he was set. "If you really want to, now's the time," Maureen
told her son. "Go right up there. It's fine with me."

So Joe-D', who with his muscular build bore a striking resemblance to
Joe, walked up to the lectern. Looking out, he saw the faces of those who
always had been there for him: beloved aunts who were like second and
third and fourth mothers; cousins who were rough and ready playmates
and confidants; uncles who worked hard but still weren't too tired for a
game of catch. He was almost a man now, and all those who had come to
pay their respects to his father had helped him grow into the kind of person he wanted to be, someone honest and fun-loving who wanted to do the
right thing. Someone a lot like Joe.

"I just wanted to thank everyone for coming here today and for all
you've done for me and my mother," Joe-D' told the assembly. "For those
of you who feel as though you never knew my father, you can look at me.
I am my father, and my father is me."

When the service was over, Maureen felt relieved. She was happy to see a
few reporters she knew and stopped to chat with them on the way out. Because Joe's case and Maureen's work had been in the news for so long—she
had even appeared on NBC's *Today Show* a few times—and because of Joe's
status as the last Navy MIA from Vietnam to be declared dead, the service
drew coverage.

After Maureen answered a few questions, one reporter lingered. As Maureen turned to go, he spoke up.

"You know Maureen, if there was anyone we would have wanted to
come back, it was him," he said. "You worked so hard."

Maureen was touched, but she knew it wasn't just Joe that had kept her
going. Her conviction that the nation be accountable to the men and women
who fought its wars had only grown with time. She looked at the reporter.
"Well," she said, "I did it for everybody."

The snow was coming down hard as the last few people made their way
out of the church and piled into cars for the ride down to South Weymouth, where Maureen was hosting a reception. Inside, Paul Gallagher was
still searching for the Schlitz.

Paul was sure he'd tucked it under a pew just before the start of service,
just as Maureen had asked. But now he couldn't find it. Maureen, watch-

ing him kneeling on the hard floor, looking under pew after pew, asked him what was wrong. But when he told her, she just gave him an odd smile. Sure, someone could have taken the beer and, thinking it was for the reception, packed it into one of the cars that was heading to the base. But ever the Irish mystic, Maureen preferred another explanation.

"Don't you see, Paul?" she asked. "He really wanted to take it with him."

Beer wouldn't be the only thing to disappear that day. After Maureen arrived on base and was helping to set up tables in the officer's club, she realized that she had left the guest book in her car. She wanted people to leave messages that she could have as a keepsake, so she threw on her coat and dashed outside, not bothering with a hat or gloves even though it was still snowing. Pulling out her car keys, Maureen opened the passenger door and grabbed the book, which was on the front seat. But as she slammed the door shut, her wedding band, which always had been a little loose, flew off her left ring finger and disappeared into a thick, soft blanket of snow.

Maureen gasped. She didn't wear the band much, preferring her diamond engagement ring, but she didn't want to get rid of it either. Base officials were summoned. With shovels and plows, they carefully moved drifting piles of new-fallen snow. Someone hooked up a floodlight, and they looked harder. But it was no use. The wedding ring had vanished.

Two months later, Maureen felt depressed as she sat in Arlington cemetery listening to the mournful tones of taps as the formal military memorial service for Joe drew to a close. There had been no burial because there was nothing to bury; Joe's remains hadn't come back. There was only a simple white marker etched with his name and rank, and dates of birth and death.

Maureen felt sadder than she had back in December at the Boston church service. The military rite was solemn, to be sure, but it was more than that.

The day had started out badly. Maureen had thought she was done with bureaucratic mistakes. But when she entered the Arlington chapel before the ceremony and looked through the program, she froze. Joe's birthday was listed wrong, and it said he was missing in Vietnam, not China. Maureen angrily pulled aside the Navy official in charge of the service. "No wonder you can't find him," she said. "You don't know what country he's in and you don't know when he was born."

It was aggravating, but it wasn't what was really bothering her. Maureen wanted to give Joe a real burial. She wanted him to rest in hallowed ground according to Catholicism's dictates. She wanted somewhere to go every year on February 14, someplace to lay a flower. It would have given her comfort. The marker site somehow felt empty. Still, she would have to make do with what she had. A cemetery marker. A flag folded into a triangle. And still no real answers.

With little more to do on Joe's case except figure out when and how to get to China, Maureen turned her attention to more tangible matters. She worked with other POW/MIA families to restore education benefits for the children of men killed in war after they fell victim to a major 1981 federal budget law. She tried to keep the MIAs in the public eye by organizing events such as candlelight vigils at the Old North Church. While such work went on, the League enjoyed greater attention from the Reagan administration. Defense Secretary Caspar W. Weinberger, addressing the League's national meeting in July 1982, called the POW/MIA issue "a matter of highest national priority."[19] The League also planned to send a four-person delegation to Vietnam and Laos. While it had met previously with officials in Vientiane, Hanoi never before had let the families of missing men visit.[20] With progress on these fronts, the hopes of some families began to rise that a best possible accounting of the missing someday would be made.

In late 1983, when Reagan announced plans to go to China the following spring, Maureen decided to ask him if she and Joe-D' could go along on Air Force One. She had put off the trip to deal with the Navy hearing, and later to be with her family while her sister, Mary, was dying from a brain tumor. But now, she was ready to take on the issue again. She felt comfortable with Reagan, who in a January 1983 speech to the League had invoked highly patriotic terms to describe his administration's commitment to investigating live-sighting reports and achieving an accounting.

"Today I want you to know that your vigil is over," he said. "Your government is attentive and intelligence assets of the United States are fully focused on this issue."[21]

Maureen, in asking Reagan about the China trip, told him that she didn't think her request was presumptuous, as many had warned her. "I do not feel that it is, because if I could pursue, persuade, etc. a foreign country into agreeing to my requests, why should I feel self-conscious about expecting the same warm, compassionate concern from my own country and its concerned leader?" she asked.[22]

Maureen, Joe-D', and U.S. Navy Capt. Richard Stratton, a released POW, march in South Boston's annual St. Patrick's Day parade to draw attention to the MIA cause. After the return of the American POWs from Vietnam in 1973, the POW/MIA movement focused on getting an accounting of the Vietnam War's missing. (Photo courtesy of Maureen Dunn)

While Maureen waited for word, Joe-D' was reaching two milestones. In 1984, he graduated from high school and became the youngest person ever elected to the League's board of directors.

On the brink of adulthood, Joe-D' felt ready to take on the work of pressing for an accounting of those still missing from the Vietnam War. He never had chosen to be an activist; the role had been thrust upon him through his mother's activism. Now he could make his own decisions. He could walk away, but he wasn't ready to do that. He didn't want future generations, including his own children, to have to deal with the issue of the missing. Because, as strong as his mother was, he knew that the years of fighting and demanding and pushing had taken a toll.

As Joe-D' stood to address the League in the summer of 1984, he could still remember how angry his mother had become last year after being presented with a heavy medal commemorating the missing, commissioned by

Congress, ten years after the U.S. withdrawal from Vietnam. Maureen looked at the medal and saw that "Vietnam," "Laos," and "Cambodia" all had been inscribed. No China. She almost gave it back.

Then there was the time she had made an entire contingent of POW/MIA relatives and concerned citizens lay down in the middle of the street, signs and all, before the start of a parade.

Maureen thought her marchers belonged with the first group of military units. But they had been placed toward the rear, near a contingent of clowns and some spangle-clad dancers. That placement, she thought, didn't connote the right level of respect. When parade organizers refused to shift the POW/MIA group to the front, Maureen acted.

"OK, everybody, listen up!" she shouted out. "We are going to get down on the ground right now, all of us. We are going to lay down here right in the street. And we are not moving until these people let us march up front with the rest of the military!"

Sure enough, the families and supporters lay down right then and there on the hard, bare ground, signs and placards beside them. If the parade went on, it would go on right over their bodies. The organizers eventually relented, and Maureen was gratified. But Joe-D' had seen her cry all the way home. She knew she had to be tough and unyielding for the sake of the men she was fighting for. But sometimes she hated it.

Now, as Joe-D' looked out at the POW/MIA families in his audience, some of whom he had known his entire life, he didn't necessarily see himself stopping parades. He thought, though, that he possibly could help the movement by attracting more young people who had lost their fathers in the war. And he felt a personal responsibility. It was his father who had been shot out of the sky. It was his job to do something about it.

✳✳✳ **9** ✳✳✳

China

It had been a long trip, and Joe-D' felt weary as he stood in the dusty village courtyard, sweating under the rim of his Red Sox cap as shirtless children crowded him, eager to see what would happen next.

Traveling with his cousin, a naval intelligence officer, Joe-D' had spent over a day searching villages like this one on Hainan Island, looking for answers to the mystery of what had happened to his father after he parachuted into the clouds twenty-three years before and was never seen again. Finally, in this village, they had found a single spoon. A flat, dull, gray spoon that looked like it was made out of the same aluminum used to make airplanes.

It was July 1991. Joe-D' hadn't ever planned to go to Hainan. But that changed when China, after a decade of delays, granted his mother a visa so she finally could travel to the country where her husband had disappeared so long ago and see things for herself.

Maureen had thought she was getting the visa back in 1981. Chinese officials had said it was approved, but when she tried to follow through, she found they had backed off because the pilots who had attacked Joe didn't want to meet with her.[1] After deciding not to pursue the option of traveling with Reagan on the grounds that she might intimidate Chinese officials and the pilots by arriving in Beijing in the company of the U.S. president, she renewed her push for approval to make a private trip.

Maureen reached out to anyone who conceivably could help. She wrote to Massachusetts Governor Michael Dukakis, who in turn contacted the U.S. Ambassador to China, Arthur W. Hummel, Jr., who tried to intervene on Maureen's behalf. She wrote to Dukakis's wife, Kitty. She wrote to Chinese officials who had been helpful in the past, especially Chai Zemin, who was by now a high-ranking official in Beijing.

"I decided to write to Ms. Wang Hong Bao at the Foreign Ministry, and yourself, because you were both so kind and concerned when we met at [the] Chinese Embassy in Washington, D.C.," Maureen wrote to Chai in May 1985, five years after their embassy meeting. "We will never be a complete family at peace with ourselves until our husband and father has been accounted for. Please, Mr. Vice-President intervene for us as you did in the past and help us achieve this meeting I have so long fought for."[2]

The visa came through in 1991. The minute Maureen heard, she began telephoning family and friends with the exciting news.

"Joe, you're never going to believe this," she told her son, who was now working in the Boston area as a manager for a restaurant group. "We finally got clearance to go to China."

Joe-D' was pleased for his mother. But he also was concerned that the trip would be too taxing for her, emotionally and physically. At the same time, he desperately wanted to help her get answers to the questions that had consumed her life. And nearing twenty-five—the same age as Joe when he was shot down—he knew he wanted his own life to be more than a quest for a lost father.

Not that the POW/MIA activism of his mother and so many like her hadn't done a lot of good. Joe-D' had grown up with it and had even assumed a leadership role, serving on the board for six years. But he was tired of it dominating his life. So many of the people he knew were associated with the movement. His entire family had participated, piling into buses bound for Washington to march down Pennsylvania Avenue and through the halls of Congress. His mother was practically a local celebrity. He couldn't finish the school day when his father was declared dead. The issue even had followed him into work.

One night a few years back, Joe-D' was tending bar at Matt Garretts in Boston and was chatting with a friend who had stopped by, when one of the waitresses brought him a cryptic message from a group of men at the corner table.

Joe-D' had wanted the table cleared so it could be set for the dinner service, which would be starting soon, but he didn't want to offend anyone.

He thought one of the guys looked like a veteran he knew from South Boston. So he called over a waitress and asked her to ask the men politely if they wouldn't mind moving to the bar. But when she went over to talk to them, they gave her a message to bring back to Joe-D'.

"Hey Joe, that guy over there wants to know how your mother liked the plaque," the waitress said.

Joe-D' looked up. He couldn't imagine what she was talking about. He looked over at the corner. Then it hit him.

Years before, a tree had been planted in Southie in Joe's honor. A plaque identified it as honoring Cmdr. Joseph P. Dunn of Hull, who was missing in the Vietnam War. But just two days later, Maureen and Joe-D' were angered when both the tree and plaque were stolen.

Some years later, Joe-D' found himself complaining about the old theft during a conversation at a local veterans' hall with his mother and a group of men that included Boston FBI agent John Connolly, a Southie native. Connolly had made his mark in the bureau by cultivating criminal informants from the old neighborhood, including gangland kingpin James "Whitey" Bulger. The association later would prove to be his undoing. But back then, chatting at the American Legion post, he was still a guy with powerful connections, listening to how this poor kid who had lost his dad in Vietnam couldn't even keep a tree in the ground for him.

"I'm going to tell you something that shocked me, when they stole my father's tree and plaque," Joe-D' had said. "That's what Southie did to us."

Soon after that conversation, a knock came at Maureen's front door. When she opened it, a man she didn't recognize handed her a brown paper bag. He didn't say a word. After he handed over the bag, he quickly walked away and got into a waiting car. The bag was fairly heavy, and Maureen couldn't imagine what was inside. She opened the top and cautiously peeked in. It was the plaque.

Joe-D' and Maureen couldn't believe they had gotten the plaque back after so long. Still, they didn't think much about how it had happened. They figured it had been taken in the first place by local delinquents and stashed away. Somebody probably stumbled across it and, seeing the inscription, felt bad. It wouldn't have been too hard to track down Maureen. She was well known in the area and kept the black-and-white POW/MIA flag flying in front of her house day and night.

Joe-D' hadn't thought any more about the plaque until he got the mys-

terious bar message. Then he put it all together. Connolly must have been
so offended by the theft that he had talked about it around the old neighborhood, where someone influential must have put out the word that who-
ever stole Joe Dunn's plaque better get it back to his kid ASAP. It took just
one more look at the corner table to complete the puzzle.

"Jesus, Joe, do you know who that is?" asked Joe-D's friend, who had
turned his head when he heard the waitress' question. "That's Whitey Bulger."

Joe-D' wasn't angry about all the years that had been spent on the movement. He didn't mind that his mother had kept Joe's memory so vividly
alive. In fact, he always had enjoyed the stories about his father. And while
he wasn't under the illusion that he really knew the man, he had a sense of
his tough-guy nature, romantic heart, and adventurous soul. The down
side was that it was an image he felt he never could live up to.

So when the Chinese visa finally came through, Joe-D' got an idea for
how he could put Joe's ghost to rest.

The next time he saw his mother, she was chatting excitedly about the
trip. She was talking about raising money and when to go, when he interrupted her in mid-sentence.

"Mum, I want to do this," he said.

"What?" Maureen asked. "What do you mean, you want to do this?"

"I want to go to China."

Maureen just stared. Her first thought was that it was out of the question. She had worked so hard for this opportunity. She was the one who
had made the meeting with the Chinese ambassador happen back in 1980.
Without that initial, early contact, and years of persistence, Maureen felt
sure the visa never would have come through. But looking at her son standing before her, a replica of his father with his no-nonsense manner and
strong physique, she wasn't sure how to react. She hadn't prepared for this
possibility.

"Let me think on it, Joe, OK?" she asked.

The next morning, things looked different. As much pain as Maureen
had endured over the years, thinking of how she and Joe were just getting
started on their wonderful life together when all was lost, at least she had
memories. Joe-D' didn't even have those. He hadn't had his father at his
First Communion, his drum and bugle corps competitions, or his high
school graduation. They had never shared opening day at Fenway, talked

about girls, or worked on model airplanes together. The more she thought, the more she realized that, for her son, this trip was it. It was every experience Joe-D' had ever missed with his father rolled into one. It was a poor substitute for having his father with him, true, but it was all he had. And it was something Maureen could do for him. She couldn't give him Joe. But she could give him this chance. She called the Chinese embassy to tell them that plans had changed.

The trip was planned with meticulous attention to detail. Joe-D' would travel to China that summer with his cousin, Dan Gallagher, a Navy lieutenant who the year before had completed his master's thesis for the Defense Intelligence College on Joe's case and knew Chinese. Dan had analyzed how the case pitted the national interest of not provoking China, at the potential cost of more American lives, against the interests of one individual, Joe. Most of the $10,000 cost of sending both Joe-D' and Dan would be raised through donations.

Joe-D's goals for the trip were far less dramatic than those represented by his recurring childhood dream, when he would slash through the jungle to spring his father from a hidden POW camp. Now he just wanted information so he and his mother could put the case to rest.

Joe-D' had no illusion that his father was alive, and he didn't want anyone to think that he did. If anything, he was uncomfortable with the more radical wing of the POW/MIA movement that had sprung up in recent years and believed that live Americans were still being held captive from the war. That view was fueled in part by the hundreds of "live sighting" reports that had come out of Southeast Asia since the 1970s. Despite these reports, since the end of the war only one U.S. military prisoner—a defector— ever returned alive from Southeast Asia. Robert Garwood was convicted of enemy collaboration by the Marines after his return in March 1979 and dishonorably discharged. (A *civilian* pilot, Emmet Kay, was released in September 1974 after sixteen months of captivity.)

Joe-D' didn't have much use for conspiracy theories. So whenever he talked about his coming China trip to news reporters, friends, or family, he tried to convey that he was taking a rational, fact-finding approach. In that way, he was as pragmatic as his mother years before, when she had tried to look as professional as possible in asking Congress to help.

With military precision, Dan helped craft an agenda, even sketching a flow chart of strategy and objectives. The goal was clear. Maureen had always tried to determine Joe's fate by pressing the U.S. government and the Chinese government for information. This effort had to be renewed consistently over the years, whenever she hit a dead-end. Over time, she had gotten information out of the Americans. But China had given up virtually nothing. It was time to close the gap.

The trip itself would be undertaken with tremendous care. Small gifts such as cigarettes, candy, and books would be presented to officials of the People's Association for Friendship with Foreign Countries, the trip's Beijing sponsor. Conversations would be kept brief and cordial. Anything negative would be avoided. They would mention the favorable U.S. news coverage the trip had received. The intent was to make the People's Association, an organization founded in 1954 for the purpose of making contacts and developing exchanges with outside groups and individuals, feel obligated to ensure that the trip was productive.

For their meeting with the pilots, they prepared five pages of questions. They would stress that Joe-D' had no animosity toward them. If the pilots seemed amenable, they would begin with basic questions, showing them pictures of U.S. war planes and a chart of the island to refresh their memories. On southeastern Hainan, a remote area where people spoke various dialects and lived in isolated villages, they drafted a message in Chinese and English to distribute on small white cards:

> My father was lost at sea a few kilometers from shore in this area. His aircraft crashed into the sea in the winter of 1968. He was seen in a parachute by another aircraft. Do you recall any villagers ever finding things belonging to an American pilot or his airplane in that time? If you do, please contact us immediately with your story. We will be most grateful and eager to show our appreciation.

Underpinning their journey would be the eastern philosophy of Tai Chi, a martial art that is part movement, part meditation, and prized by the Chinese for physical as well as mental benefits. Practitioners of Tai Chi believe that it helps to control impulses, and that greater self-control enhances communication with others. That was important. Joe-D' and Dan knew they wouldn't get anywhere in China by being provocative and demanding. They couldn't struggle with people. They had to set their minds to working with them or they risked coming away with nothing.

On July 14, 1991, Dan and Joe-D' left Washington for Hong Kong on the first leg of their eleven-day trip.

Maureen was teary as she hugged her son at the airport and wished him well. "Be careful," he told him. Then she turned to Dan. "Don't let anything happen to him," she pleaded. "Take no risks." As they turned to leave, she had one final thought. If Joe-D' got as far as the beaches of Hainan, she wanted him to do something for her.

"Say hello to him," she said.

The departure was exceedingly hard for Maureen, who was overwhelmed by memories of another painful July parting at an airport. The last time she had seen Joe, he was boarding a plane for California at Logan in July 1967. Now her only son was going to China, where his father had died, and she and the dog were left to worry like before. Watching Joe-D' and his girlfriend say goodbye also brought back bittersweet memories of how hard it had been for her to be apart from Joe. Maureen's feelings were so intense that she began a daily chronicle.

Sunday, July 14, 1991
Washington, D.C.
It's so hard to be separated when you're in love, and even harder when the one you love is going on such a potentially dangerous trip. Certainly an emotional one—as much as I wish I had Sligo here with me, I'm glad I'm not home because everyone would be calling to see if everything was OK, if Joe-D' got off all right, etc., I really am too tired physically and emotionally to deal with that right now.[3]

Hong Kong and Beijing were uneventful. Joe-D' had an upset stomach. A People's Association official was assigned to accompany them for the trip's duration as an interpreter and facilitator, as was a Marine colonel attached to the U.S. embassy in Beijing. The itinerary was packed with official meetings and meals. They were taken to tourist sites, including the Great Wall of China and a sprawling open market, where Joe-D' and Dan walked along grimy streets taking in the incredible variety of wares, from slithery eels swimming in shallow buckets to rows of caged opossums.

Dan began to worry that people back home might expect too much from the trip. He had trouble sleeping and kept a detailed journal of their activities day and night. "I figure it is 1 in 10,000 we'll come up with anything," he wrote.[4]

Back home, Maureen hoped Joe-D's health would hold out under the stress of what he was trying to accomplish.

Tuesday, July 16, 1991
Randolph, Mass.
"I can't dwell on it because I've always had that nightmare I was in China, got sick and couldn't come home. I'd go nuts if I kept thinking this was going to happen to him."[5]

A week after leaving Washington, Joe-D' and Dan arrived in Shanghai for the pivotal meeting with the Chinese pilots, who in 1968 had been members of the "Sea Eagle Regiment" based on Hainan. On one level, Dan wanted to take control of the meeting because of his intimate knowledge of the case's technical details. He would have been a natural questioner. But he held back, knowing it was Joe-D's place to take the lead. He was the son, and it was important to convey to the pilots the personal nature of their inquiry.[6]

When the pilots arrived in the room of the Shanghai office of the People's Association where Joe-D' and Dan were waiting, Joe-D's first reaction was how utterly ordinary they looked. He wasn't sure what he'd expected. After reading the Chinese propaganda accounts in his mother's possession that painted them as great warriors for blowing Joe's plane out of the sky, perhaps he thought they would make a more dramatic entrance. But they looked like any of the middle-aged Chinese men that Joe-D' had passed on the street since his arrival.

Joe-D' shook the pilots' hands. They all took their places with interpreters at a large table. Joe-D' looked at them. Just as he had expected, he felt no anger. He always had taken a black-and-white approach to life, especially where matters of love and war were concerned. What was done was done, and these pilots were charged with defending their country's borders, just as his father had been charged with rescuing Americans and killing communists in Vietnam. It was that simple.

But the meeting, because of its unusual nature, did strike him as somewhat surreal. Most people who lost loved ones in war never got to meet the man or woman who actually detonated the bomb or pulled the trigger. But here he was, faced with the two men who had altered the course of his life profoundly.

He was a bit nervous, too. He was acutely aware that he had but one chance to make this work. A misstep could cost them cooperation and valuable information. Then his mother would never be able to put this behind her. He also was afraid of what he might hear. While he wanted information, he didn't want to find out that his father's death had been far different from what they had thought all along. Joe-D' basically agreed with Dan's conclusion in his thesis, that Joe most likely had died from hypothermia before rescuers reached Hainan. But what if they learned that Joe had made it to shore and was killed there, and that people knew but had never said anything? What if Joe hadn't been missing after all? He couldn't imagine breaking his mother's heart with that news.

As the meeting day approached, Maureen grappled with her own anxieties. She sought solace at midday Mass and wondered if Joe-D' would experience any strong feelings of anger or sadness once he faced the pilots. She also hoped her relatives who had worked for years on the case wouldn't be disappointed by the trip's outcome, whatever it was.

Thursday, July 18, 1991
9 A.M., Randolph, Mass.
I keep feeling as though I'm in a dream, suspended, because I'm waiting again! For info on Joe, just like that first week after shootdown in '68. Thirsty for just one morsel to nourish me. I've been numb all day . . . I don't have any expectations that they have any answers for us. Again, this is a pat answer I've had for everyone, but right now, at this minute, I want to have hope, I want [to] let down my guard, break through the wall I've built around myself, and say, I'm hoping they'll shed some light on the conclusion, just a glimmer. Then my pessimism surfaces, and I think, it's like playing the lottery, you've got a million in one shot, very rare, maybe if you were a lucky person, you'd have a shot, but I'm just not lucky enough . . .[7]

The pilots seemed uneasy. They said nothing and one of them frequently looked down. Deputy Group Leader Chen Wu Lu, who had risen to the rank of wing commander, was now retired. He wore civilian clothes. Airman Wang Shun Yi, who was still on active duty as chief of staff for an unspecified military command, wore a uniform. Joe-D' pushed photographs of the Skyraider, Joe, and the family across the tabletop. He and Dan hoped that, if the pilots could see Joe as a person and not just as an enemy airplane, they would be more forthcoming. They also were hoping to foster some sympathy for Joe-D'.

"We were hoping that you would tell us what you remembered about the incident," Joe-D' asked. The pilots seemed tense and defensive. Joe-D' and Dan assured them they hadn't come to make accusations.

"You were just doing your job," Joe-D' told them. "My father was doing his job. I just need to know what happened. And we can go from there."

The pilots seemed to relax a little. Slowly, through an interpreter, they began recalling the events of February 14, 1968, in basic detail. They told how they had taken off as soon as the alarm sounded and looked for enemy aircraft through thick clouds. Wang spotted one and fired a cannon. Immediately, the aircraft exploded in flames. They quickly turned to find the second aircraft, but not before catching a glimpse of an inflated parachute descending into the clouds below. They didn't stay long. The pilot disappeared into the clouds, and they went after the other aircraft.

Their presentation seemed tightly scripted, which wasn't surprising. Eager to refresh their memories and more precisely pinpoint where they should go on Hainan, Joe-D' and Dan began asking questions. They had at least thirty prepared questions, ranging from what the weather was like on the day of the engagement to what method of navigation the pilots had used to approach their targets.

Even so, the pilots divulged virtually nothing that wasn't known already. The only item of potential interest was that they suggested, in the course of describing events, that Joe's plane might have crashed into the water closer to shore than previously thought. Other than that, there was nothing new, although Dan and Joe-D' were relieved that the pilots hadn't contradicted any existing information. They also felt sure that they really had spoken to the pilots in question, not just to two random men brought in by authorities to humor Joe's family. The pilots' level of discomfort and their familiarity with the arcane facts of the case would have been hard to fake.

There was just one spontaneous moment. When the pilots heard that Joe had been unarmed, they were taken aback. After the incident, they had been treated as great heroes for felling an American aggressor. But now the aggressor, whom they had shot without warning, didn't look so aggressive. After this aspect of the case came up, the pilots exchanged a few words back and forth with their interpreter and then fell silent. Joe-D' thought they seemed embarrassed.

After the meeting ended, Joe-D' immediately telephoned Maureen, knowing she would be waiting for word. He told her he didn't have much time to talk, that Dan would call her later with more specifics, and that the only thing the pilots had said of note was that Joe's plane may have crashed closer to shore. That was enough to let Maureen hope.

Thursday, July 18, 1991
11 P.M. EST, Randolph, Mass.
. . . it may have been closer to shore, which may be good for his body having been washed ashore. I didn't want to get even a glimmer of hope up, but maybe, just maybe his body did reach one of the islands. Dear God let it be so, please let me bring him home.[8]

The next day, Joe-D' and Dan climbed out of an airplane on a small landing field. It was very hot, and they could see palm trees around the airport perimeter on this tropical island in the South China Sea.

Near the end of their China journey, Dan and Joe-D' finally had arrived on Hainan. The next morning, they immediately headed four hours south to Wanning County, where Dan had calculated that Joe's remains or airplane wreckage would have come ashore—a location that the pilots had confirmed. As they headed to Wanning City to pick up an interpreter familiar with the local dialects, Joe-D' realized how tired he was. This part of the trip would be the most grueling, and he considered that it was good his mother hadn't come, especially in her heightened emotional state.

Dan, meanwhile, considered the Hainan portion of the trip to be their top priority, even more so than the pilot meeting. It was on Hainan that they stood the best chance of having a spontaneous encounter with someone who might remember the incident or, if they got really lucky, could provide an eyewitness account that ultimately would lead to the recovery of Joe's remains. There was much at stake, and Dan found himself plagued by doubts that maybe he hadn't done quite enough, that maybe his analysis and preparation were inadequate to the task:

July 19, 1991
Shanghai, China
"I don't want to wish the man dead, but if he is dead, I want no evidence that he survived to make it to land. That would only make things worse. I want the truth but I want it over, with no avenues of false hope for them . . . This is a mission, as my thesis was. I want them to move on with their lives. The dream

I had of Anna the other night helped me somewhat. I honestly feel that hers and Joe's love for Maureen and Joe-D' guided me in my thesis and are guiding me now. I hope so dear God."[9]

The basic plan for Hainan was to get to the coast and go from village to village along a targeted stretch thought to have the best prospects for success. They would ask older residents if they remembered when an American plane was shot down during the war.

Hainan's southeastern coast was accessible only by boat or by the motor bikes, tractors, and four-wheel-drive passenger vehicles that could negotiate its muddy, unpaved roads. Joe-D', Dan, and their companions got through mostly on foot or by making use of the local version of a taxi, a three-wheeled motorized scooter with a top-heavy rear space enclosed by tarp where passengers sat.

As they approached the coast, Joe-D' had the sense of being transported back in time. Far away from China's urban centers and more-developed areas, this corner of the island seemed poor and cut off. The men could see pigs and chickens running around, barefoot children, bicyclists in straw hats, simple houses of cement, and piles of silvery fish waiting to be turned into the day's next meal.

Fishermen lived and worked in the same villages, generation after generation, and often had no idea what went on in neighboring counties, much less further away. That would be evidenced years later when a government team following up on Joe's case canvassed residents of nearby Lingshui County. Not only could they not provide any information about Joe's case, none of them had even heard of it.[10]

The first time Joe-D' and Dan stopped in a small village to ask questions, they noticed they were a major curiosity. Men congregating in doorways or under shade trees to talk and smoke would stop and stare in stony silence as the foreigners walked by. But once they approached someone, and explained why they had come, they found people willing to help. Joe-D's group typically would be brought to one of the village's nicer buildings, possibly the home of an elder or some central meeting place. Within minutes, word would spread that strangers were in town and people would begin trickling into the house and adjacent yard to hear what was going on. On one such visit, Joe-D's interpreter learned that villagers initially had mistaken Joe-D' and Dan for missionaries. Those were apparently the only westerners who ever came through.

Their first potential lead came in Wu Chang, when an old fisherman remembered that an airplane had been snagged underwater southeast of Dah Zhou Island. "The fishermen of Lingshui could find it," he told them. But when Dan considered the information, he concluded that it was too far south to be Joe's plane. More likely, it was a Chinese airplane from a nearby naval airfield.

Further along, in Xin Long Cun, villagers had more promising information.

One man, the former head of the local militia, immediately recognized the story and recalled that a man who regularly scavenged for debris on the beach had found an airplane wing during the war years. But the man had died ten years before. "His village is north of here," he said.

They went to that village, Yen Wing, about five miles away, but didn't find any clues. A cadre leader said that the village wouldn't have played any role in the case. After grilling their taxi driver, who said that as a child he had played with the wing at the beach scavenger's house, they returned to Xin Long Cun.

By now, word was out that a group of Americans already had been through once. When Joe-D' and Dan appeared a second time, it seemed as if the entire village was waiting for them in the street. With a trail of folks behind them, Joe-D', Dan and their interpreters were led to a building. Dozens of people crowded in, some fanning themselves in the stifling air as a conversation ensued in a jumble of Chinese and English. Slowly, a partial story emerged of what had transpired twenty-three years before:

It was overcast on February 14, 1968. Villagers were going about their business, unaware that anything out of the ordinary had taken place. Fishermen were already out for the day when government officials contacted members of the local militia.

"An American spy has been shot down," they said, ordering the men to search the beach and outlying islands.

The men did as they were told, going down to the beach to seek the downed airman, the remnants of his parachute, or the wreckage of his airplane. They found nothing. They took boats out across shark-infested waters to a couple of islands visible from shore. The islands presented a challenge. They were uninhabited, and many locals were fearful of entering the dark, mysterious caves there. The men looked but again found nothing.

Some time later, Cai Yi Xue was walking the beach as he usually did, trying to find something of value to sell. He was fortunate to find a large slab of aluminum. Metal would bring good money, and Cai sold the largest part for scrap. He kept the rest, forming it into a rice bucket and three flat eating utensils.

"If you have a piece, yes, we want it," Dan chimed in loudly, as one of the villagers mentioned that the utensils were probably still in the kitchen of one of Cai's descendants. Someone was dispatched. Soon after, a woman with long dark hair and a white blouse came in with a piece of flattened aluminum, no more than five inches long. It had a curved handle and a rounded top that ended in a point like a spade. The wife of a local leader, her family was using the utensil in their kitchen. But she was willing to part with it.

"We would very much like to have them, " Dan said. "They are the only things he has left of his father. We would like to show our appreciation to the village."

At that point, the entire crowd went into the courtyard, where Joe-D', quintessentially American in his white Nike T-shirt with green swoosh, khaki shorts, and sunglasses, stood across from the Chinese woman who peered at him pleasantly from under a fringe of dark bangs.

"I present this to you on behalf of our village," she said, handing over the ladle.

Joe-D' handed her some money, which she initially refused. He insisted. He gave her money for her family, and then about $100 so the village could have a banquet.

"We would like to present this out of appreciation for myself and my entire family," he said. They had helped him, a stranger on a sad quest very far from home.

Armed with the utensil, Joe-D' and his party went back to Ying Wen. There, they discovered another two utensils and a rice bucket, all reputedly made from the same piece of the recovered wing.

Back in Randolph, Maureen hadn't heard from Joe-D' in two days. As he and Dan were making their way around the Hainan villages, she was worrying about Typhoon Amy, which was headed for China.

On China's Hainan Island, Joe-D' holds cooking implements fashioned from metal that washed ashore and may have come from his father's airplane. Local families were using the utensils and rice bucket and gave them to Joe-D' on a 1991 trip to China. (Photo courtesy of Maureen Dunn)

Sunday, July 21, 1991
Randolph, Mass.
I awake anxious and nauseous, two other feelings that were with me the first weeks after Joe's shootdown. Now it's because I haven't heard from Joe-D' and I'm frightened something has happened to them because of [the] storm. I feel so much like '68 again. I'm just existing, getting up, showering and going through motions of life, not living it. I just came back from Mass and priest prayed for Joe-D' and Dan . . . we do need all the prayers possible. I feel myself going into a shell again like I did the first year of Joe's shootdown and I've to fight it because it was a long fight back the last time and I don't know if I've it in me this time. I just about have the energy to brush my teeth. The fight has just left me.[11]

On Hainan, Joe-D' had gotten more than he had hoped for. There was just one thing left to do.

After their last village visit ended, Joe-D' and Dan made their way down a dirt road toward the beach. At the end of the road, they came to a patch of rough, hilly terrain. Dan stood back as Joe-D' picked his way over rocks and stubby roots. He gingerly made his way down, avoiding prickly bushes and thick vines that threatened to trip him up, until he reached a sandy clearing. The scene wasn't exactly pretty but it was dramatic, with rocky, arid mountains tumbling down to the dark water's edge.

With his eyes on the horizon and the breaking waves, Joe-D' walked across the sand toward the sea. He could see fishing boats and islands that looked closer than they really were. The waters out there were full of sharks, so everyone said. That was what Joe's father, Henry, had latched onto in his later years, as he tried to sort out what had happened.

"The sharks must have gotten Joe," he had told his daughter, Hennie, just before he died.

Joe-D' turned and walked down the beach for a bit. He stopped and squatted, picking up a stick so he could write in the sand. He poked around for a few minutes then walked back to his original spot, where he stood once again looking out at the murky water where his father had drifted so many years before.

Joe-D' felt calmer than he had at any point during the trip. A peaceful sensation overcame him. It was as if his father were right there beside him.

"This is it," he said to himself as he gazed out at the sea. "I've done all I can do for you. I wish I could do more, but I can't."

Slowly, Joe-D' took off the POW/MIA bracelet bearing his father's name. He held it for a minute or two. It was utterly silent, without so much as the call of a bird to break the stillness. The only thing he heard was the sound of the surf against the shore. Taking a deep breath, Joe-D' slowly brought his arm up and back. In a split second he let go, sending the bracelet flying through the air. It dropped into the water and vanished beneath the surface.

The next year, the U.S. Army Central Identification Laboratory in Hawaii (CILHI) found that the cooking utensils carried away from Hainan by Joe-D' and Dan may not have come from Joe's plane.

The laboratory, established in Hawaii in May 1976 for the purpose of recovering and identifying the remains of U.S. military personnel killed in wars, grew out of the mortuaries set up by the Army in South Vietnam during the war. After the U.S. withdrawal, the recovery and identification work moved to Thailand. After Saigon fell, it moved to Hawaii, where investigators also worked on identifying those killed in such terrorist acts as the 1983 bombing of the Marine Corps barracks in Beirut, Lebanon.

When CILHI analysts looked at the serial numbers on the cooking implements Joe-D' brought back from Hainan, they found that the numbers were inconsistent with the format of A-1H Skyraider serial numbers, based on a comparison with government and manufacturer's records. They also said the aluminum didn't appear to be aircraft-grade. Because of one marking that read, "5″ TANK MKI5NS 1944," analysts concluded that the items may have been made out of a World War II–era shipping container for five-inch naval guns.[12]

The analysis didn't jibe with the accounts of the Hainan villagers, whom Joe-D' and Dan had believed. The people had seemed honest, freely describing how the cookware had been fashioned from a wing recovered around the time of Joe's shootdown. Dan and Joe-D' realized that the villagers may have been mistaken, but the laboratory work still wasn't enough for them to discount completely the notion that the utensils might have come from Joe's plane. Maureen, for her part, wondered about the thoroughness of the lab work. Regardless, the CILHI report was certainly enough to prevent the conclusive link to Canasta 404 they all wanted.

In 1994, the Pentagon undertook its own review of Joe's case as part of a new initiative to review every case involving an American serviceman or civilian unaccounted for from the Vietnam War.

In April 1994, six witnesses were interviewed on Hainan, including the pilots who shot down Joe. They again said that they had seen a fully deployed parachute go into the clouds. Other witnesses spoke about the unsuccessful search-and-rescue effort that ensued. The team tried to corroborate reports of local people finding wreckage soon after the incident but was unsuccessful.

The second part of the investigation took place in October 1996, when a team from the United States and China spent four days in Wanning and Lingshui counties. They interviewed twenty-seven residents between Dahua Point and Lingshui Point and on Dazhou Island, all of them lifelong residents of the area and most of them fishermen. Just two of those witnesses corroborated the 1968 crash of a U.S. airplane into the South China Sea. Neither of them had seen a parachute nor had any information on the fate of the pilot. No one had ever seen or heard of a Caucasian body washing ashore.[13]

Six months after getting back from China, Joe-D' moved to the island of Jamaica to work in a restaurant. He had grown to like the restaurant business because no one cared where you came from or who your family was. You were judged on your business skill and performance, and that was what he wanted. He worried that he would never find happiness unless he could stand and succeed on his own, without relying on his mother's prominence and connections.

Until that point, Joe-D's life had revolved around his family, not just because of his father's case but also because of misfortunes like his Aunt Anna's 1987 death from pancreatic cancer. When Anna got sick, Joe-D' left Assumption College in Worcester during his junior year and never went back. He moved home and took her to chemotherapy every day until she died. Now it was time to see the world.

He stopped working on the POW/MIA issue entirely, except for helping Maureen to raise money for her pet project, the creation of a permanent POW/MIA "eternal flame" memorial in Boston. But while he took his life in a new direction, his hope that his mother would do the same, and put Joe's case behind her, did not materialize.

Maureen was thrilled with the utensils from Hainan. But she implored Dan not to say publicly that the family now considered Joe's case closed. She wanted the Navy someday to send a ship after the wreckage of Joe's plane. She knew Joe's body was long gone, consumed by nature. But she couldn't forget that he wore a metal helmet and steel-toed boots. Something would be left, and she didn't want to preclude the possibility of a future search.

She also wondered about those two remote islands. Although the local militia had searched there, even Dan wondered how thorough the search had been, given how afraid the locals were of entering those caves. Maureen wondered too. If Joe had made it to one of those islands, would something be left?

Then there was that haunting serial number on one of the cooking pieces that now occupied a display shelf in Maureen's living room. One of the pieces bore a code containing the letters "JRD" in a row. But the "R" was partially worn away. It looked more like a "P." Maureen knew that the CILHI analysis had cast serious doubts on the bucket's origin. But she also knew what her mother, with her mystical Irish heart, would have said. She would have told her that the letters resembling Joe's initials contained a message. Joe was trying to say that he knew about all they had done for him. "I know you were here," he was telling them. "I know you came."

✳✳✳ **10** ✳✳✳

Aftermath

On April 25, 1995, Maureen stepped up to the microphone at Harvard University's John F. Kennedy School of Government to ask a question of Robert S. McNamara, the former Defense Secretary who was speaking about his new book, *In Retrospect: The Tragedy and Lessons of Vietnam.* Maureen didn't have a question about the book, though. She was thinking about another set of printed words she had tucked into a plain brown envelope—words that were spoken at a secret mid-day meeting in Washington in the winter of 1968.

Three years before, long after Joe-D' and Dan had returned from China, a large envelope came in Maureen's mail. When she opened it, she saw a few sheets of paper. Later, she would learn that they had emerged as a result of research Dan had done for his thesis.

Reading them for the first time, she wasn't sure where they had come from. But it didn't take long to figure out what they were.

The top page had been typed on White House letterhead. In the top left corner of the top page, the word "MEMORANDUM" was in all capital letters. The date was February 14, 1968. Under the date was stamped, again in all capitals, "TOP SECRET-EYES ONLY."

"Mr. President:" the memo began. "Attached are the notes of your meeting February 14, 1968 in the President's Office on the violation of Chinese Air Space."

Maureen walked over to a small sofa and took a seat. This was a memo sent directly to President Johnson about Joe's case on the day he was shot down. She remembered that early news story said that high-level meetings had taken place concerning the attack, but she had never gotten the specifics.

The list of attendees, which was printed below the one-sentence intro-
duction, read like a "Who's Who" of one-time leading foreign policy and
military advisers.

In addition to Johnson, there was Vice-President Hubert Humphrey
and Secretary of State Dean Rusk. McNamara, who would leave office in
two weeks, was present, as was his replacement, Clark Clifford, and General Earle Wheeler, the chairman of the Joint Chiefs of Staff. Others present
included General Maxwell Taylor, George Christian, Johnson's press secretary, and Tom Johnson, deputy press secretary, who would go on to become
chairman and Chief Executive Officer of the Cable News Network.

Maureen flipped the page. As she read, she became absorbed by the en-
suing discussion of what to do about Joe.

The meeting started at 1:14 P.M. By then, the Navy's fruitless search of
the Gulf of Tonkin was long over. A destroyer was already on the scene off
the Hainan coast. The carrier USS *Kearsarge* was about four hours away.[1]

Johnson first had heard about the case early that morning. As soon as
McNamara had gotten word, he had telephoned the president:

"Are you familiar with the loss of the plane to Chinese fighters off
Hainan?" he asked. Johnson hadn't heard. McNamara went on.

"During the night a plane moving from the Philippines to one of the
carriers in the Gulf of Tonkin apparently violated Hainan Island airspace.
They claim 12-mile territorial waters and hence 12-mile airspace . . ." he
said. "There were two planes flying together from the Philippines to the
carrier. One of them was shot down. The pilot apparently parachuted out
of it. The other plane with its pilot went into Da Nang airfield. We haven't
had proper interrogation of him yet . . ."

Johnson wondered what the airplane was doing going from the Philippines to the carrier. McNamara explained that it was a typical method for
replacing planes that could make such a long flight, picking them up from
the base and then bringing them back to the carrier.

"What, were they off course or something?" the president asked.

"Yes, off course," McNamara replied. "It looks to be a navigational error,
as best we can tell. But we just don't have good information at the moment."

"How close were they to the border?" Johnson asked. McNamara told
him he wasn't sure, but that they hoped to be getting better information
from the debriefing of the Robinson 777 pilot at Danang.

"In the past when this has happened, and I recall one occasion and more

President Lyndon B. Johnson (center right) gathered with top advisers, including Defense Secretary Robert S. McNamara (back to camera) and Secretary of State Dean Rusk (seated far left on couch), at the White House on February 14, 1968, to discuss Joe's shootdown by China earlier in the day. (Photo courtesy of the LBJ Library)

than one . . . one if we violated the airspace, we indicated so, in a news report, the incident has just passed away," McNamara said. "I don't believe this would cause serious trouble here assuming we believe and do say we violated the airspace."

"It's awfully important then that we find out what this boy says," Johnson concluded.

McNamara agreed. They should find out what the Robinson 777 pilot had to say before they could decide how to proceed.

"It's very important," McNamara told Johnson. "We'll do it immediately. We've already sent out special requests for it. And we'll keep you informed . . . be sure the White House is informed."

"Good," Johnson replied. Then the call ended.[2]

White House aides tried all that morning to contact the Seventh Fleet. But communication problems made it impossible. Now time was growing short. The plan was for Deputy Defense Secretary Paul Nitze, a former Navy secretary, to keep trying. But in the meantime, Johnson had to start considering just how far he wanted the Navy to go in getting its downed pilot back.

Walt Rostow, Johnson's special assistant for national security affairs, sent him a confidential memo at 12:20 P.M.[3]

"You may wish to make your decision on the basis of present evidence, given shortness of time," he wrote.

Nitze finally reached the Seventh Fleet. The report was promising. Bringle felt confident he could rescue the pilot if they picked up another beeper signal to narrow down his location, even though the job would have to be done at night. He planned to hold a protective cap of fighter aircraft far from shore—25 miles—unless the rescue helicopter was attacked. Everyone had been advised in strictest terms not to initiate any hostile action toward the Chinese.[4]

When the meeting began, Admiral Bernard Clarey spoke first, essentially recapping Bringle's plan to send in a chopper low and at night if Joe's location could be ascertained.

"There would be no retaliatory action against MiGs," said Clarey, one of the Navy's top officials.

Johnson said there were two basic questions to answer. Would the United States come to Joe's rescue? If so, what method should be used?

Clarey pointed out that Joe was thought to be well within Chinese territory, approximately six miles off Hainan's eastern shore.

"What if the chopper were attacked?" Johnson asked.

"In that case," Clarey responded, "the chopper would pull back."

Rusk appeared troubled by the scenario.

"It is not unusual for our commanders in Vietnam to consider rescue of pilots downed. It would be a mistake if any aircraft other than the proposed chopper went inside the 12-mile limit," he said. Then he stressed, again, "The fighter cap could not be inside the 12-mile limit."

Johnson asked what the purpose of the fighter cap was if it couldn't get close. Clarey said the idea was to maintain a protective presence, possibly to ward off any MiGs that might come after the rescue helicopter.

"How many men are there on a chopper?" Rusk asked. Clarey said three or four.

"Do you want to risk three or four men for one? Do you want to go into Chinese airspace?" Rusk asked. "I have no objection to going in an unarmed chopper to attempt to rescue the man at night. I do not want to do it in the daylight."

Clarey again stressed that Bringle, the Seventh Fleet commander, thought that they stood a good chance of rescuing Joe if they could find out where he was.

McNamara had listened the entire time. He reluctantly had come to a conclusion.

"I hate to say this Mr. President, because this pilot is one of my men," he said. "But I recommend against this action for the following reasons: There is a very high chance of losing three or four men in an effort to save one. The chances are better than fifty-fifty, perhaps sixty to forty that this would involve us in a conflict with the Chinese."

McNamara continued, pointing out that China watched U.S. aircraft and ships on radar very carefully.

"This was how they could detect this aircraft and decide to shoot it down," he said. "In addition, this may be an ambush. The Chinese will have heard the beeper and they will be forewarned of any planes which would be launched from one of our carriers.

"I do not want us to get in a dog fight with MiGs where we could lose more than we would gain by the action," he stressed. "Because the risks are so high, I would recommend against this action."

Wheeler wondered if, in the event of a MiG attack, a rescue helicopter could be warned to pull back. Clarey said there would be communications with the helicopter. But because of the island's land mass and its mountain ranges, it would be hard to pick up the presence of MiGs on radar until they were airborne and well clear of land—in other words, well on their way to attack the helicopter. Clarey pointed out on a map where Hainan, Joe's beeper sequence, and a MiG air base were all located.

"We lose fighter pilots each week when commanders decide that the risks are too great for rescue operations to be undertaken," said Rusk. McNamara's recommendation had convinced him.

"I have very great concern about the fighter cover," he said.

Johnson wanted Wheeler's opinion. Wheeler had to agree with Rusk's pessimistic assessment.

"I would recommend against it," he said. "There is a high risk. The MiGs are near. We cannot adequately protect the chopper. The chances are high that we would lose the chopper along with this man. We could lose three men in a high risk operation to save one."

He said the situation might be different if they could be sure of detecting the MiGs in time to warn the chopper. But that was not the case.

Johnson asked about other ways to detect the MiGs. But the right planes weren't in the area.

Clarey suggested that maybe Joe had been swept further out to sea. He thought the risk of a helicopter being detected at night by Chinese radar was quite high, especially since China would be on the lookout for Joe and for search-and-rescue craft. They couldn't understand why the Chinese hadn't picked him up already. But a boat could go up to the 12-mile limit to check.

"We could send out an electronic plane to determine the pilot's location," Rostow said. "Could we do this without violating airspace?"

Clarey said a plane could certainly stay outside the 12-mile limit. But if it found Joe and he was hurt, a man would have to go in to help rescue him.

Again, the conversation turned to how a rescue helicopter might be protected.

"Can you shoot down a chopper easily at night flying in a jet?" asked Rusk.

Clarey said it would be difficult if the helicopter knew the MiGs were on their way, but easy otherwise.

"I would not do this in daylight," said Nitze. "It might be worth going to the 12-mile limit and if an attack is flushed, we could withdraw immediately."

Rusk warned that China would have a "pretext" for attacking any aircraft carrier that launched a helicopter into its territory.

"I do not want to come out of this with greater losses than we already have," McNamara stressed.

Clifford seemed the most torn of the group. He realized the airplanes had violated Chinese airspace inadvertently. But he also felt that China could have taken a different course, at least providing a warning before shooting. He wanted to rescue the pilot, but the risks just seemed so high.

"At first I felt it might be worth trying to rescue [him]," he said. "Now I feel uneasy about it. They chose to shoot this plane down. They will see the chopper. They will hear the beep. They will see the ship if it turns in that direction. And of course, they will know of the air cap," he said.

"The Chinese also don't know what our intention might be. There is a very strong element of danger here," he said. "They may conclude that this is a retaliatory action by us. We may send planes. So I grudgingly conclude that we must let this man go. I would not even start an action toward the 12-mile limit . . ."

"I conclude that we are better off not doing anything rather than taking a risk of doing something that would involve a major incident," he said. "Our position is unfounded although this would be a mission of mercy. I am afraid we would not get the support we would need to defend the action we would take."

Wheeler had to agree. But he still wanted the electronic aircraft to go and check to see if Joe had drifted further out, so long as it didn't get within Chinese territory.

"Is there any objection to taking this action?" the president asked. Nobody objected.

"Okay, let's send an electronic plane," he said.

The only final point was why the airplanes had crossed into Chinese territory in the first place.

"This was a 30- to 40-degree navigational error," Rusk said. "I know it may be a little inappropriate to ask, but can't we keep these guys on course?"

McNamara said there was no way to guarantee it.

"There is no radar in the Philippines that would keep this from happening," he said.

The meeting was over in just under a half an hour. The order—to leave Joe if he was found inside Chinese territory—was transmitted to the Seventh Fleet, which wanted to launch a helicopter from the *Kearsarge* before dawn if Joe was found while aircraft from the *Coral Sea* provided the protective fighter cap.

Rostow sent Johnson another memo at 5:30 P.M. Daylight would soon break over the South China Sea, and still the Navy had not found Joe.

"Mr. President: The orders have been communicated successfully to the Seventh Fleet and are fully understood," Rostow wrote. "No word yet on the position of the pilot."

Bringle, of course, had kept his search-and-rescue party far away from China's 12-mile territorial line the entire time. But many years later, in an interview before his death, he indicated that he would have ignored the White House order had he had the chance. That is, if the Navy had located Joe, and he was inside Chinese territory, they would have gone to get him no matter what Washington said.[5]

The next day, Rostow sent one final memo about Joe's case to Johnson.

"No beeper heard from the downed flier off Hainan," he wrote to the president just before noon on February 15, 1968. "Makes the decision of yesterday easier."[6]

Maureen put down the papers, stunned by what she had read. She understood the risks of the rescue as laid out by Rusk, McNamara, and the others. But it was still chilling to read how the nation's highest officials had calmly debated letting Joe drift to his death in a cold sea.

In practical terms, Johnson's decision probably didn't have any impact. Bringle, the Seventh Fleet commander, was only willing to breech Chinese territory in the first place for a rescue operation once Joe's location was determined. But the Navy never found out where Joe was. So the White House order to stay outside the 12-mile limit, and not send a rescue helicopter inside Chinese territory, was moot. It never came into play because no rescue was ever attempted.

That didn't matter to Maureen. She was offended by the entire tenor of the discussion about whether rescuing Joe was worth it. She saw it as a betrayal and a breech of loyalty. Joe had been committed to his country, right or wrong. He had volunteered for Vietnam because of professional ambition but also because he believed in what his government had told him, that the fight against communism in Southeast Asia was just. That view was reinforced by his own dealings with the South Vietnamese pilots he had trained briefly in Florida. He believed in the cause and was willing to play a role, even after he saw first hand the horrific destruction, the waste of life on both sides in the long, bloody conflict. So why were Johnson's men so dead set against a rescue? Intellectually, Maureen understood. Johnson, as Commander in Chief, had to consider the risks to the entire country and to other men under his command. But she also knew that military men traditionally carried their dead and injured off the battlefield. Why not here?

To Joe's wife, the scenario was unthinkable. Bringle had seemed so sure a night rescue could work. Couldn't searchers have gotten closer to shore? Was there no way of conveying to China that the searchers weren't attacking, that they just wanted their pilot back? Joe had been willing to risk everything for his country. But the reality was that his country had been unwilling to take a risk to get him back.

Maureen kept busy on POW/MIA policy work throughout the early 1990s, before and after the emergence of the transcript. It was a busy time, as the

League of Families had branched out far beyond Southeast Asia and China.

In 1991, the League had tried to help secure humane treatment for Americans and Allies being held by Iraq as a result of the Persian Gulf War by using the same argument Iraq had made against Iran.

Back in 1989, the Iraqi embassy in Washington had asked for the League's help in facilitating the exchange of about a hundred thousand POWs between Iraq and Iran "and to end their suffering and their families' plight.

"The Iranian regime has been using this issue as political hostage in a manner clearly violating the Third Geneva Convention of August 12, 1949," the embassy wrote to the League. "The Embassy avails itself of this opportunity to renew to the National League of Families the assurances of its highest consideration."[7]

Armed with that letter, the League issued a public reminder to Iraq to treat its Allied and American prisoners with the same consideration that it once had asked of Iran. That is, to treat them humanely in accordance with the Geneva Conventions.[8]

Maureen, who was again serving as the League's northeast regional coordinator, also got involved. At statewide POW/MIA events, information tables typically included petitions to all countries connected with outstanding POW/MIA cases, dating back to Korea. Iraq was added during the Gulf War. Maureen also telephoned the Iraqi embassy in Washington. Twice, she received no answer. The third time, to her amazement, she was connected to the ambassador. She urged him to respect the Geneva Conventions on POWs.

That same year, just eight days after Joe-D' and Dan's return from China, a special congressional committee, the Senate Select Committee on POW/MIA Affairs, was established to try to lay to rest the controversy that had swirled around the POW/MIA issue for nearly twenty years.

At the heart of the issue were questions of whether Americans remained alive in captivity from past wars, especially Vietnam, and whether the U.S. government had done everything possible to try to get them back.

The committee's formation was sparked by several controversies, including the resignation of a top U.S. POW/MIA official and the emergence of photographs, later shown to be fraudulent, purportedly of American POWs in Southeast Asia. Also, President George H. W. Bush's administration had called for greater progress and cooperation on such POW/MIA matters as resolving reports of live sightings and repatriating remains as some of the necessary steps toward eventually normalizing relations with Vietnam.[9]

But numbers were at the root of its task.

When the committee was formed, 2,264 Americans were unaccounted for from Vietnam. That was roughly a thousand more than the number believed to be "missing" at the end of Operation Homecoming in 1973.

That did not mean that the fate of thousands was actually in question. Rather, it reflected an administrative change that had taken place in the late 1970s, when those POW/MIAs who had not returned from the war, and who were considered dead administratively, were lumped together with those who had been killed but whose remains had not come back (KIA/BNR). The new category reflected "unaccounted for" cases. There was no real evidence that any of these men were alive. But neither had they been proven dead by means of physical evidence.[10]

That was precisely what had kept Maureen and other POW/MIA relatives going for close to two decades. They had never wavered from their desire to find out what had happened to these men and they still believed it was possible, in many cases, to find out. It wouldn't happen, though, unless the right U.S. policy compelled the governments of Southeast Asia to be more forthcoming with information and cooperation.

"The real measure—results—depends on those who control the territory and the answers," the League's executive director, Ann Mills Griffiths, testified before the select committee. "Serious responses to U.S. initiatives by Hanoi, Vientiane, and Phnom Pehn could rapidly achieve the fullest possible accounting for missing Americans. The lack of greater results is simply not due to lack of priority, effort, resources or dedication by the U.S."[11]

The committee understood the families' quest. As it acknowledged in its final report, "It is only human nature to hope, in the absence of contrary proof, that a loved one has survived. And it is only to be expected, in such circumstances, that the American people, would demand the fullest possible effort to establish the truth."[12]

But if anyone thought the committee would prove that live American prisoners were still in Southeast Asia, or anywhere else, they were mistaken.

Under co-chairs Senator Kerry of Massachusetts and Republican Senator Bob Smith of New Hampshire, the committee concluded that there was no compelling evidence proving any Americans remained alive in captivity in Southeast Asia. It did find evidence indicating the possibility that some POWs may have survived beyond the end of "Operation Home-coming" in 1973. But it also found no willful abandonment of living men by the U.S. government.[13]

While thousands of men were listed as unaccounted for from the Vietnam War, progress had been made on accounting for some dead and missing since the U.S. withdrawal from Vietnam in 1973. However, it had come slowly, with sets of remains trickling out from year to year.

Over about twenty-two years, since the end of U.S. involvement in the war through early 1995, 377 Americans dead or missing from the war had been accounted for by South Vietnam, Laos, Cambodia, and China by way of unilateral repatriations by governments and local peoples and joint field activities. Much of the progress had come after Reagan appointed General John W. Vessey as a special emissary to Vietnam for POW/MIA Affairs in 1987.[14]

Prior to Vessey's appointment, there had been regular meetings and con-sultations with Vietnamese officials over the POW/MIA issue, in some of which the League was involved directly. But there had been no dramatic improvement.

Vessey focused on getting cooperation for resolving the highest priority cases, or those with the best potential sources of information. These were "discrepancy" cases involving men who once were known to be alive in cap-tivity, lost under circumstances where survival seemed possible, or about whom a Southeast Asian government was thought to know something.[15] From 1985 to 1988, 146 Americans were accounted for, nearly fifty percent more than the total number accounted for during the first decade after the war.[16]

In 1991, Republican Senator John McCain of Arizona, a former North Vietnam POW, traveled to Vietnam to discuss with officials the prospect of setting up a permanent POW/MIA office there. He wanted to secure com-mitments that U.S. investigators would have better access to Vietnam's mil-itary archives, something Vietnam previously had been reluctant to give be-cause of concerns for national security. McCain also laid out the steps being proposed by the Bush administration as precursors to normalized relations.[17]

The League backed Bush's "road map" toward better relations with Viet-nam on the grounds that it was based on reciprocity. That is, that Vietnam wouldn't be rewarded until it made serious progress on accounting for outstanding POW/MIA cases, especially by turning over records. It was staunchly opposed to normalizing relations until the POW/MIA cases were settled as much as possible. Maureen argued that once relations were normalized, Vietnam would lose any incentive to open its archives fully and to support the forensic teams who had begun combing the countryside for teeth, bits of bone, and old dog tags.

Emotions were running high. At a League meeting in the summer of 1992, a small group of hecklers who wanted more radical action shouted down Bush, who was addressing the group. Bush got so rattled that, when one man began shouting again after the crowd had quieted down, he yelled out for the man to be silent.[18]

The antics infuriated Maureen. Joe-D' considered it a defining moment that permanently damaged the League's credibility. Maureen immediately sent a three-page, single-spaced newsletter to the Massachusetts families after the meeting, asking them to pray that the League would stay together long enough to see the country through normalization, as there were still MIAs to be accounted for. If radical members gained control of the organization, "It is all over for the League," Maureen wrote. "The public, and the government, will view us as a bunch of irrational wackos."[19]

The League apologized to Bush, who was praised by the next speaker, Kerry, for his commitment to the POW/MIA issue and by McCain in a letter. He didn't hold a grudge.

"I assure you that I am not angry at those who interrupted my speech," Bush wrote in response to a Detroit, Michigan, woman who had contacted him about the incident. "In fact, I sympathize with their pain and frustration, and I pledge to them, as well as to each family of one of our missing, the continuing commitment of my Administration to achieving the fullest possible accounting of their loved ones."[20]

Meanwhile, the League had asked Bush's 1992 Democratic presidential opponent, Arkansas Governor Bill Clinton, for his position on the POW/MIA issue. Members wondered if Clinton would follow the example of Bush's "road map" or take a different approach to normalization.

One year later, with President Clinton in office, Maureen believed normalization was inevitable. Ever practical in matters of politics, she argued that the League should try to secure for itself a role in a rapidly changing environment before it got shut out and became irrelevant. She argued that the League should pass a resolution supporting normalization in exchange for financial support from companies doing business in Vietnam. The companies also would be required to have U.S. government-trained protocol officers on staff to keep them informed of POW/MIA developments.[21]

It was an audacious suggestion, and Maureen never had a chance to push fully for its implementation. Soon after she floated the concept, she faced the most serious health crisis of her life.

In 1994, doctors discovered a tumor on one of the salivary glands on the side of Maureen's face. Such growths are usually benign. But when a fairly routine surgery to remove the growth stretched on for nine hours, Maureen's family knew something was wrong.

The tumor turned out to be a rare cancer. Faced with daily radiation treatments, Maureen took on her illness with characteristic directness. When doctors tried to explain aspects of her illness and treatment, she made it clear that she didn't want to spend a lot of time mulling things over.

"Tell me what we're going to do and let's start doing it," she would say.

Maureen had thirty-eight days of radiation treatments and, three years later, would spend over two hours a day for three months isolated in a hyperbaric oxygen chamber to treat complications from the radiation. But she never thought the cancer would kill her. Nor did she ever launch into a reevaluation of her life and its goals, as is sometimes typical in the face of a potentially life-threatening sickness. She simply believed she would get through it. If Joe's case had taught her anything, it was to persevere.

During the period Maureen was battling cancer, the United States took crucial steps toward normalization.

On February 3, 1994, Clinton lifted the trade embargo that had been in place on Vietnam for nineteen years, and on North Vietnam for thirty years. The policy had the backing of Clinton's top Cabinet officials, the Joint Chiefs of Staff, and the U.S. Senate. Vietnam had returned over sixty-seven sets of remains the year before, and although just three had been identified positively as belonging to U.S. servicemen, it had granted more access to records and more help in resolving live sightings. Clinton wanted to acknowledge such cooperation and believed that lifting the embargo was the best way to ensure future progress on resolving the fate of the missing. But veterans groups, including the American Legion, were opposed. When the administration held a briefing for them, Griffiths, the League's executive director, didn't go.[22]

The United States and Vietnam normalized relations the next year, 1995. A new U.S. embassy opened in Hanoi with a former North Vietnam POW, Pete Peterson, installed as the first ambassador. Many POW/MIA families, Maureen among them, believed that the decision was premature. Despite progress, over two thousand Americans were still unaccounted for from the war.

While Maureen considered the ramifications of normalization, something happened a few months before the scheduled opening of the new embassy that pulled her back into the past. She heard McNamara would be speaking at Harvard in April 1995 as part of a promotional tour for his book. He would take part in a panel discussion on the war with other experts and take questions from the audience. Maureen dug out the old transcript of the 1968 White House meeting and looked it over once more. It was time to face the former Defense Secretary.

A handful of people already had stepped up to ask questions when Maureen's turn came. In her hand was the envelope containing the transcript. She began nervously.

"Mr. McNamara, you don't know who I am but you certainly—from my entire—you posited a situation which created the rest of my adult life. My name is Maureen Dunn. I don't know if you remember the incident of February 14, 1968, the China incident . . ."

Maureen was shaking as her voice trailed off. Then she read the names of those who had met for that twenty-six-minute meeting to discuss Joe's fate.

"Do you remember that?" she asked McNamara.

McNamara responded, but Maureen couldn't hear what he said.

She went on.

"It was a pilot that was shot down over Hainan Island. Do you remember the incident?" she asked again.

"I'm sorry, I don't," McNamara said.

Maureen explained that she had gotten hold of a top-secret document that showed McNamara and the others had discussed Joe in the White House. They hadn't referred to him by name.

"He was twenty-five years old," she said. "So, you never had a face to see, or to know that he had a . . . wife and a baby, a one-year-old baby.

"This is very emotional for me. I didn't think I would be. But, I'm that guy's wife," Maureen went on. She wanted McNamara to apologize for deciding, in essence, that Joe wasn't worth rescuing.

"All these years, Mr. McNamara, I wanted someone from those ten people who were at that meeting to say to me, 'I am sorry'," she said, trying to hold back tears. "And I'd like you to say that in front of all these people to me, 'I am sorry'. I just want you to say, 'I am sorry'."

Some in the audience clapped. But McNamara couldn't remember.

"I have no recollection of the meeting and I can't . . ." he began.

Maureen interrupted.

"It's right here," she said, holding out the envelope.

"I haven't seen it and I'd like to see it. But, let me just say this," McNamara said. "If I said it, I'm not sorry, I'm horrified. I'm absolutely . . ."

But Maureen couldn't hold back. It was as if all the waiting and frustration and disappointment of twenty-seven years was erupting within her, forcing its way to the surface through her angry tears. She felt as if she might choke.

"Say, 'I'm sorry, Maureen'," she implored.

"Well, I'll say I'm sorry but that's not enough," McNamara responded. "I am absolutely horrified."

"Well, it's right here, sir, on the 12th page [of the] document," she said.

"Well, if you let me have that I'll . . ." McNamara started. Before he could say more, Maureen interrupted.

"I certainly will," she said. "And my son is here . . . And he'd like to present you with a letter. Joe, would you do it please. I waited twenty-seven years for you to say that."

Joe-D' and Maureen gave McNamara the envelope. They didn't hear from him again.

In the decade since Maureen's confrontation with McNamara, an elaborate federal apparatus has grown up around the issue of achieving the fullest possible POW/MIA accounting from past wars.

The issue is virtually unrecognizable from the days when POW/MIA families were urged by their government to keep quiet. Today, U.S. officials routinely invoke their commitment to the "fullest possible accounting" of those missing in past wars, not only to fulfill the country's pledge to those who fought in the past but to demonstrate to current military forces that their government will back them, no matter what.

"Today we also remember the Americans who are still missing," President George W. Bush said at a Memorial Day commemoration at Arlington National Cemetery in 2005. "We honor them. And our nation is determined to account for all of them."

Today, the U.S. government spends about $105 million per year on MIA recovery efforts across four federal agencies employing more than six hundred people.

On the scientific side, the Pentagon stores millions of DNA samples from active-duty and reserve personnel in a repository so those killed in duty can be identified readily. In December 1992, a six-person team was dispatched to Fort Drum in New York to collect fifty-six hundred samples over three days from personnel about to deploy to Somalia. The urgency highlighted the new importance the nation's military leaders placed on having a system in place for accounting for its men and women.

A laboratory for processing DNA information, the Armed Forces DNA Identification Laboratory established in 1991, has assisted in identifying remains from Korea and Vietnam, including those buried as unknowns at the National Cemetery of the Pacific in Hawaii and at Arlington National Cemetery. It has worked on identifying victims of airplane crashes, terrorist bombings, and events such as the FBI's raid on the Branch Davidian compound in Waco, Texas. In 1995, it helped Russia confirm the remains of Czar Nicholas II and his family.

In 2003, the thirty-year-old CILHI and the eleven-year-old Joint Task Force—Full Accounting, which grew out of the Joint Casualty Resolution Center set up during the Vietnam War, were merged into a new Joint POW/MIA Accounting Command (JPAC) headquartered in Hawaii. The JPAC analyzes records, conducts interviews, negotiates with foreign officials, deploys field investigators and recovery teams, and identifies remains. Of the JPAC's eighteen recovery teams, ten work on cases in Southeast Asia, five are dedicated to Korea, and three try to recover missing Americans from World War II, the Cold War, and the Persian Gulf War.

Other governmental efforts to account for missing servicemen include the 1992 creation of a U.S.–Russia Joint Commission, a post–Cold War initiative to determine if any missing Americans were held in the former Soviet Union.

As of June 1, 2005, more than eighty-eight thousand Americans remained unaccounted for from World War II, Korea, the Cold War, Vietnam, and the 1991 Gulf War. World War II accounted for all but ten thousand. Of those remaining, Korea accounted for more than eight thousand. There were 1,833 unaccounted for from Vietnam.

Private and international interest in the issue has soared since the League of Families helped to make the goal of accounting for America's wartime missing a national priority.

Today there are myriad POW/MIA organizations, newsletters, and web sites. When Korean and Cold War families organized in the early 1990s, they sought advice from the League, as have foreign nations seeking to account for their own war-time missing, including Russia, Kuwait, Israel, and Croatia. In recent years, the Defense POW/Missing Personnel Office has seen an increase in the numbers of Korean and World War II families at the monthly briefings it hosts around the country. While the interest shows how far the issue has come, some in government worry that there is a down side, that families will expect too much in the way of accounting for some who never will be found due to the ravages of time and poor record-keeping.

There are, too, private initiatives rooted in the Vietnam-era POW/MIA campaigns that benefit today's military. HeroBracelets.org (www.herobracelets .org), based in Austin, Texas, took its inspiration from the original Vietnam POW/MIA bracelets. Launched in December 2004, the organization sells bracelets with the names of military personnel deployed, wounded, or killed in the line of duty, including those lost in Vietnam. Proceeds go toward the creation of a new facility to train and rehabilitate military personnel severely disabled or burned in Iraq, Afghanistan, or during the normal course of military duty.

After so many years of uncertainty, some who have received the remains of their loved ones from the Vietnam War speak of the relief and peace the experience brings, a feeling that has eluded Maureen.

Barbara Cleary O'Connor of South Hadley, Massachusetts, who worked with Maureen on the MIA cause in the 1970s, buried the remains of her first husband, Air Force Capt. Peter Cleary, at Arlington just a few years ago.

Peter Cleary disappeared on the last flight of his last tour. His crewmates were waiting on the ground to douse him with champagne, but he never

212 The Search for Canasta 404

materialized. All his wife knew was that a plane with him and his navigator aboard had vanished from the radar screen.

Barbara Cleary spent nearly thirty years praying. At first, she prayed that Peter would come home. She didn't know if he had died in the crash or if he had survived and been captured. But after a few years, she accepted that he probably was gone. He flew high-risk missions, and half a dozen men from his squadron had died. Barbara Cleary kept praying, but her intention changed. Now she just hoped to God that Peter's death had come fast, that he hadn't suffered.

One day, there was news. A Vietnamese man had found a St. Michael's medal and had led American investigators to the crash site. Peter Cleary had worn the medal toward the end of his tour, against regulations. There was more at the site. When Barbara heard what they had discovered, she felt emotional but comforted. The news was all she had been hoping for.

"That had been my prayer for all of those years, that it was quick. That he died in the crash," she said last year. "This answered that. His remains were found in the crash site. He wasn't tortured. He wasn't captured. He didn't eject. That was tremendous. That's peace of mind."[23]

Barbara had a more tangible benefit, too. Her children didn't remember their father but had witnessed the controversy generated by the war and the role of those who had fought it. But when Peter's remains were laid to rest at Arlington, they saw something else. Close to two hundred people turned out for a majestic military burial to pay their respects.

There was just one last thing to do to close Peter's case fully. Barbara knew Peter's remains never would have come back without the presence of federal investigators in Southeast Asia, part of the U.S. government's commitment to accounting for the missing. And that, she believed, never would have come about without the persistent work of the POW/MIA families. Some had pushed for years, even as their own cases went unresolved. So after Peter Cleary was laid to rest, Barbara decided to say thanks. She went home, took out a pen and some paper, and wrote a long, heartfelt letter to Maureen.

Maureen, though she never has received Joe's remains, continues with her public policy and POW/MIA work.

In 1993, she accepted an invitation from the Institute of Politics at Harvard's Kennedy school to lead an eight-week study group. The aim of the institute, which was established in honor of President Kennedy and doesn't offer formal courses or grant degrees, is to stimulate students' interest in public service by bringing them together with activists, politicians, and others who influence public policy. Maureen talked about her own work and brought in such speakers as Henry Kissinger; Richard Childress, a former Reagan administration official, Asian policy specialist, and League adviser; and Everett Alvarez, who was the longest-held POW in North Vietnam.

In recent years, Maureen has strived to incorporate the two Americans unaccounted for since Vietnam, Navy Capt. Michael "Scott" Speicher from the Gulf War and Army Pfc. Keith Matthew Maupin from current operations in Iraq, into speeches like the one she gave at a 2005 roast for a Massachusetts American Legion commander. She told the crowd to keep pressing for an accounting, not just for Vietnam-era families but for Speicher, Maupin, and those who may join their ranks in future conflicts.

Maureen organizes the yearly "POW/MIA Race for Freedom" in Massachusetts. Now in its twenty-third year, it draws hundreds of participants and raises funds for statewide POW/MIA activities. Runners typically wear red ribbons with names of the Massachusetts missing, plus Speicher and Maupin. Maureen also helps run events for the yearly POW/MIA Recognition Day—a nationwide commemorative event—in Massachusetts.

All over Massachusetts, meanwhile, is evidence of the work Maureen and others have done over the years to keep the POW/MIA issue alive in the public's mind and heart.

The black POW/MIA flag flies every day over the Boston State House and Boston City Hall. The state requires every city and town to fly the flag over at least one municipal building every day. The flag flies at Fenway Park during every home game. And a state law requires that a POW/MIA decal be affixed to all state vehicles.

The flag still flies, too, outside of Maureen's house. These days there aren't many congressional hearings on POW/MIA issues, but Maureen is no less committed than she was two decades ago, when she took the stage during a candlelight ceremony at the Vietnam Veterans Memorial in Washington to try to stop a riot from breaking out.

It was 1984. The bronze statue of the Three Servicemen was being dedicated near the Wall, which had been dedicated two years before. Maureen had never been a big fan of the V-shaped black granite Vietnam memorial, thinking it too funereal. But now, with thousands of people holding candles, the Wall looked alive. The candles' flickering flames were lighting up its dark, sleek surface, as if bringing to life the fifty-eight thousand names of American war dead etched there, including Joe.

Maureen sat on the stage as one of the League's regional directors, seeing members of her own family, who had come down with her on a bus for the commemoration, in the first few rows. There was a restless atmosphere. All sorts of rogue factions had sprung up in the POW/MIA movement, and speakers were being shouted down. When an admiral got up, the noise grew so loud that he couldn't address the crowd, which began shifting and surging forward.

Maureen panicked briefly, thinking her family, caught in the unrest of the moment, would be crushed against the stage. She looked over at the Wall. She had hoped this dramatic candlelight ceremony would invigorate the POW/MIA issue, which she thought had stagnated of late. But now everything seemed to be falling apart. The lights were still bouncing off the Wall. It looked as if Joe's name and the names of all the others were coming at her. She wanted to do something.

Maureen stood then and walked over to the admiral on the podium.

"If you don't mind, sir, I'd like to say something," she said. He stepped aside, and she looked out at the crowd. Their lights seemed to stretch all the way down to the white-domed U.S. Capitol.

"This is not going to happen," she thought to herself. "These people are not going to embarrass our organization and all those names over there."

"Look, some of you have no idea who I am, some of you do," she began. "My husband's name is on that Wall. I never embraced the Wall. But when it's raining, they're crying. When it's snowing, they're cold."

She stopped and took a breath. She said she knew everyone there had different opinions, whether on the war, the POW/MIAs, President Reagan's policies, or the memorial itself. But shouting each other down at a solemn ceremony wouldn't accomplish anything.

"There is no way a small number of people are going to take this over and say, 'We won!'" Maureen said. "This isn't about winning. For you to scream and yell at this admiral, I don't even know this admiral. I'm not protecting him. I'm protecting the names on that Wall. This is to honor them."

She pointed to the Wall, and the thousands of lights that burned in its reflection.

"This is for *them*," she said.

A few protestors screamed out, but enough others had quieted down so that the ceremony could wrap up. Maureen's sister-in-law Leona, who had helped her in the earliest days of the Joe Dunn Committee, was so touched that, that same night, she wrote a letter to her own father, a disabled World War II veteran. Before, Leona had never pictured her father as a young man. Now she saw him standing on the deck of a ship, scared and unsure, as cannons exploded around him. She wanted to say thank you.

Maureen was never quite sure why everyone had listened to her that day. Perhaps they knew she had spoken from the heart, as she typically did, preferring the strength of raw feeling over the smoothness of prepared text. And Maureen's feelings really hadn't changed much in the years since Joe had left for Vietnam. It was just as she had told the crowd. No matter what, she felt honor-bound to do what she could for the men on the Wall, especially for those whose cases had never been resolved fully. She couldn't forget them, any more than she could forget Joe. It was what fueled her, year in and year out. It was just as she'd told Joe more than year after he had vanished on that cloudy morning off the coast of China.

It was March 5, 1969, and Maureen was composing a letter. She wanted to fill Joe in on all the news, starting with how nicely everyone in Washington had treated her during her recent trip. She told him they had had three snowstorms. His old dog, Laddie, had disappeared in one of them. But now they had a new puppy. She told him that Joe-D', not yet three, was already over three feet tall and spoke of Joe always. Every plane he saw was "Daddy's plane." Then it was time to close. Maureen said she wouldn't write again until she knew some of her letters were getting through to Joe. As always, she sent her love and prayers.

"Again, honey, I love you & miss you terribly & have never and will never give up hope," she said. "We're waiting for you like I told you I would the night before you left."

Epilogue

Since the Vietnam War ended thirty years ago, not one American missing as a result of enemy action has ever returned home alive from Southeast Asia. Garwood, the defector who returned in 1979, started out as a POW. Additionally there were a few anomalous cases of men who deserted, went absent without leave, and/or voluntarily stayed in Southeast Asia who turned up alive after the war.

Over eighteen hundred American men remain unaccounted for in Vietnam, Laos, Cambodia, and China, along with hundreds of thousands of Vietnamese who are still missing from the war. The remains of 750 Americans have been repatriated and identified.

Thirty-five years after its incorporation as a nonprofit group to draw attention to the POW/MIA issue, the Arlington, Virginia–based National League of Families of American Prisoners and Missing in Southeast Asia continues to advocate for the fullest possible accounting of personnel from the war. The League's challenge will be keeping the issue alive and relevant as new U.S. officials take over from those who have worked it, in some cases, since the war years. The League also will need to attract younger members to pick up where parents, siblings, and wives began.

Joe Dunn's remains have never been found. The A-1H Skyraider he flew on his last mission on February 14, 1968, is believed to be somewhere at the bottom of the South China Sea. Maureen still hopes the Navy will someday send a search crew to locate the wreckage.

Dorchester, Massachusetts, where Joe and his brothers and sister grew up, is today home to a thriving Vietnamese community. In 1996, after the community contributed to the creation of a POW/MIA memorial in

Boston, Maureen spoke at the re-dedication of Vietnam Veterans Memorial in Dorchester. "I say to you, I lost a husband, you lost an entire country and you lost whole families," she told a community delegation. "Whenever I have a chance to acknowledge your sacrifice, I will."

Joe's surviving sibling, Henrietta Dunn Kelly, still lives in the greater Boston area with her husband and near many of their children and grandchildren.

Joseph P. Dunn II, known as Joe-D', and his wife Beverly own the Island Merchant, a restaurant in Hyannis, Massachusetts. When they married in 1998 at the Newport Naval Station, a location selected in honor of Joe, a destroyer happened to cruise by during the reception, prompting Maureen's brothers to joke that she had ordered it for the occasion.

Joe-D's cousin who accompanied him to China, Dan Gallagher, retired from the Navy. He is the Chief Information Officer for Cape Cod Community College and lives in Massachusetts with his family.

China's Hainan Island, where Joe was shot down, is today being marketed as a tropical resort island.

Maureen Dunn still lives in Randolph, Massachusetts, where the black POW/MIA flag flies daily in the front yard. Among her activities, she is trying to raise funds for the construction of a $485,000 "eternal flame" POW/MIA national monument in Boston's City Hall Plaza.

In April 2003, Maureen was named as one of the Boston Celtics' "Heroes Among Us" for her POW/MIA work. Maureen still works as an interior designer and enjoys following politics and the Red Sox. She remains close to her sprawling family, including nearly forty nieces and nephews and almost ninety grandnieces and -nephews. Maureen can be spotted driving a car with a vanity license plate that reads, "Lt. Dunn."

Notes

Prologue (pp. 1–3)

1. "China Downs Lost U.S. Plane; Unarmed, Propeller-Driven Craft Strays; 2d Escapes," Associated Press, February 14, 1968.

1. Love (pp. 4–23)

1. Kennedy speech at Boston College centennial ceremonies, April 20, 1963.
2. Letter from Dwight D. Eisenhower to Ngo Dinh Diem, October 23, 1954.
3. Letter from Joe Dunn to Maureen Hoey, January 28, 1964.
4. Letters from Joe to Maureen, January through February, 1964.
5. Letter from Joe to Maureen, postmarked January 20, 1964.
6. Letter from Joe to Maureen, January 28, 1964.
7. Letter from Joe to Maureen, January 18, 1964.
8. Ibid.
9. Letter from Maureen to Joe, March 2, 1964.
10. Letter from Maureen to Joe, February 18, 1964.
11. Letter from Joe to Maureen, August 7, 1964.
12. Ibid.
13. Ibid.
14. Ibid.
15. Gulf of Tonkin resolution, August 7, 1964.
16. Stanley Karnow, *Vietnam, A History* (Annapolis, Md.: Naval Institute Press, 1983), 357.
17. Letter from Joe to Maureen, postmarked March 11, 1965.
18. Ibid.

19. Letter from Joe to Maureen, July 27, 1965.
20. Letter from Joe to Maureen, August 20, 1965.
21. Letter from Joe to Maureen, postmarked August 18, 1965.
22. Letter from Joe to Maureen, July 27, 1965.

2. War (pp. 24–45)

1. Letter from Joe to Maureen, August 29, 1967.
2. Lyndon Johnson, Annual Message to the Congress on the State of the Union, January 12, 1966.
3. http://www.wpafb.af.mil/museum/modern-flight/mf12.htm.
4. Interviews with Jay Stone and Bruce Marcus, former members of VA-25 aboard *Coral Sea,* 2005.
5. http://www.wpafb.af.mil/museum/air_power/ap49.htm.
6. Interview with Stone.
7. Interviews with Stone and former A-1 pilot Zip Rausa, 2005.
8. Interview with Coley and Eddie Conneely, Hartford, Connecticut, 2002.
9. Letter from Joe to Maureen, September 22, 1967.
10. Letter from Joe to Maureen, August 19, 1967.
11. Ibid.
12. Letter from Joe to Maureen, August 24, 1967.
13. Letter from Joe to Maureen, January 18, 1968.
14. Letter from Joe to Maureen, November 15, 1967.
15. Letter to Joe from Maureen, postmarked August 9, 1967.
16. Letter from Joe to Maureen, August 24, 1967.
17. Ibid.
18. Rausa interview, January 2005.
19. Letter from Joe to Maureen, August 29, 1967.
20. Letters from Joe to Maureen, August through October 1967.
21. Letter from Joe to Maureen, August 9, 1967.
22. Letter from Joe to Maureen, December 16, 1967.
23. Letters from Joe to Maureen, October 1967 to January 1968.
24. Letter from Joe to Maureen, September 26, 1967.
25. Letter from Joe to Sister Mary Agnita, December 28, 1967.
26. Letter from Joe to Maureen, October 24, 1967.
27. Letter from Joe to Maureen, October 15, 1967.
28. Letter from Joe to Sister Mary Agnita, December 28, 1967.
29. Hubert Humphrey statement, PBS American Experience on Vietnam, October 1967.

30. Letter from Joe to Maureen, January 4, 1968.
31. Letter from Joe to Maureen, postmarked February 1, 1968.
32. Letters from Joe to Maureen, January 1968.
33. Letter from Maureen to Joe, February 8, 1968.
34. Letters from Joe to Maureen, January to February 1968.
35. Letter from Joe to Maureen, February 10, 1968.

3. Last Flight (pp. 46–66)

1. AP and UPI accounts of China shooting down a Navy A-1 aircraft, February 14, 1968.
2. Interview with Jay Stone, former VA-25 intelligence officer, 2005.
3. Interviews with Stone, and with former A-1 pilots Zip Rausa and Bruce Marcus, 2005.
4. Ibid.
5. Statement of Lt. Robert B. Stoddert, pilot of Robinson 777, U.S. Navy records.
6. Incident chronology and Stoddert statement, Navy records.
7. Stoddert statement.
8. March 4, 1968, memo from Commanding Officer Church to Chief of Naval Personnel.
9. Ibid.
10. Ibid.
11. Navy summary, Stoddert statement, message from Commander Task Group (CTG) 77.3 to National Military Command Center, 140746 February 1968.
12. Stoddert first-person account of flight, Navy records.
13. Message from Commander Task Group (CTG) 77.3 to National Military Command Center, 140746 February 1968.
14. Stone interview.
15. Stoddert statement.
16. Message from CTG 77.1.2 to RUMFCR/CTG 77.0, 140432 February 1968.
17. Interview with Dan Gallagher, January 2005, and message 140756Z from CTG 77.3 regarding "collateral info."
18. Message from CTG 77.0 to RUHGUL/COMSEVENTHFLT 140638 February 1968.
19. Distance calculation from Dan Gallagher, "When National Interests Conflict with Individual Interests: Command Decisions Relating to the Loss of LTJG Joseph P. Dunn," master's thesis submitted to faculty of Defense Intelligence College, August 1990.

20. Message to *McCard* from COMSEVENTHFLT 140540 February.

21. Message from CTF 77 to RUHGUL/COMSEVENTHFLEET 140833 February.

22. Message from COMSEVENTHFLEET to RUMFCR/CTF 77.

23. Message from CTG 77.3 to RUYSUK/CTG 77.0.

24. Message from USS *McCard* to RUMFUE/CTF 77 141126 February 1968.

25. Secret message to CTG 77.3 from CTG 77.0 141334 February 1968.

26. Zip Rausa journal entry, February 14, 1968.

27. Stone interview.

28. Message from CTXYGSEVEN SEVEN to RUPJUL/COMSEVENTH FLT 141223 February 1968.

29. Message from COMSEVENTHFLT 141334 February 1968.

30. Rausa journal entry, February 15, 1968.

31. Messages from CTG 70.4 to RUMFCR/CTG 77.3 141738 February 1968; from CTG 77.9 to ZEN/COMSEVENTHFLT 141756 February 1968; and from CTG 77.0 to RQHHBRA/CINCPACFLT 142258 February 1968.

32. Gallagher and Rausa interviews, 2005.

33. Message from COMSEVENTHFLT to CINCPACFLT 141808 February 1968.

34. Ibid.

35. Joint message from Secretary of Defense to CINCPAC et al., February 15, 1968 1816Z.

36. Ibid.

37. East Asian and Pacific Affairs press briefing paper, and State Department transcript of press and radio news briefing, February 14, 1968.

38. Message from CTG 77.9 to CTG 77.0 141918 February 1968.

39. Message from COMSEVENETHFLT to CTG 70.9 142122 February 1968.

40. Messages from CTG 77.0 to CINCPACFLT 142258 February 1968 and from CTG 70.4 to CTG 77.0 142332 February 1968.

41. Stone interview.

42. Rausa journal entry.

43. *Boston Globe,* February 15, 1968.

44. Various Boston newspapers, February 15, 1968.

45. Interviews with Sister Mary Ellen Bettencourt and Pat Barnes, 2005.

46. Western Union telegram, February 16, 1968.

47. *Boston Globe,* February 16, 1968.

48. "OK To Retrieve Pilot Is denied", AP story datelined San Diego, California.

49. Transcript and press release from WEEI Radio, Boston, Massachusetts, February 16, 1968.

50. Cmdr. Clifford Church letter to Maureen, February 27, 1968.

51. Cdr. James B. Linder letter to Maureen, February 27, 1968.

52. Church letter to Maureen, March 4, 1968.

53. Letter from Comité International De La Croix-Rouge, Genève, to Mrs. J.P. Dunn, Randolph, Massachusetts, May 21, 1968.

54. Church memo to ONP, March 4, 1968.

55. Message from CTG 77.3 to RUMFUF/CTF 77, 150655 February 1968.

4. Where is Lt. Joe Dunn? (pp. 67–86)

1. Letter from Maureen to Joe, June 8, 1968.

2. Interviews with Rose Bucher, 2005; www.usspueblo.org.

3. Letter from Rose Bucher to Capt. E. R. Williams, November 12, 1968.

4. Text of Ch'en Tung's letter as transmitted via telegram from U.S. embassy, Warsaw, to State Department, Washington, D.C., March 5, 1968.

5. Letter from Walter E. Jenkins to Ch'en, transmitted from the State Department to the U.S. embassy in Warsaw, June 11, 1968.

6. Telegram from the U.S. embassy, Warsaw to the State Department, November 15, 1968.

7. State Department memo, December 5, 1968.

8. Letter from Rose Bucher to Maureen, November 19, 1968.

9. Bulletin from VFW Post No. 1848, Jackson, Tennessee.

10. Letter from William J. Connor to Senator Edward Brooke, January 27, 1969.

11. "Missing Pilot's Wife Confident," *Boston Herald Traveler*, January 8, 1969.

12. Ibid.

13. Massachusetts constituent letters to Congress, January 1969.

14. Constituent letter to Burke, February/March 1968.

15. Letter from William B. Macomber, Jr., to Representative James A. Burke, April 10, 1968.

16. http://www.pbs.org/wgbh/amex/vietnam/series/pt_06.html (Clifford statement, others).

17. President Johnson's address to the nation, March 31, 1968;http://www.lbjlib.utexas.edu/johnson/archives.hom/speeches.hom/680331.asp.

18. Letter from Brooke to Secretary of State Dean Rusk, November 12, 1968.

19. Letter from Macomber to Burke, January 9, 1969.

20. Letter from Senator Edward Kennedy to Secretary of State William Rogers, February 5, 1969.

21. Massachusetts State Senate resolution, February 5, 1969.

22. "Please Help Me Get My Son's Daddy Back From Red China," release from "Where is Lt. Joe Dunn, U.S.N.R." committee, 1969.

23. *Boston Sunday Globe,* February 16, 1969.

24. "Release of Three Imprisoned Americans Certain to be Discussed," *Boston Sunday Globe,* February 16, 1969; remarks of CIA Director George Tenet on presentation of director's medal to John T. "Jack" Downey and Richard G. Fecteau, June 25, 1998; Ted Gup, *The Book of Honor: Covert Lives and Classified Deaths at the CIA* (Doubleday, 2000).

25. http://www.pownetwork.org/bios.

26. Memo from Ambassador Brown to Ambassador Johnson, February 11, 1969.

27. Paul Kreisberg's notes on the meeting between Maureen and Johnson, February 14, 1969.

28. Compilation of stories transmitted by Peking NCNA International Service in English, February 14–15, 1968.

5. The League of Families (pp. 87–110)

1. "Ex-P.O.W.'s Charge Hanoi with Torture," *New York Times,* September 3, 1969.

2. http://www.vietnamwar.com/POWHonorBound.htm.

3. Constituent letter to U.S. Senator Claiborne Pell (D-Rhode Island), March 10, 1969.

4. Letter from Leona Hoey to Secretary of State William Rogers, February 24, 1969.

5. Letter from Winthrop Brown to Leona Hoey, March 21, 1969.

6. Memo from Paul Kreisberg on a telephone conversation with Maureen Dunn, February 25, 1969.

7. Text of Rogers' letter to Chinese ambassador, Warsaw, as transmitted in a State Department telegram, February 15, 1969.

8. Letter from Alexis Johnson to Frank McGee, February 28, 1969.

9. Maureen Dunn's typed remarks, Lt. Joseph P. Dunn Benefit Dance, June 27, 1969.

10. Letters from Republican Howard Baker and Democrat Richard Russell to the State Department, February 1969; Massachusetts Senator McIntyre letter to Nixon, Boston City Council resolution, March 1969.

11. Undated story from *Quincy Patriot Ledger,* 1969; "Where Is Lt. Joe Dunn, U.S.N.R.?" *Randolph High School Blue and White Banner,* October 1969.

12. Letter from Carole Hanson to Maureen Dunn, May 22, 1969.

13. U.S. Defense Secretary Melvin Laird statement from a Pentagon news conference, May 19, 1969, taken from the Report of the Senate Select Committee (SSC) on POW/MIA Affairs, January 1993, 245–46.

14. SSC report; http://www.pbs.org/wgbh/amex/honor/timeline/timeline2.html.

15. SSC report.

16. "P.O.W. Became Pawn In a Complex Struggle," *New York Times,* February 13, 1973.

17. Joint Statement on Vietnam POWs signed by forty U.S. senators, undated; SSC report, 244–46.

18. "The Geneva Convention Relative to the Treatment of Prisoners of War with Reservations, if any, by Governments Participating in Hostilities in Vietnam, Cambodia and Laos," U.S. House Foreign Affairs subcommittee on national security policy and scientific developments' report, May 1970.

19. SSC report, 244–47; http://www.vietnamwar.com/Timeline69-75.htm.

20. Congressional record for Wednesday, September 17, 1969.

21. Ibid.

22. *San Diego Union* editorial, May 20, 1969.

23. "POW Wives Break Lonely Silence," *San Diego Union,* June 4, 1969.

24. Ibid.

25. http://www.pbs.org/wgbh/amex/honor/sfeature/sf_stockdale.html.

26. Louis R. Stockstill, "The Forgotten Americans of the Vietnam War," *Air Force Magazine* 52, no. 10 (October 1969).

27. SSC report, 246–47; Gerald Posner, *Citizen Perot: His Life and Times* (New York: Random House, 1996).

28. Interview with Carol Bates Brown, April 2005.

29. "Wives Organizing to Find 1,332 G.I.'s Missing in War," *New York Times,* July 31, 1969.

30. Congressional record, September 17, 1969.

31. Program for "Appeal for International Justice," Washington, D.C., May 1, 1970.

32. League of Families' background fact sheet, June 2004.

33. Bureau of Naval Personnel memo, "U.S. Navy Personnel Believed Lost Over Communist China," March 13, 1970.

34. Letter from Maureen to Joe, postmarked December 10, 1969.

35. Maureen Dunn letter to the editor, March 20, 1972.

36. State memo of conversation, February 24, 1970.

37. Navy memo, March 4, 1970.

38. Letter to Maureen Dunn from Navy Capt. Dean E. Webster, special assistant for POW matters, July 24, 1970.

39. Letter to Henry Dunn from Webster, August 11, 1970.

40. League news release to cities and towns in Massachusetts, January 1971.

41. Letter from Kevin White to North Vietnam, January 15, 1971.

42. "Thousands Mail Letters to POWs' Captors," *Boston Globe,* undated story.

43. Advertisement, "An open letter to the citizens of Needham," *Needham Chronicle,* January 21, 1971.

44. "Needham Mails Hanoi 3,000 POW Letters," *Herald Traveler,* undated story.

45. *Boston Globe,* January 30, 1971.

46. *Boston Herald Traveler,* January 31, 1971.

47. Statement of Eleanor Myerson, January 18, 1971.

48. Ibid.

49. *Boston Record American,* January 31, 1971.

50. *Boston Globe,* January 31, 1971.

51. Ibid.

52. Report of the Senate Select Committee on POW/MIA Affairs, January 1993, Chapter 5.

53. League of Families report, undated, probably summer 1970.

54. Ibid.

55. Nixon's address to the nation, "A new peace initiative for all Indochina," October 7, 1970, and letter to Maureen Dunn, October 14, 1970.

56. Adm. E. R. Zumwalt letter to Maureen Dunn, November 25, 1970.

57. *Boston Sunday Advertiser,* December 20, 1970.

58. Ibid.

59. Department of Defense commanders' digest, May 23, 1970.

6. Peace (pp. 111–135)

1. *Boston Herald Traveler,* "POW Salute at Fenway Great but . . . ," July 6, 1971.

2. Statement of Cora Weiss to the House Foreign Affairs subcommittee on national security policy, March 31, 1971.

3. *Boston Sunday Advertiser,* December 20, 1970.

4. Ibid.

5. Minutes of League board meeting, Bolling Air Force Base, Washington, D.C., May 7–8, 1971.

6. Ibid.

7. Vietnam Veterans Against the War web site, www.vvaw.org.

8. Testimony of John F. Kerry of VVAW, Senate Foreign Relations Committee, April 22, 1971.

9. Ibid.

10. http://www.vvaw.org/about/.

11. Transcript of Senate Foreign Relations Committee hearing, April 22, 1971.

12. Weiss statement to House Foreign Affairs subcommittee.

13. "Lt. Dunn's Alive In Family's Heart," *Boston Herald Traveler,* August 1971.

14. PBS "Return with Honor" web site, http://www.pbs.org/wgbh/amex/honor/.

15. Email from MIA wife/former League office manager Mary Jane McManus, May 2005.

16. "Pawns in the Game of Peking Chess," *New York Times,* December 19, 1971.

17. The National Security Archive, "Negotiating U.S.-Chinese Rapprochement," http://www.gwu.edu/~nsarchiv/NSAEBB/NSAEBB70/.

18. *Patriot Ledger,* December 15, 1971.

19. Note from White House to Maureen Dunn, December 24, 1971.

20. Letter from Representative James A. Burke to Nixon, December 8, 1971.

21. State Department memo, January 4, 1972.

22. Newspaper clip, unidentified source, February 14, 1972.

23. *New York Times,* March 11, 1972.

24. Ibid.

25. State telegram from the U.S. Mission, United Nations to Secretary of State, Washington, D.C., March 24, 1972.

26. Ibid.

27. Ibid.

28. *Providence Journal,* March 30, 1972.

29. Ibid.

30. Maureen Dunn's letters and questionnaires to 1972 candidates/delegates, and Hubert Humphrey announcement of presidential candidacy, January 10, 1972.

31. Letter from Maureen Dunn to Humphrey, March 17, 1972.

32. "Families of War Prisoners Denounce Nixon's Policies," *New York Times,* May 8, 1972.

33. Ibid.

34. Ibid.; and http://www.pownetwork.org/bios/m/m131.htm.

35. "Families of War . . . ," *New York Times,* May 8, 1972.

36. *New York Times* and *Washington Post,* May 16, 1972.

37. Transcript of White House press conference with Dunn, Sybil Stockdale, and Phyllis Galanti, May 15, 1972.

38. http://www.washingtonpost.com/wp-srv/politics/daily/sept98/wallace.htm.

39. *Patriot Ledger,* May 17, 1972.

40. Paul Cole, *POW/MIA Issues,* vol. 1 (RAND, 1994), taken from www.korean warpowmia.net, "Background on Lists 944/450/389."

41. United States of America Korean War Commemoration fact sheet.

42. Cole *POW/MIA Issues.*

43. Massachusetts chapter of the National League of Families advertisement, "Don't Leave Us Behind," *Boston Sunday Globe,* October 8, 1972.

44. "Mrs. Dunn Has Doubts About Viet Policy," *Quincy Patriot Ledger,* May 17, 1972.

45. The American Presidency Project at UCSB, Nixon's remarks to League, October 16, 1972.

46. PBS American Experience, http://www.pbs.org/wgbh/amex/vietnam/series/pt_09.html.

47. *Herald Traveler* and *Boston Record American,* October 4, 1972.

48. *Suffolk Journal,* Suffolk University, Boston, October 10, 1972.

49. "Freedom Tree Dedication" invitation, November 16, 1972.

50. http://www.pownetwork.org/bios/m/m004.htm.

51. *Herald Traveler* and *Boston Record American,* Monday, December 4, 1972.

52. Ibid.

53. *Boston Globe,* December 29, 1972.

54. Nixon broadcast announcement of peace in Vietnam, January 23, 1973.

55. Ibid.

56. Ibid.

57. "POW Families Temper Optimism With Caution," *St. Paul Dispatch,* January 24, 1973.

58. Kissinger remarks on peace in Vietnam, January 24, 1974.

59. Ibid.

60. Letter from Representative Hale Boggs to Mrs. James Wiley, July 19, 1972.

61. Letter from U.S. Navy Captain T. F. Rush, special assistant for POW matters, to U.S. Representative Robert L. F. Sikes, March 14, 1973.

62. http://www.check-six.com/lib/Famous_Missing/Boggs.htm.

63. Phyllis Galanti email response to questions, October 2005.

7. The Missing (pp. 136–156)

1. "Home Town Honors Pilot Listed Missing," Associated Press, February 14, 1973.

2. "POWs Need Time for Re-culturation," *Boston Evening Globe,* November 17, 1972.

3. Ibid., and "The POW: A Stranger Coming Home," *Boston Herald Traveler,* November 7, 1972.

4. *Boston Herald Traveler,* November 7, 1972

5. Ibid.

6. Vietnam peace accord, Article 8.

7. "Hanoi to Aid U.S. Seek the Missing," *New York Times,* March 28, 1973.

8. Ibid.

9. Ibid.

10. "U.S. Teams Search for Missing G.I.'s," *New York Times,* July 1, 1973.

11. Ibid.

12. Report of the U.S. Senate Select Committee on POW/MIA Affairs, 1993.

13. Ibid.

14. Ibid.; and statement of Henry Kissinger before the SSC, September 22, 1992.

15. Report of the U.S. Senate Select Committee on POW/MIA Affairs, 1993, 67.

16. "Washington Assures Mrs. Dunn of Full Accounting of POWs," *Patriot Ledger,* undated; and "Reds Will Be Made to List POWs, Says Randolph Wife," *Brockton Enterprise,* January 1973.

17. "Wife of an MIA Pleads For Complete PW Lists," *New York Post,* February 2, 1973.

18. Advertisement, "Have You Forgotten Him," *Boston Globe,* February 8, 1973.

19. Ibid.

20. Statement of the Massachusetts chapter of the League of Families, January 1973.

21. "Home Town Honors . . . ," Associated Press, February 14, 1993.

22. "For Joe Dunn Jr., Cards Keep Returning," *Patriot Ledger,* February 1973.

23. "Home Town Honors . . . ," Associated Press, February 14, 1993.

24. "Wife of An MIA Pleads for Complete PW Lists," *New York Post,* February 2, 1973.

25. *The Book of Honor* by Ted Gup; letter from Marshall Wright to Senator Alan Cranston, May 4, 1973.

26. Ibid.

27. Transcript of State Department press, radio, and television news briefing, December 7, 1973.

28. Ibid.

29. "Joseph P. Dunn . . . M.I.A.," ad sponsored by Randolph selectmen, February 1973.

30. Memo from the deputy secretary of defense to the president, July 17, 1973.

31. Ibid.

32. Department of Defense status determination fact sheet.

33. Memo from the deputy secretary of defense to the president, July 17, 1973.

34. SSC report, 1993.

35. Memo from the deputy secretary of defense to the president, July 17, 1973.

36. Ibid.

37. "The Kin of Missing Servicemen Push for Action on Their Status," *New York Times,* May 26, 1973.

38. Ibid.

39. Ibid.

40. U.S. District Court for the Southern District of New York, *Ellen P. McDonald et al. vs. John McLucas et al.,* counter-proposed final decree, March 5, 1974.

41. "MIA Kin Unlights Yule Tree," unidentified newspaper clipping, December 1973.

42. "Families of Mass. MIAs Plan State House Rally," unidentified newspaper clipping, January 22, 1974.

43. "POWs' Kin in Demonstration," *Boston Herald American,* January 28, 1974.

44. "MIA Families Vent Frustration," *New York Times News Service,* January 29, 1974.

45. *Washington Post* story, "Kin of Missing Servicemen Reproach Nixon, Congress," ran in *Boston Globe,* January 29, 1974.

46. Statement of Maureen Dunn before the Senate Foreign Relations Committee, January 28, 1974.

47. Statement of E. C. Mills before the Senate Foreign Relations Committee, January 28, 1974.

48. *Washington Post* story, "Kin of missing servicemen . . ."

49. Statement of Frank Sieverts before the Senate Foreign Relations Committee, January 28, 1974.

50. *Washington Post* story, "Kin . . ."

51. Statement of Scott Albright, executive director of the League, before the Senate Foreign Relations Committee, January 28, 1974.

52. Ibid.

53. Carole Hanson Hickerson, email response to questions, June 2005.

54. Albright statement, January 28; and "MIA Families Vent . . ." *New York Times News Service,* January 29, 1974.

55. Letter from the Pakistan Council for Repatriation of Prisoners of War to the League of Families, April 2, 1973; "Pakistani POWs: 'The New Forgotten People'," *Washington Post,* January 18, 1973; "Tension Rising in Indian POW Camps," *Washington Post,* December 23, 1972.

56. U.S. District Court decree, March 5, 1974.

57. Ibid.

58. State Department telegram to the American Embassy in Saigon et al., July 1, 1974.

59. Ibid.

60. "Official Sees Tougher Stand On Men Missing in Vietnam," *Omaha World-Herald,* June 28, 1974; and "POW Group Vows Strengthened Stand," *Omaha World Herald,* July 1, 1974.

61. "Quan Doi Nhan Dan" commentary, August 4, 1974, translated from a Vietnamese publication.

62. Private correspondence to Maureen Dunn, 1974.

63. Letter from White House Press Secretary Ronald L. Ziegler to Maureen Dunn, May 21, 1974.

64. "Ford Urges Leniency for War Resisters," *New York Times,* August 20, 1974.

65. Nixon statement on amnesty, October 1972.

66. *Boston Sunday Advertiser,* February 13, 1972.

67. President Ford's remarks on amnesty for Vietnam-era draft evaders, September 16, 1974.

68. Ibid.

69. Editorial by Maureen Dunn, "Where is Justice for 1,300 Missing Servicemen?" September 1974.

70. Text of memo as transmitted by State to Defense departments, December 24, 1975.

71. "Dunn Family's Drama Began Eight Years Ago Feb. 14," *Quincy Patriot Ledger,* February 9, 1976.

8. Acceptance (pp. 157–176)

1. U.S. House Select Committee on Missing Persons in Southeast Asia, final report, December 13, 1976.

2. SSC report, January 1993.

3. Letter to Chai Zemin from Maureen Dunn, March 9, 1979.

4. Letter from Maureen Dunn to Navy Capt. G. W. Horsley, March 8, 1980.

5. Ibid.

6. *Boston Herald American,* August 7, 1980.

7. Letter from Maureen Dunn to President Reagan, October 26, 1983.

8. SSC, January 1993.

9. Western Union mailgram from Maureen Dunn to Ronald Reagan, January 26, 1981.

10. Letter from Donald S. Jones to Maureen Dunn, February 18, 1981.

11. Letters from the Navy and the PRC embassy to Maureen Dunn, May 19, 1981.

12. Letter from Maureen Dunn to Navy Cmdr. Sullivan, June 1, 1981.

13. Correspondence between Maureen Dunn and the U.S. Navy, June to August 1981.

14. Letter from Navy Secretary John Lehman to Maureen Dunn, November 19, 1981.

15. Letter from Navy Secretary John Lehman to U.S. Representative Brian Donnelly, January 20, 1982.

16. Memorandum from Capt. John G. Colgan, hearing officer, to the Status Review Board, September 11, 1981.

17. Ibid.

18. Letter from John Lehman to Maureen Dunn, November 19, 1981.

19. National League of Families newsletter, August 2, 1982.

20. Ibid.

21. Remarks of Ronald Reagan to the League of Families, January 28, 1983.

22. Letter from Maureen Dunn to Ronald Reagan, October 26, 1983.

9. China (177–194)

1. Letter from U.S. Ambassador Arthur W. Hummel, Jr., to Massachusetts Governor Michael Dukakis, September 4, 1985.

2. Letter from Maureen Dunn to Chai Zemin, May 8, 1985.

3. Maureen Dunn journal entry, July 14, 1991.

4. Dan Gallagher, China trip diary, July 14, 1991.

5. Maureen Dunn journal entry, July 16, 1991.

6. Gallagher China diary, July 19, 1991.

7. Maureen Dunn journal entry, July 18, 1991.

8. Ibid.

9. Gallagher China diary, July 19, 1991.

10. Summary report of the third JTF-FA field activity in China, October 1996.

11. Maureen Dunn journal entry, July 21, 1991.

12. Letter from JTF-FA commander, Brig. Gen. Thomas H. Needham, to Alan C. Ptak, deputy assistant defense secretary for POW/MIA Affairs, June 19, 1992.

13. JTF-FA summary report, October 1996.

10. Aftermath (pp. 195–215)

1. Navy chronology of highlights of A1-H downing, February 1968.

2. Audio recording of telephone call between Robert McNamara and Lyndon Johnson, February 14, 1968.

3. Memorandum from Walt Rostow to Lyndon Johnson, 12:20 P.M., February 14, 1968.

4. Ibid., 12:40 P.M., February 14 1968.

5. Interview with Dan Gallagher, 2005.

6. White House memorandum from Walt Rostow to Lyndon Johnson, February 15, 1968.

7. Letter from the Embassy of the Republic of Iraq to the National League of Families, August 4, 1989.

8. League press release, February 7, 1991.

9. Senate Select Committee on POW/MIA Affairs report, January 1993, 45, 320–24.

10. Ibid., 158–59.

11. Testimony of Ann Mills Griffiths before SSC, November 7, 1991.

12. SSC report, 44.

13. Ibid., 7–9.

14. U.S. POW/MIA statistics from the National League of Families, status report 1995.

15. SSC report, 370–83.

16. Statistics from League, 1995.

17. SSC report, 379–80.

18. Letter from the White House to F.T. Runyan, August 26, 1992.

19. Maureen Dunn statement, August 8, 1992.

20. Letter from George H. W. Bush to Eileen Thompson, August 17, 1992.

21. Letter from Maureen Dunn to League's Northeast regional members, August 5, 1993.

22. "No Formal Ties Yet," *New York Times,* February 4, 1994.

23. Interview with Barbara Cleary O'Connor, August 2005.